Italian Manuscript Sources
of 17th Century Keyboard Music

Studies in Musicology, No. 18

George Buelow, Series Editor
Professor of Musicology
Indiana University

Other Titles in This Series

Italian Manuscript Sources of 17th Century Keyboard Music

by
Alexander Silbiger

RESEARCH PRESS

Produced and distributed by
UMI Research Press
an imprint of
University Microfilms International
Ann Arbor, Michigan 48106

Library of Congress Cataloging in Publication Data

Silbiger, Alexander, 1935-
Italian manuscript sources of 17th century
keyboard music.

(Studies in musicology ; ser. 2, 18)
Bibliography: p.
Includes index.
1. Harpsichord music—Bibliography. 2. Music, Italian
—Bibliography. 3. Music—Bibliography—Manuscripts.
I. Title. II. Series.
ML128.H35S5   016.7864   79-25558
ISBN 0-8357-1075-0

Contents

v

Contents

Tables

Musical Examples

Abbreviations and Other Conventions

MANUSCRIPTS

Manuscripts are referred to by a short title usually consisting of the present location followed by an identifying number, e.g.:

Florence 115 = Florence, Biblioteca Nazionale Centrale, Fondo Magliabechiano XIX. 115.

Full titles are listed in the *Key to Manuscript Short Titles.*

16TH- AND 17TH-CENTURY EDITIONS

16th- and 17th-century editions of Italian instrumental music, except for editions of Frescobaldi's works, are referred to by short titles (in capitals) followed by sigla. The siglum indicates the entry in Sartori's *Bibliografia* (to which the reader is referred for further bibliographical information), e.g.:

Mayone, CAPRICCI I, Sa. 1603b = PRIMO LIBRO DI DIVERSI CAPRICCI PER SONARE DI ASCANIO MAYONE . . . MDCIII, catalogued by Sartori under 1603b (hence date of publication = 1603).

Since Sartori's listings of Frescobaldi editions are not entirely in agreement with more recent bibliographic findings, his sigla are not used for these publications— see the *Key to Short Titles of Frescobaldi Editions.*

References to early publications not falling in the above categories follow conventional bibliographic practice.

OTHER REFERENCES

In all other references the name of the author is given, followed by an underlined short title, e.g.,

Testi, *Musica* II, 321-65 = Flavio Testi, *La musica italiana nel seicento* (Milan: Bramante, 1972), Vol. II, pp. 321-65.

Full titles and further bibliographical information are given in the *Bibliography.*

STAFF-RULING SYSTEMS

In referring to two-staff keyboard notation the number of lines in the upper and lower staves is represented as a fraction, e.g.:

6/7 = 6 lines in the upper staff, 7 lines in the lower staff.

The number of systems per page is indicated as follows:

2 × 6/7 = two systems of 6/7 lines per page.

ITALIAN GENRE DESIGNATIONS

When a reference is made to the title of a specific composition as given in a source, the original spelling is preserved, e.g., *Tocata, Tochata, Recercar, Canzon*. In all other cases conventional modern spellings are used, e.g., toccata, ricercare, canzone, and the terms are not underlined. The Italian forms of the plurals will be employed (toccate, canzoni).

COMPOSERS' NAMES

Variant versions of composers' names are common in the sources, for example, Pasquini, Pasquino. The names will be standardized according to present-day usage except in the quotation of a specific attribution. In such quotations misspellings and other variants will not be corrected, nor provided with editorial comment.

MUSICAL EXAMPLES

The musical examples are notated on five-line staves and are transcribed to G_2 and F_4 clefs, according to present-day usage. In all other aspects, such as time and key signatures, accidentals, barlines, note values, and beaming, the notation of the sources is followed. In the transcription of two-staff scores the division between the two staves preserves that of the original text; four-staff scores are notated on two staves with the soprano and alto parts placed on the upper stave and the tenor and bass parts on the lower stave. All editorial changes or suggestions are noted in the musical text.

Key to Manuscript Short Titles

Manuscripts preceded by an asterisk are included in the Annotated Catalogue.

SHORT TITLE	MANUSCRIPT
Antoniano	*Rome, Biblioteca del pontificio Ateneo Antoniano (no signature)
Assisi	*Assisi, Archivio musicale del Sacro convento (no signature)
Bagnacavallo	*Bagnacavallo, Biblioteca comunale Giuseppe Taroni, Codice C.M.B. 1
Barb. lat. 4181	*Rome, Biblioteca Apostolica Vaticana, Ms. Barb. lat. 4181
Barb. lat. 4182	*Rome, Biblioteca Apostolica Vaticana, Ms. Barb. lat. 4182
Barb. lat. 4288	*Rome, Biblioteca Apostolica Vaticana, Ms. Barb. lat. 4288
Bauyn Ms.	Paris, Bibliothèque nationale, Mss. Rés. Vm^7 674 and Vm^7 675
Berlin 40316	Berlin, Staatsbibliothek, Ms. 40316 (lost, photostat copy at Isham Memorial Library, Harvard University)
Berlin 40615	Berlin, Staatsbibliothek, Ms. 40615
Berlin L.215	Berlin, Staatsbibliothek, Ms. L.215
Bologna 53	*Bologna, Civico museo bibliografico musicale, Ms. DD/53
Bologna 258	*Bologna, Civico museo bibliografico musicale, Ms. BB/258
Bologna 270	*Bologna, Civico museo bibliografico musicale, Ms. Z.270
Bologna 360	*Bologna, Civico museo bibliografico musicale, Ms. AA/360
Bologna Q 21	Bologna, Civico museo bibliografico musicale, Ms. Q 21
Bologna Q 34	*Bologna, Civico museo bibliografico musicale, Ms. Q 34

Castell'Arquato	*Castell'Arquato, Chiesa Collegiata, Archivio (no signature)
Cecilia 400	*Rome, Biblioteca Conservatorio di musica Santa Cecilia, Ms. A/400
Chigi 4	Rome, Biblioteca Apostolica Vaticana, Ms. Chigi Q.IV.4
Chigi 23	Rome, Biblioteca Apostolica Vaticana, Ms. Chigi Q.IV.23
Chigi 24	*Rome, Biblioteca Apostolica Vaticana, Ms. Chigi Q.IV.24
Chigi 25	*Rome, Biblioteca Apostolica Vaticana, Ms. Chigi Q.IV.25
Chigi 26	*Rome, Biblioteca Apostolica Vaticana, Ms. Chigi Q.IV.26
Chigi 27	*Rome, Biblioteca Apostolica Vaticana, Ms. Chigi Q.IV.27
Chigi 28	*Rome, Biblioteca Apostolica Vaticana, Ms. Chigi Q.IV.28
Chigi 29	*Rome, Biblioteca Apostolica Vaticana, Ms. Chigi Q.IV.29
Chigi 205	*Rome, Biblioteca Apostolica Vaticana, Ms. Chigi Q.IV.205
Chigi 206	*Rome, Biblioteca Apostolica Vaticana, Ms. Chigi Q.IV.206
Cologny T.II.1	*Cologny/Geneva, Biblioteca Bodmeriana, Musik T.II.1
Como 820/40	*Como, Archivio musicale del Duomo, Ms. 820/40
Como 820/55	*Como, Archivio musicale del Duomo, Ms. 820/55
Doria 250 A	*Rome, Biblioteca Doria-Pamphilj, Ms. 250 A
Doria 250 B	*Rome, Biblioteca Doria-Pamphilj, Ms. 250 B
Elizabeth Rogers Virginal Book	London, British Library, Ms. Add. 10337
Faenza 117	Faenza, Biblioteca Comunale, Ms. 117
Fitzwilliam Virginal Book	Cambridge, Fitzwilliam Museum, Music Ms. 32.G.29
Florence 106b	*Florence, Biblioteca Nazionale Centrale, Ms. Magl. XIX 106bis
Florence 115	*Florence, Biblioteca Nazionale Centrale, Ms. Magl. XIX 115

Florence 138	*Florence, Biblioteca Nazionale Centrale, Ms. Magl. XIX 138
Florence 641	*Florence, Biblioteca Medicea Laurenziana, Ms. Acquisti e Doni 641
Florence 2358	*Florence, Biblioteca del Conservatorio di musica Luigi Cherubini, Ms. D.2358
Garofalo	*New York, formerly private collection of Carlo Giorgio Garofalo (present location unknown)
London 2088	*London, Royal College of Music, Ms. 2088
London 14246	*London, British Library, Ms. Add. 14246
London 30491	*London, British Library, Ms. Add. 30491
London 31422	London, British Library, Ms. Add. 31422
London 31501	London, British Library, Ms. Add. 31501
London 36661	London, British Library, Ms. Add. 36661
London 40080	*London, British Library, Ms. Add. 40080
Lübbenau, Ly A1, A2	Berlin, Staatsbibliothek, Mss. Lynar A1, A2
Milan 53	*Milan, Biblioteca del Conservatorio di musica Giuseppe Verdi, Riserva mus. 53
Modena 491	*Modena, Biblioteca Estense, Ms. App. Campori 491
Munich 1581	Munich, Bayerische Staatsbibliothek, Ms. 1581
Naples 48	*Naples, Conservatorio di musica San Piètro a Majella, Ms. Mus. str. 48
Naples 55	Naples, Conservatorio di musica San Piètro a Majella, Ms. Mus. str. 55
Naples 73	*Naples, Conservatorio di musica San Piètro a Majella, Ms. Mus. str. 73
Nuremberg 33748-V	*Nuremberg, Germanisches Nationalmuseum, Ms. 33748-V
Oxford 1113	Oxford, Christ Church College Library, Ms. 1113
Paris 674-675	See Bauyn Ms.
Paris 6771	Paris, Bibliothèque nationale, nouv. acq. fr. 6771
Parville	University of California at Berkeley, Music Library (no signature)

Ravenna 545	*Ravenna, Biblioteca Comunale, Ms. Class. 545
Spello	*Spello, Archivio di Santa Maria Maggiore (no signature)
Ste. Geneviève 2348	Paris, Bibliothèque de Ste. Geneviève, Ms. 2348
Trent	*Trent, Private Collection of Laurence Feininger (no signature)
Turin	Turin, Biblioteca Nazionale, Mss. Foà 1-8, Giordano 1-8
UCLA 51/1	*University of California at Los Angeles, Music Library, Ms. 51/5
Vall. 121	*Rome, Biblioteca Vallicelliana, Ms. Z.121
Vat. mus. 569	*Rome, Biblioteca Apostolica Vaticana, Ms. Vat. mus. 569
Venice 1227	*Venice, Biblioteca Nazionale Marciana, Cod. It. IV-1227
Venice 1299	*Venice, Biblioteca Nazionale Marciana, Cod. It. IV-1299
Venice 1727	*Venice, Biblioteca Nazionale Marciana, Cod. It. IV-1727
Verona MCXXVIII	Verona, Biblioteca capitolare, Cod. MCXXVIII
Verona MCXXIX	*Verona, Biblioteca capitolare, Cod. MCXXIX
Vicenza 2.7.17	*Vicenza, Biblioteca civica Bertoliana, Mus. Ms. FF 2.7.17

Key to Short Titles of Frescobaldi Editions

The publishing history of Frescobaldi's keyboard works is complex; no complete bibliographical study, covering all surviving copies of the various editions, is available. Fortunately, for the purposes of this study there is in most cases no need to distinguish between editions that are substantially identical. In general, reference is made to the first edition in which the musical text under discussion appears. This procedure is followed even when subsequent editions involve addition or deletion of musical materials, unless such changes are of concern to the discussion. In the following table concordances are given to three bibliographies: Sartori, *Bibliografia*; RISM, A/I/3; and Newcomb, *Frescobaldi*. Newcomb's listing is the most comprehensive and accurate, but has not yet appeared in print.

Short Title	Sartori	RISM	Newcomb	Notes
FANTASIE (1608)	1608i	F 1855	A.1	
TOCCATE I (1615)	1615a	F 1856	A.3	
	1615-1616b	F 1857	A.4	a
	1615a bis }	—	A.4b	b
	1615f }			
	1628k	F 1858	A.4c	
	1637f	F 1859	A.4d	c
RECERCARI (1615)	1615g	F 1860	A.5	d
	1618g	F 1860	A.5b	
CAPRICCI (1624)	1624b	F 1862	A.6	
CAPRICCI (1626)	1626i	F 1863	A.5c/A.6b	d
	1628l	F 1864	A.5d/A.6c	
	1642h	F 1865	A.5e/A.6d	
TOCCATE II (1627)	1627b	F 1866	A.7	
	1637g	F 1867	A.7b	

Key to Short Titles of Frescobaldi Editions

Short Title	Sartori	RISM	Newcomb	Notes
CANZONI I (1628i)	1628i	F 1869	A.9	e
CANZONI I (1628j)	1628j	F 1868	A.8	e
ARIE I (1630)	—	F 1854	B.10	
ARIE II (1630)	—	F 1854	B.11	
CANZONI I (1634)	1634	F 1870	A.10	e
FIORI (1635)	1635a	F 1871	A.11	
AGGIUNTA (1637)	1637f	F 1859	A.12	c
CANZONI IV (1645)	1645a	F 1872	A.13	

a. According to Newcomb, published in 1616.

b. According to Newcomb, probably published sometime between 1617 and 1626. Not listed in RISM.

c. To the 1637 edition of TOCCATE I a substantial new segment was added, headed "Aggiunta." In this study the added segment is treated as a separate source with title AGGIUNTA (1637).

d. The entire content of RECERCARI (1615) was incorporated in the 1626 edition of CAPRICCI and subsequent editions.

e. The three listed editions of CANZONI I—1628i, 1628j, and 1634—differ in many aspects; hence separate titles are used.

Preface

This edition presents essentially the text of my dissertation "Italian Manuscript Sources of Seventeenth-Century Keyboard Music" (Brandeis University, 1976). However, some additional information has been incorporated, based on recent work by myself and others, and a few sections have been slightly revised.

The present study drew my attention to a group of manuscripts which appeared to be of major importance for an understanding of the development of keyboard music in Rome during the middle and late seventeenth century. As a result, I have since turned towards a more thorough investigation of the Roman keyboard tradition, on which I report in a forthcoming article, "The Roman Frescobaldi Tradition: 1640-1670." This article supplements the material on the Roman manuscripts found in the present volume. In order to keep duplication to a minimum both studies contain a number of cross-references. A more extended project on Roman musical institutions (churches, patronage), keyboard players, and keyboard music is currently in progress.

Among studies in related areas that have appeared since the completion of my dissertation, one of the most welcome has been Bruce Gustafson's monumental survey of the sources of 17th-century French harpsichord music, enabling me to add references to his comprehensive lists of concordances for popular French dances and tunes (see Gustafson, *Sources*, in the Bibliography). I should also mention here a Master's thesis by Lyle Anderson on the manuscript Cecilia 400, completed under my supervision at the University of Wisconsin-Madison, which made several contributions to our understanding of this intriguing collection (Anderson, Cecilia 400).

In spite of all my efforts to make the survey of manuscripts in my dissertation as complete as possible a few additional items have "surfaced" since its completion. During my visit to Bologna in 1979 Oscar Mischiati brought these to my attention, and, with his customary generosity, put microfilms and other materials at my disposal. I am grateful to him for making it possible to incorporate these manuscripts in my revision (they have been entered as Bagnacavallo, Bologna 270, Garofalo, Modena 491 and Spello).

A number of small slips, which somehow managed to escape all earlier scrutiny, have been corrected here. I am indebted to Lyle Anderson for bringing some of these to my attention.

The National Endowment for the Humanities and the American Council of Learned Societies provided grants enabling me to return to Italy during the

Preface

summer of 1977 and the spring semester of 1979 for further studies on 17th-century keyboard music.

A.S.
Madison, July 1979

Acknowledgments

I am deeply indebted to the many people, both here and abroad, who have helped me during the course of my work. First and foremost I must thank Professor Paul Brainard whose advice guided me through many phases of this project and whose support and encouragement was to a large extent responsible for its completion. I also am most grateful to Professor Joshua Rifkin who provided many illuminating comments on various problems that I encountered, and who, in fact, first suggested that I extend this study, which was originally conceived as an investigation of the manuscript sources of Frescobaldi's keyboard music, to a general survey of seventeenth-century Italian keyboard manuscripts.

Of the several people in Italy who provided help in one form or another I should like to thank especially Oscar Mischiati, with whom I spent several delightful mornings exchanging thoughts and information on various manuscripts, Claudio Sartori of the Ufficio Ricerche musicale in Milan, who made available to me his extensive catalogue of Italian sources, Mons. José Ruysschaert of the Biblioteca Apostolica Vaticana, who arranged for me to examine some uncatalogued manuscripts, Professor Francesco Degrada of the Conservatorio di musica Giuseppe Verdi in Milan, who provided me with a description of a manuscript in the Conservatorio's library, and finally, the Prince and Princess Doria Pamphilj of Rome and the late Father Feininger of Trent, who permitted me to examine some manuscripts in their collections.

I am also grateful to Professor Anthony Newcomb of the University of California at Berkeley, James Ladewig of Berkeley, and Etienne Darbellay of Fribourg, Switzerland, who provided me with information from their researches.

Several friends and colleagues at the University of Wisconsin in Madison came to my aid during the final stages of this project. Charlotte Greenspan and Marion Gushee commented on portions of my preliminary drafts, Lenore Coral gave valuable advice on bibliographic and organizational problems, and Kathy Reynolds provided extensive editorial help with the preparation of the final draft.

To the trustees of the Martha Baird Rockefeller Fund I wish to express my gratitude for a dissertation grant that allowed me to visit Italy during 1972-73 in order to obtain materials for this study.

I cannot close these acknowledgments without mentioning my late wife, Gian. She was my companion only for the earlier stages of this project, during which she shared with me the happy excitement of research and discovery.

Acknowledgments

Nevertheless, the memories of those years continue to provide my work with a source of inspiration.

Introduction

Studies in 17th-century Italian keyboard music have been based on an incomplete knowledge of the surviving repertory. There are several reasons for this. Some of the sources transmitting the repertory form part of collections that are not easily accessible; other sources simply have escaped the notice of scholarly investigators. But most important: while a catalogue of 17th-century editions has been available for some years,[1] a comprehensive guide to the manuscript sources—most of them containing as yet unpublished materials—has been lacking.

This study hopes to provide such a guide. For these sources, however, a descriptive catalogue would be of limited use. Most of the manuscripts contain no precise information regarding their provenance, such as dates, place-names, names of copyists or original owners. Nor in general are the sources of the manuscripts' content acknowledged. In some cases a group of pieces or even the entire contents were clearly copied from a contemporary publication, but for most of the repertory no concordances to printed editions have been found. Only one of the manuscripts considered here names a composer with every composition (London 30491); the contents of several manuscripts are entirely anonymous. Furthermore, when a composer is named, his connection with the composition in question, and with the text of the composition as given in the manuscript, cannot be accepted uncritically. It is clear that a mere listing of the manuscripts, and of the composers and compositions contained in them, would not adequately serve the student of 17th-century keyboard music.

If one turns to the scholarly literature one will find few answers to the basic questions regarding these manuscripts—questions such as: Where do they come from? How do they relate to other sources of the period? What is the authority of their contents? A few discussions of some individual manuscripts have appeared in recent years, but these rarely venture beyond providing some descriptive information.[2] The need for a comprehensive study of the manuscript sources, a study that will attempt to place them in a larger historical context, seems clear.

I have excluded from this study consideration of non-Italian manuscripts containing compositions attributed to Italian composers. Such sources are better dealt with in the context of studies similar to this one on the manuscripts of the countries in question.[3] Furthermore, the repertory in the foreign sources is essentially independent from that found in the Italian manuscripts. I have also not considered manuscripts presently residing in Italy which clearly are of foreign origin. On the other hand, I have included in my study manuscripts in foreign libraries which are apparently of Italian provenance.

Part Two of this study contains an annotated catalogue of Italian keyboard manuscripts from c. 1500-1700.[4] Of the fifty-three items included in this catalogue only twenty-two are mentioned in Willi Apel's *Keyboard Music* (many only in passing reference, as a source of a composition), to date by far the most comprehensive reference work on early keyboard music.[5] Several manuscripts are, in fact, not listed anywhere in the scholarly literature, or appear only in library catalogues. These little-known manuscripts include several compositions attributed to important composers such as Frescobaldi, de Macque, Ercole and Bernardo Pasquini, which have appeared neither in the modern editions of the collected keyboard works of these composers nor elsewhere.[6]

A study of the sources of a repertory cannot proceed independently of a study of the repertory itself; frequently the history of the repertory provides indispensable assistance in estimating the origin of a manuscript. To some extent the reverse is also true. Studies of a repertory—including studies on the works of specific composers or on the development of specific genres—carried out without thorough knowledge of the contents and reliability of the surviving sources have tended to produce results that can be accepted only provisionally.[7]

The manuscript sources are especially important for our knowledge of keyboard music after c. 1640, the music of the generations following Frescobaldi. The almost continuous stream of publications that appeared during Frescobaldi's lifetime slowed to a mere trickle during the remainder of the century. As a result, past studies of Italian keyboard music have devoted comparatively little attention to this later period. For example, Apel, in his *Keyboard Music*, devotes 75 pages to the period 1600-1650, but only 23 pages to the period 1650-1700 (by comparison, the ratio in his book for the same periods in German keyboard music is 62 pages to 130 pages). The manuscript repertory from this period has scarcely been investigated. A recent dissertation—Monroe, *Italian Keyboard Music in the Interim Between Frescobaldi and Bernardo Pasquini*—is based, with one exception (Naples 73), exclusively on printed sources.

Yet it is from this period that the largest number of manuscripts have survived. Whereas the printed collections tend to be backward-looking,[8] the manuscripts reflect to a much greater extent the new developments taking place in keyboard music, developments paralleling those found in instrumental ensemble music (and, no doubt, stimulated by them). I am convinced that further study of the manuscript repertory will show that the vital traditions of Italian keyboard music did not slacken during the second half of the century, but were maintained, to be carried to the next century by Alessandro Scarlatti and passed on to his son, Domenico.

The manuscripts discussed in this study form a comparatively well-defined and homogeneous group with respect to both appearance and content; for this reason they lend themselves to study in isolation from other source groups, such as manuscripts from other countries or from adjacent periods. To be sure, there are some manuscripts for which it is not clear whether they properly belong to the group defined by our chosen geographical and chronological limits, especially since the provenance of most sources can be only roughly estimated. For example, two manuscripts discussed here, Bologna 53 and Cecilia 400, were heretofore believed to date from the 17th century, since they contain for the most part 17th-century repertory and follow 17th-century notational traditions; in all likelihood, however, they were not compiled until well after 1700.

On the other hand, I have excluded from detailed consideration the Bernardo Pasquini autographs, dated c. 1700; their provenance is relatively unproblematical and their repertory is not linked directly to that of the earlier sources.[9] Neither will the manuscript sources of the keyboard music of Alessandro Scarlatti—most if not all of which appear to date from the 18th century—be considered here.[10] The study of these sources (at least some twenty manuscripts are involved) forms one of the major areas towards which future research in Italian keyboard music must be directed.[11]

The decision to include in the catalogue the small number of surviving 16th-century manuscripts was based on the fact that these share many characteristics with the manuscripts of the following century. They are not considered in detail—individual studies are already available for most of them—but will be dealt with as a group in Part One in order to provide a background for the discussion of the later manuscripts. The provenance of some of the early sources will be briefly discussed, since I believe that previous conclusions with respect to their dating require some revision.

In addition, I have included a few manuscripts that perhaps do not properly belong to the category of sources chosen as the subject of this study—in fact, this very issue will form an important aspect of the discussion. For some of these, doubt exists as to whether they date from the 17th century or whether they are of Italian provenance (London 40080 and Nuremberg 33748-V); for others, there is some question whether they were in fact intended for keyboard instruments (Florence 106b, Bologna Q 34, Antoniano).

Part Three of this study surveys the works of the most significant composers represented in the manuscripts. The possible relation of the composer to the source is explored, and the credibility of the attributions—a problem dealt with in more general terms in Part One, Chapter X—is evaluated.

Few composers are encountered with any regularity in the manuscripts. Not too surprisingly, attributions to Frescobaldi far outnumber those to any other composer, although for various reasons many of these must be questioned— more so than is the case with other authors. Although Frescobaldi's dominating role in 17th-century keyboard music remains uncontested, a second composer, Ercole Pasquini, emerges from the manuscripts as having generated much interest among musicians of the period. So far as we know, none of his keyboard works appeared in print, but numerous compositions are attributed to him in several manuscripts of diverse regional origin, dating from throughout the century. A third composer with a number of attributions to his name—mainly in Neapolitan sources—is Giovanni de Macque; he, too, is not represented in any Italian keyboard publications of the period.

Since this study deals with a large amount of material, inevitably some problems are not pursued to the fullest extent. One will not find here a detailed description of the physical characteristics and musical content of every manuscript; such descriptions must await future studies of individual manuscripts or groups of manuscripts. A thorough stylistic analysis of the extensive repertory contained in the manuscripts was, of course, even more out of the question. It is my belief that, considering the present state of knowledge, the gains derived from a broad survey outweigh the benefits that could be obtained from a more intensive investigation of a single source or a restricted group of sources—and, indeed, that a survey of this type ideally should precede such investigations. I have confidence that the present study will bear out this belief.

PART ONE

THE ITALIAN MANUSCRIPT SOURCES

I

The Printed Source Tradition

As a prelude to the discussion of the manuscripts I shall review the better-known printed source tradition. During the 16th and the first half of the 17th centuries the printed collections undoubtedly were of prime importance for the dissemination of Italian keyboard music. Most other countries, for example, England, France, and Germany, produced only a handful of publications during this period, and our knowledge of the repertory from these regions is derived primarily from manuscripts. In Italy, however, publications appeared in ever-increasing numbers from c. 1520 onward, the production reaching its peak during the years 1590-1620.[1] A leading role was played by the Venetian publishing houses such as those of Gardano and of Vincenti, whose multi-volume series of the works of Merulo and the Gabrielis gained wide distribution. Yet publishing flourished also in several other cities such as Naples—where mostly local authors were published—and Rome, a center for elegantly engraved volumes. The Italian publications reached libraries all over Europe, and their contents were copied into numerous foreign manuscripts.

The period c. 1615-1650 was dominated by the publications of Frescobaldi's keyboard music; in fact, during the latter part of the period little else was published. These publications apparently found an even larger international market. Of the various editions and reprints of his TOCCATE I (published between 1615 and 1637), fifty-two copies have survived in libraries in thirteen countries (some of these, to be sure, may have been acquired long after their publication); of the second volume, TOCCATE II (published between 1627 and 1637), forty-four copies survive.[2] Their popularity is further attested by the number of extant manuscript copies. A list of Italian copies is given in Table 8; if the foreign copies were included the list would no doubt be considerably longer.[3]

It is interesting to examine some statistics on the number of publications issued during successive periods. The increase in publishing activity during the 16th and early 17th centuries and the subsequent decline is evident from Table 1a.[4] This decline shows up even more tellingly when smaller time intervals are used (Table 1b).

The figures in Tables 1a and 1b may reflect to some extent a general decline in music publishing during the latter part of the 17th century, but not entirely so. An examination of Sartori's *Bibliografia* reveals that the publication of instrumental music in general showed no such falling-off: the decrease in keyboard-music publication is counterbalanced by an increase in publications for string ensemble. Neither was the decline in the publication of keyboard music an international phenomenon; the trend in England and especially in France was very much in the opposite direction.

The Italian keyboard publications are generally devoted to the work of a single composer. Only two collections, one dating from the beginning and one from the end of our period, are exceptions to this rule: Diruta's treatise, TRANSILVANO (Sa. 1593b and 1609-1610), and Arresti's SONATE (Sa. 1697?m). Both publications include a selection of compositions by various authors.

Many publications contain dedications and prefaces signed by the composer, suggesting that the latter was directly involved in their preparation. In the case of some Frescobaldi publications there is other evidence indicating that the composer invested his time as well as his money in seeing them through the press (see pp. 152-53). We have every reason to believe that such editions closely correspond to the intentions of the composer with respect to contents, organization, and musical text.[5]

Not all publications were prepared under the supervision of the composer. Some were edited posthumously, or even during the composer's lifetime, by a relative (e.g., Claudio Merulo's CANZONI II, Sa. 1606d, prepared by his nephew Giacinto), a pupil (Frescobaldi, CANZONI I, 1628i, prepared by Bartolomeo Grassi), or by the publisher himself (Frescobaldi, CANZONI IV, 1645, prepared by Alessandro Vincenti). Even though these editors may have stood in close relation to the composer, editions of this type do not carry the same authority as the publications prepared by the composers themselves. Several examples bear out this contention. Whereas the texts of Frescobaldi's editions appear to be remarkably free of errors, Gardano's posthumous publications of Andrea Gabrieli's works contain a considerable number of misprints. Some of the works contained in the only two Frescobaldi publications not prepared by the composer, CANZONI I (1628i) and CANZONI IV (1645), are problematical insofar as their relation to Frescobaldi is concerned.[6] These are exceptional cases, however. For most of the printed repertory the attributions and the text can be regarded as entirely trustworthy.

With respect to content one can classify the printed collections as general or specialized. The specialized collections are devoted to a particular type of music, such as intabulations of vocal music, music with explicit liturgical function (e.g., organ Masses), contrapuntal models (stile antico ricercari), or dance music. The general collections contain a variety of types; some, in fact, seem to make a point of including a sampling of different genres. The two well-known Frescobaldi collections, TOCCATE I and TOCCATE II (containing toccate, canzoni,

Table 1a
The Number of Publications of Italian Keyboard Music
(Excluding Reprints) Between 1500 and 1700 in 50-Year Intervals

1500–1549	1550–1599	1600–1649	1650–1699
5	20	37	11

Table 1b
The Number of Publications of Italian Keyboard Music
(Excluding Reprints) Between 1590 and 1680 in 30-Year Intervals

1590–1619	1620–1649	1650–1680
34	14	7

intabulations, plain-chant versetti, arie with partite, dances, etc.), are of the general type. Nevertheless, among printed editions general collections are rare and, except for these Frescobaldi editions, are found mainly among the Neapolitan publications, where, in fact, they constituted a long tradition leading from Valente's INTAVOLATURA, Sa. 1576, to Strozzi's CAPRICCI, Sa. 1687h. I shall later propose an explanation for the prevalence of specialized collections among the publications.

Except for two Neapolitan publications, all printed collections of the later 17th century are of the specialized type; furthermore they are virtually all devoted to stile antico ricercari or to liturgical music.[7] For examples of North and Central Italian toccate, canzoni, balli, and partite we must turn to the manuscripts of the period.

II

The Manuscript Sources
Before 1600

Our knowledge of the history of Italian keyboard music begins with the large collection of intabulations in Faenza 117.[1] Here we meet for the first time some features that are to become characteristic of Italian keyboard sources: double-staff notation with regularly placed barlines and planned organization of the contents. In Faenza 117 the organization involves a division into segments containing pieces based on Latin (plain-chant), French, and Italian vocal models. The tradition of including as distinct genres Latin pieces (plain-chant settings, motet intabulations—the latter uncommon in Italian sources), French pieces (chanson intabulations), and Italian pieces (intabulations of frottole, and later of madrigals; also settings of popular song and dance tunes) is maintained throughout the 16th century. After 1600, intabulations of chansons and madrigals become rare, although in a sense one can see in the newly popular canzoni and toccate a continuation of these two traditions.[2] On the other hand, chant settings, in the form of Mass, Magnificat and Hymn versets, continue to flourish, as do song and dance settings, sometimes expanded by means of long chains of partite.

Another feature of the keyboard settings in Faenza 117 which can be linked to a later tradition is the practice of omitting the contrapuntally independent inner voices of the models. In the 15th-century settings the original cantus is turned into a highly florid upper voice, and the tenor, functioning generally as the structural foundation, is left in more or less unaltered form; the contratenor, if present in the model, is omitted altogether. Many of the keyboard settings of popular songs and dances in the later aria and ballo collections, from those in Venice 1227 (early 16th century) to those in Bologna 360 (from the 1660s), follow the same principle, with the difference that the bass of the aria (frequently still called tenore, see Chapter VII) is often amplified by 5-3-1 and 8-5-1 chords.[3] As a result of this chording one encounters frequent parallel fifths and octaves. Through much of the 17th century such parallels—which occur only within the left-hand accompaniments, generally not between the upper voice and the bass—continue to be part of the "low art" Italian keyboard idiom and even make an occasional appearance in the keyboard music of "high art" composers such as Merulo and Frescobaldi.

Table 2 summarizes some information on the surviving 16th-century manuscripts.[4] These manuscripts form a valuable addition to the printed sources, especially for the earlier part of the century, documenting developments not represented in the publications (see Jeppesen, *Orgelmusik*; Slim, *Ricercar*).

Table 2
The 16th-Century Manuscripts

Short Title	Estimated Dates[a]	Repertory
Venice 1227	1530-1550 (probably c. 1540)	settings of popular arie, balli, and hymns
Castell'Arquato (10 fascicles)	dating of individual fascicles varies between c. 1540 and c. 1600	variety of repertory, incl. balli, arie, intabulations, organ Masses, ricercari
Florence 641 "Intavolatura di M. Alamanno Aiolli"	1565-1600	intabulations of popular madrigals and chansons
London 2088 "Libro d'Intavoladura ..." (Marco Facoli)	c. 1586	balli, arie, and accompaniments (?) of madrigals and chansons
Chigi 206, ff. 156-179	1565-1575	fantasie, plain-chant versetti

[a]The estimated dates do not agree in every case with those given in the literature for reasons explained in the text.

Venice 1227 is the oldest representative of the aria and ballo collections. Jeppesen believes it to date from c. 1520 on the basis of the similarity of its notation to that found in a contemporary vocal manuscript (*Tanzbuch*, 254) as well as to that of early 16th-century Italian keyboard tablatures (*Balli*, ix). He does not specify which tablatures he means, but he must have had in mind the two printed collections FROTTOLE (Sa. 1517) and Cavazzoni, RECERCHARI (Sa. 1523), the only surviving keyboard sources from the first decades of the century. These are indeed quite similar to Venice 1227 with respect to notation. Nevertheless, the repertory suggests that this dating may be rather early; settings of traditional arie and balli found in this manuscript such as the two passamezzi and *la cara cossa* (= *la gamba*) do not appear in other Italian sources until several decades later. In fact, the repertory is close to that found in the Venetian publication BALLI (Sa. 1551b), which includes settings of at least half a dozen arie and balli found in the manuscript (among which, in addition to the three popular ones mentioned above, are *Tu te parti, la Comadrina,* and the *Saltarello del Re*). Furthermore, this publication follows the same notational practices as the two printed tablatures mentioned above (published c. 30 years earlier) and as Venice 1227; hence the notation of the manuscript provides no basis for its early dating. The date 1520, although not inconceivable, would certainly have to be taken as an earliest limit. I would propose as a probable range the years 1530-1550, with c. 1540 as the most likely date.[5]

The large and varied collection of manuscripts from Castell'Arquato (near Piacenza) is—to some extent by default—a source of the first importance; no similar collections have survived from possibly more influential musical centers. Only the fascicles containing the earliest materials (from c. 1540) have been discussed at length in the literature, but a study and edition of the entire collection (by Colin Slim) is in progress (see Part Two, Castell'Arquato). The later repertory in this collection includes keyboard scorings of Florentio Maschera's CANZONI (Sa. 1584a) as well as settings of popular arie and balli, intabulations of chansons and madrigals, and liturgical music.

The recently rediscovered Florentine collection, Florence 641 entitled "Intavolatura di M. Alamanno Aiolli [= Layolle]," is devoted entirely to intabulations of popular chansons and madrigals. The manuscript contains contributions by two distinct hands; D'Accone (*Aiolli*) has established that the earlier hand belonged in all likelihood to Alamanno Layolle (in Florence from 1565 to his death in 1590). Since the later hand contributes portions of Emilio Cavalieri's famous "O che nuovo miracolo" (which provided the model for the aria *la Fiorenza*), first performed in 1589 and published in 1590, there is no need to assume, as D'Accone has done in his study (*Aiolli*, 58), that contributions by this hand date from Layolle's lifetime. I have extended the possible final date to 1600. The Aiolli tablature is a prototype of a genre of manuscript very common in the 17th century: a collection of settings of popular materials in adaptations that are unique to the manuscript and that probably are the work of the copyist-owner (see Chapter XII).

Like most other 16th-century keyboard collections London 2088 contains mainly settings of dances and of popular vocal compositions. The opening flyleaf contains the inscription, "Laus Deus M. D. LXXXVI./Libro de Intavoladura di arpicordo./F. A. P." Brown, who describes this collection and provides an inventory (*Instrumental Music*, 343), suggests that the first composition, headed "Passmezo di nome anticho di marcho facoli veneto," probably was taken from the lost *Primo Libro* of Marco Facoli's *Intavolaturo di Balli* (1586?). This would also appear to be true of the second piece (f. 10': *Pavana detta la Paganino*), which, like the first, bears close stylistic resemblance to the dance settings in the surviving *Secondo Libro* (Facoli, INTAVOLATURA II, Sa. 1588c). The remainder of the pieces in London 2088 probably do not derive from this publication. Whereas the first two compositions have rather thick textures and abound with written-out ornaments, the subsequent dances are mostly simple, unadorned soprano-bass settings. The adaptations of vocal compositions (among them settings of the often intabulated "Vestiva i colli" of Palestrina and "Ung gay bergier" of Crequillon) also are predominantly in two parts, which outline the outer voices of the models—the bass line in basso-seguente style. Brown suggests that these settings may have been used to accompany ensemble performances.

I shall not discuss here some 16th-century manuscript scores of vocal and instrumental music, although some may have been prepared for performance on keyboard (see Lowinsky, *Early Scores*). The fascicle Chigi 205-206, ff. 156-179, which contains four-staff scores possibly of original 16th-century keyboard music, is dealt with in Part Two.

III

The Seventeenth-
Century Manuscripts:
A Preliminary Survey

As background to the general discussion of the 17th-century manuscripts in the following chapters a preliminary survey is presented here; details on individual manuscripts will be found in Part Two.

The sources can be divided into several groups of manuscripts related by similar content and proximate origin.[1] The largest number of manuscripts fall into the category of general collections (i.e., collections whose content presents a cross-section of the various genres). Such manuscripts are conveniently grouped into successive periods marked by the onset and waning of Frescobaldi's influence.

(1) *The pre-Frescobaldian general collections, c. 1590-1620.* The four early collections that fall in this group—Trent, Naples 48, Spello, and London 30491—are in a sense transitional sources. Their content includes the work of composers whose active life extends back well into the 16th century, such as Ercole Pasquini and Giovanni de Macque. A few intabulations of popular chansons and madrigals—a genre prominent in the 16th-century collections—are still found in these manuscripts, although the bulk of the repertory is more typical of the new era (toccate, canzoni, etc.).

(2) *The Roman general collections, c. 1630-1670.* The manuscripts that constitute this group all show traces of the impact of the work of Frescobaldi. The repertories reflect the new styles and genres popularized by his publications (for instance, the ciaccona and the passacaglia) and several of the manuscripts contain copies of compositions from these publications and other works attributed to him. This group includes the several manuscripts in the Chigi collection, Doria 250 A and 250 B, Vall. 121, and Vat. mus. 569. Similarities in physical appearance mark these volumes as being closely related—a supposition confirmed by their repertories. Vat. mus. 569 dates from somewhat later than the other collections and shows evidence of newer trends, such as an interest in French dance music and the disappearance of settings of the older arie such as the

Ruggiero and the Romanesca. The manuscript Ravenna 545 will also be included in this group; it is not of Roman origin, but its repertory has many ties to the Roman sources.

(3) *The late manuscripts, after c. 1670.* This group contains a miscellany of unrelated manuscripts. The earliest, Naples 73, is dated c. 1675 but much of its repertory appears to be considerably older; it includes works attributed to de Macque and Ercole Pasquini. The contents of Venice 1299 also appear to date back to a somewhat earlier time. Florence 2358, probably from the last decades of the century, shows further evidence of the inroads of French traditions and of the disappearance of the standard arie and balli.

Two manuscripts are included here that almost certainly were not compiled until the second decade of the 18th century at the very earliest: Bologna 53 and Cecilia 400. They are considered in this study because of their importance as sources for repertory dating from a much earlier time. They follow 17th-century notational traditions and, in fact, their 18th-century origin had not heretofore been recognized. The manuscript London 40080 also may date from a later time, but it has been included because its contents are attributed to Frescobaldi.

(4) *The arie and balli collections, c. 1600-1670.* The collections devoted exclusively or principally to anonymous settings of arie and balli form a somewhat distinct tradition. The repertory of arie found in these volumes includes common ones such as the Ruggiero and La Monaca as well as relatively unfamiliar ones. Sometimes text incipits are given for the arie; in several cases an entire text is underlaid. Whereas the aria settings in the general collections often include several partite, in these manuscripts each aria usually appears in a single setting. These settings tend to be simple and straightforward, and almost always are unique to the manuscript. Because of the lack of attributions and of concordances, the dating of the aria manuscripts is sometimes more difficult than is the case with the general collections.

Among the earliest of the aria and ballo collections—dating from before 1630—are Florence 115 and 138, and Barb. lat. 4288. A second group, from c. 1630-1670, includes Nuremberg 33748-V (possibly not Italian), UCLA 51/1, Bologna 360, Chigi 28, and Doria 250 B, although the last three include a few pieces in different genres.

No collections of this type have come down to us from the last part of the century, a situation probably reflecting the decline in popularity of the entire genre of aria and ballo settings.

IV

Format, Binding, Collation, and Paper

The typical keyboard manuscript is of oblong format, has the dimensions c. 16 × 22 cm, and is bound in cardboard covered with parchment. The tradition of the oblong keyboard book is characteristically Italian; many contemporary German and English manuscripts use upright format.[1] Among Italian manuscripts the latter format is encountered only in a few volumes that are atypical in other respects.[2]

The dimensions are also quite uniform. The majority of manuscripts are within a centimeter or so from the average given above. This suggests that their pages were obtained from sheets measuring approximately 32 × 44 cm, cut length-wise, an assumption confirmed by the chain lines, which run vertically, and the watermarks, which, when present, usually appear in the top center in halves.[3] A few manuscripts have an appreciably larger page size; all but one of these—Ravenna 545—date from the end of the 17th century or thereafter.

The simple, usually undecorated parchment covering is characteristic of the utilitarian appearance of the keyboard collections.[4] Elegant leather bindings with stamped designs, common in many contemporary collections of other types of music, are found only in two late keyboard manuscripts, Florence 2358 and London 40080.[5] One cannot always be certain that the present bindings date back to the 17th century; some manuscripts clearly have been rebound. A more critical issue is whether a manuscript was bound before the copyist entered his music, or whether it consisted of independent fascicles, which were bound together some time after the music had been copied. There is evidence that both practices existed. Many manuscripts contain large segments of pages left blank except for music ruling; there are even volumes in which only the first few pages contain any music (Barb. lat. 4181 and 4182). The manuscript Bologna 360 provides other evidence of having been a bound volume of paper with keyboard ruling (2 × 5/8) before any music was entered. The collection opens with keyboard music, but much of the contents consists of music for which this ruling is not appropriate—that is, music for instruments such as lute, violin, and guitar. To meet this problem the copyist sometimes crossed out lines, added lines to the staff, or skipped the lower, eight-line staves. On the other hand, Chigi 205-206 contains a number of loose fascicles that show no thread holes in the folds, and which hence were never bound.

An indication that a volume is a composite of originally independent fascicles is sometimes given by the collation. Ordinarily the collation is regular, i.e., the manuscript is made up of a series of gatherings with the same number of leaves. Gatherings of four leaves (quaternions) are most common, but some manuscripts are made up of gatherings of two, six, or even eight leaves. When a gathering does not follow such a regular pattern one suspects either that the original manuscript has been tampered with (e.g., pages have been torn out, or have been rebound in different order) or that the manuscript is of composite origin. The former case is often confirmed by the presence of discontinuities in the musical text, the latter by other discrepancies between the gatherings, such as differences in paper and in dimensions of the staff-rulings (see for example the discussions of Naples 48 and Chigi 25). An analysis of the collation of such composite manuscripts is obviously necessary in any study of their origins.

The manuscripts use a heavy paper that has generally withstood the ravages of time; the paper of the flyleaves tends to be of a lighter weight. Watermarks are not always easily discernible; those that were observed could not be identified in the limited literature on 17th-century Italian watermarks. Nevertheless, even though watermarks were not used in dating the manuscripts, they proved helpful in distinguishing different papers within a manuscript.

V

Notation

STAFF LAY-OUT

Italian keyboard music uses exclusively mensural notation.[1] Two notational practices existed side by side: four-staff score notation and two-staff keyboard notation. Score notation is not uncommon in the published keyboard collections, but among the manuscripts it is rarely found. There were some commercial advantages to printing keyboard music in score, in addition to the pedagogical advantage of making it easier for the performer to follow the voice leading. Score notation expanded the potential use of the edition for ensemble performance and counterpoint study and, perhaps even more importantly, it facilitated printing from movable type. Such advantages undoubtedly offset the additional expenses incurred by the publisher for the larger quantity of paper required when using this type of notation. For the copyist of a manuscript, most of these factors were of no concern; generally, he was a keyboard player who needed the copy for his own use (see Chapter XII), and he evidently preferred two-staff notation, which, in addition to saving paper, was less cumbersome to read.

Whether a manuscript score in fact contains keyboard music is not always easy to determine; we know that printed scores, which tend to provide more information about their purposes, served several different functions. Often they contain music originally written for ensemble and put into score for the purpose of keyboard performance and counterpoint study, e.g., the MADRIGALI DI CIPRIANO DI RORE (Sa. 1577c), "spartiti et accomodati per sonar d'ogni sorte d'Instrumento perfetto, & per Qualunque studioso di Contrapunti." Some scores were prepared for use in solo as well as in ensemble performance, for example, the score edition of Frescobaldi's ensemble canzoni prepared by his pupil Grassi (1628i): "ogni Sonatore potrà sonare queste Canzoni in compagnia, è solo." Presumably, in the case of ensemble performance separate parts would be copied, as is suggested in Johann Klemm's score publication *Partitura seu tabulatura italica* (Dresden, 1631). In other cases a mixed performance was envisioned, for example, in Banchieri's PARTITURA MODERNA (Sa. 1612a), "Da Concertarsi nell'Organo con dui Stromenti Acuto e Grave." A score would, furthermore, allow an organist to support an ensemble by doubling the parts, or, with the newer music, could be used as a basis for fashioning his own accompaniment.

In this study I shall not deal with a number of late 16th- and early 17th-century manuscript scorings of vocal and instrumental ensemble music,[2] but will discuss only scores that may contain original keyboard compositions.

Three-staff scores were not used in keyboard music; the variable number of staves (two to four) found in Castell'Arquato represents a practice that did not survive. Pedal parts, when needed, were simply added to the bottom staff, sometimes with the marking "pedale" (e.g., Chigi 25, f. 5′).

Two-staff notation, i.e., the notation still used today for manual keyboard music, has been part of the Italian notational tradition since the earliest preserved manuscript (Faenza 117) and printed (FROTTOLE, Sa. 1517) sources. It is sometimes referred to as Italian keyboard tablature to distinguish it from other notational traditions, i.e., English, French, Netherlandish, German and Spanish keyboard tablatures.[3] However, with the exception of the German letter-tablatures and the Spanish number-tablatures, these forms of keyboard notation do not differ in any basic and consistent way from one another, nor, for that matter, from the keyboard notation used today. The term "Italian keyboard tablature" is misleading since the notational practice is not truly a tablature, nor is its use restricted to Italy; it was used in virtually every country of Europe, including Germany and Spain. Furthermore, the only known 17th-century use of the term—in Klemm's *Partitura seu tabulatura italica*—is in connection with a four-staff score![4] Rather than referring to Italian, French, English and Netherlandish tablatures I propose that we speak simply of two-staff keyboard notation and two-staff keyboard score.

Within this system of notation some local conventions did exist; by far the most interesting and long-lived of these had to do with the number of lines in the staves. In the preserved French sources this number never exceeds five; but in Italian sources it varies between five and eight.

The differing French and Italian practices may represent a legacy of earlier divergences in the notation of vocal polyphony. By the 14th century the five-line staff had become standard in French manuscripts; on the other hand, in Italian polyphonic sources of the 14th and early 15th century a six-line staff was employed.[5] Faenza 117 shows that Italian keyboard notation also followed the latter practice. The later 15th-century Italian polyphonic manuscripts abandoned the indigenous system of notation and, like the rest of Europe, embraced the system developed by the French Ars Nova, including the five-line staff. It is possible, however, that the six-line staff continued in use for keyboard notation; sources are lacking for the later 15th century, but we find this staff again in 16th-century sources, for example, in Cavazzoni's RECERCHARI (Sa. 1523).[6]

There was also a practical advantage in the larger number of lines. In the notation of Italian keyboard music the notes to be played by the right and the left hand were consistently divided between the upper and lower staves.[7] The larger number of lines allowed each hand a wider range without requiring ledger lines or clef changes. In fact, in 16th-century sources, one or even two lines may be temporarily added to further extend the range, although later on this practice becomes rare (probably because it can be confusing for the reader). Instead, the lower staff acquired a permanent seventh and, in some sources, a permanent eighth line. For the upper staff five or six lines were apparently regarded as adequate, probably because right-hand parts tended to be confined to a narrower range than left-hand parts. As a result we find in 17th-century Italian keyboard music four different staff systems: 5/7, 6/7, 5/8, and 6/8.

It may be that the lack of standardization in Italian staff systems is only apparent; perhaps we are dealing with a number of regional traditions. One would expect that a performer accustomed to a particular system would have been rather disoriented when faced with more or fewer lines than he was used to,[8] and hence that there was some consistency within a given area and period. In Table 3 various systems have been tabulated. The number of surviving manuscripts from most regions is not large enough to establish firmly in every case the existence of local traditions. However, the Roman practice appears well-defined; it is followed in virtually all surviving 17th-century manuscripts from that region.

MENSURATION AND BARLINES

Another notational tradition that can be traced back to the early 15th-century sources Faenza 117 and Paris 6771 is the regularly-spaced barline. In duple (imperfect) meter the barlines are usually spaced according to the imperfect breve; this remains true in the 16th-century sources, regardless of whether the signature is C or ¢. Even in the earlier 17th-century sources this practice is often followed, though spacing according to the semibreve becomes more common, especially in canzoni, arie and balli. In later sources semibreve spacing predominates. Occasionally the barring appears less consistent; usually the irregularity can be interpreted as the omission of a barline within semibreve spacing, the addition of a barline in breve spacing, or the change from one type of spacing to another.

Duple meter is indicated by the mensuration signs C and ¢; sometimes no signature is given.[9] In the 16th- and 17th-century keyboard sources the choice between C and ¢ does not seem to depend on the predominant note values; we have noted already that there is no correlation between the two signatures and the barline spacing. In 16th-century sources there is a marked preference for ¢, but during the early 17th century (i.e., in the pre-Frescobaldian sources) one observes a gradual increase in favor of C; in manuscripts after c. 1640 the latter is used almost exclusively. The change can be seen most dramatically in a comparison of the compositions of Ercole Pasquini with those of Frescobaldi. The pieces in duple time attributed to Pasquini in the major sources (Trent,

Ravenna 545, Chigi 27) virtually all use the signature ₵; in Frescobaldi's keyboard music the signature C is used almost exclusively. This distinction cannot be accounted for by different copyists' habits, since it is found even in pieces attributed to the two composers in one manuscript and by one hand (i.e., in Ravenna 545 and Chigi 27).

In triple meter the barlines in the early sources are spaced according to the dotted (perfect) breve or semibreve. In the later sources the spacing is mostly according to the dotted semibreve, occasionally according to the dotted minim, though this latter spacing remains rare and is found chiefly in correnti. The most common signature is 3; one also finds 3/2 and 6/4, never 3/4. Again, no consistent correspondence between these signatures and the barline spacing or range of note values can be observed. The old-fashioned triple-meter signatures O and ₵ still favored much by Frescobaldi do not appear in the manuscripts (except in London 30491).[10] One does find, however, occasional examples of coloration and also of what might be called ''white coloration'', i.e. ♪ = ♩ etc., a practice more commonly found in French sources.

CLEFS

Characteristic of Italian keyboard notation is the use of the combined C-F clef on the lower staff; see Ex. 1a. This usage dates back to Faenza 117 (e.g., see f. 56). The position is not standardized; the F may be placed on the third, fourth or fifth line from the bottom. The combined clef may have had the purpose of orienting the player among the large number of lines. On the upper staff a C clef (generally on the lowest line) or a G clef was used, occasionally a combination of the two, see Ex. 1b.

Example 1a

Compound bass clef

Example 1b

Compound treble clef

Table 3
Staff Systems Used in 17th-Century Italian Keyboard Manuscripts

System	Region	Manuscripts
5/7	Ravenna	Ravenna 545
6/7	Rome	Chigi 24-29 Chigi 205-206[a] Doria 250 A Doria 250 B Barb. lat. 4181, 4182 Barb. lat. 4288 Vall. 121 Vat. mus. 569 Modena 491 (keyboard segment) Spello Berlin L. 215 (B. Pasquini autograph, dated 1697-1702)
5/8	Bologna	Bologna 258 Bologna 360 Bologna 53 (18th c.)
	Faenza	Bagnacavallo
	Florence	Florence 115 Florence 641 (late 16th c.)
	Unknown	Nuremberg 33748-V UCLA 51/1
6/8	Florence	Florence 138 Florence 2358
	Naples	Naples 48 Naples 73 London 30491 (in two-staff-score segment)
	Rome	Cecilia 400 (18th c.)[b]
	Venice	Venice 1727
	Unknown	Trent
5/5	Provenance problematical	London 40080

[a]Two fascicles in Chigi 205-206 use 6/8.

[b]Only in the segment containing early 17th-century Italian materials; the remainder uses 5/5.

ACCIDENTALS

The early printed and manuscript sources (e.g., Venice 1227; FROTTOLE, Sa. 1517; BALLI, Sa. 1551b) use dots to indicate accidentals (no distinction is made between raising and lowering), a practice also found in the 1530 French keyboard publications of Attaingnant. Sometimes dots are used side by side with conventional accidental signs. In two earlier 17th-century sources, Naples 48 and Florence 115, examples of this practice can still be found.[11]

The only key signature found in the 17th-century keyboard manuscripts is a single flat, except for the very late sources Florence 2358 and Bologna 53, which extend the range to two sharps.[12] All other accidentals are added in the text, even when the pieces are effectively in other keys. In this respect the practice in the Italian manuscripts is conservative compared with that found, say, in the French sources or, for that matter, in Italian music for other media.

VI

Instrumentation

A specific instrument is rarely mentioned in the manuscripts. The title "Toccata per organo" is found in Chigi 25 (f. 5', 13, 31, 37), in Vat. mus. 569 (p. 1), and in Doria 250 A (f. 1', 31). Trent contains pieces with a similar title, "Entrate d'organo" (f. 13, 16). Such designations with individual pieces might be taken to imply that the other compositions in the collection were not intended exclusively for organ. The inscriptions found on the covers and flyleaves of some of the late sources include specifications such as "per cembalo" and "per organo," presumably applicable to the entire contents (see the entries of London 40080, Bologna 53, Naples 73, Vat. mus. 569, Vall. 121, and Venice 1299 in Part Two). Few, if any, of these inscriptions appear to date from the 17th century.

Specifications of instruments are more common in the published collections; in fact, the only collections likely to omit them are publications in four-staff score, such as Frescobaldi's FANTASIE (1608) and Cifra's RICERCARE (Sa. 1619b, d). Some publications give a general designation, such as "Stromenti da tasti"; others are more specific (see Table 4). As might be expected, editions that only mention organ often specialize in liturgical music, and dance collections frequently name only stringed keyboard instruments, but for most genres the publications do not provide consistent evidence to associate them primarily with either organ or harpsichord. For example, the notion that the abstract genres such as the ricercare and the toccata were primarily conceived for organ is contradicted by the exclusive specification "per cembalo" in Valente, RECERCATE (Sa. 1576), and in the 1615 edition of Frescobaldi, TOCCATE I.

When considering the matter of instrumentation one must distinguish a performance practice issue and a stylistic issue. It is one matter to assert that performers played the same music indiscriminately on any keyboard instrument, and quite another to assert that a composer never had a specific instrument in mind when writing a particular work. Since most keyboard players were organists as well as harpsichordists (specialization did not become common until the advent of the pianoforte), it appears likely that they performed the same composition on either instrument, provided the work was suitable to the occasion. Nevertheless, composers often wrote for a specific instrument, as witnessed by such indications as "Toccata per l'organo," "per cembalo cromatico," "per l'arpa," and one would expect the character of the designated instrument to be reflected in the style of the composition. It is my belief that styles more appropriate to one or another instrument can be recognized already in many 16th-century compositions, even if such works were frequently played on different types of instruments.

Few manuscript collections appear to have been compiled exclusively for one kind of instrument. The aria and ballo collections were probably intended primarily for stringed keyboard instruments, but most of the other manuscripts include liturgical pieces side by side with dances and settings of secular songs, suggesting that the owners performed from them on organ as well as on harpsichord.

SONG SETTINGS WITH TEXT UNDERLAY

A special problem in terms of intended mode of performance is posed by the song settings with complete text underlay found in the manuscripts Florence 138, Bologna 360, and Barb. lat. 4288.[1] Except for the texting, these compositions have the appearance of keyboard music; they may have a full-voiced texture, and they are notated on staves of more than five lines. Music for a single voice and basso continuo was also notated on a two-staff score, but such scores use only five-line staves and have a single melodic line on each staff, often with figures above the bass line.

Were the texted keyboard settings intended for performance by voice and keyboard, or are they keyboard settings of songs, with the text inserted for some other reason? The answer may depend on the individual setting. For example, Barb. lat. 4288, f. 2′ presents a line of florid monody in the upper staff (including little echoes marked "forte" and "piano") accompanied by chords in the lower staff. Vocal performance appears likely for this setting. However, the next piece in the same collection, f. 6′, also texted, has in the treble staff two voices moving in parallel thirds; here one would have to assume performance either by two voices or by one voice with the keyboard playing the second part. The texted settings in Florence 138 contain chords with varying textures in both hands and characteristically instrumental ornaments in the upper voice, suggesting that for these settings performance on keyboard was the primary intention.

Table 4
Some Specifications of Instruments in 17th-Century Italian Keyboard Publications

I. **General Designations**

"ogni sorte di Stromenti da Tasti," Andrea Gabrieli, RICERCARI (Sa. 1595b)
"organi, et istromenti da penna," Diruta, TRANSILVANO (Sa. 1593b)
"qualsivoglia stromento, ma più proportionemente ne gli Organi, e ne i Cembali," Trabaci, RICERCATE I (Sa. 1603c)
"cimbalo et organo," Frescobaldi, TOCCATE II (1627)

II. **Organ**

"organi," FROTTOLE (Sa. 1517), cut shows picture of harpsichord
"organo," Merulo, MESSE (Sa. 1568a)
"organo," Merulo, TOCCATE (Sa. 1604a)

III. **Stringed Keyboard Instruments**

"arpichordi, Clavicembali, Spinette et Manichordi," BALLI (Sa. 1551b)
"arpicordo," Facoli, BALLI (Sa. 1588c)
"cimbalo," Valente, RECERCATE (Sa. 1576)
"cimbalo," Frescobaldi, TOCCATE I (1615)
"clavicordo," in connection with tuning instructions, Cima, RICERCARI (Sa. 1606a)
"arpa," in Trabaci, RICERCATE II (Sa. 1615c)
"cembalo cromatico," in Trabaci, RICERCATE II (Sa. 1615c)
"spinettina sola," in Frescobaldi, CANZONI (1628i)
"Clavecembali, Arpa, Violini & altri Stromenti," Pistocchi, CAPPRICCI PUERILI (Sa. 1667c)

VII
The Repertory

One of the most fascinating and perhaps most "Baroque" aspects of keyboard music of the period is the broad diversity of genres. In the previous era most compositions that could not borrow their titles from vocal or dance models were called simply "Ricercare." The 17th-century composer, however, could choose among a wealth of titles: Toccata, Intrata, Ricercare, Canzone, Fantasia, Capriccio, etc.—each presumably reflecting a different genre of composition. This wide choice was to disappear again during the course of the following century, when most keyboard compositions came to be called "Sonata."

The importance attached to genre classification in 17th-century keyboard music is evident from the printed collections; the contents of these usually are organized according to genre, and the titles of the publications often consist merely of an enumeration of these genres. Manuscript copies from the prints almost always included the title of the composition, even when the name of the composer has been omitted, suggesting that a knowledge of the genre of a composition was considered more important than a knowledge of the author.

Whereas anonymous compositions are common in the manuscripts, untitled compositions are comparatively rare. An examination of the genres, therefore, forms an attractive approach to the study of the manuscript repertory. Such an approach will not, however, be fruitful if it is based on too rigid a definition or description of the individual genres, or if the genres are seen principally as forerunners of 18th-century forms such as the fugue and the sonata with undue emphasis on the features shared with those forms. The point is not that it is impossible to formulate defining characteristics for the 17th-century genres, but rather that one must allow such formulations to be sufficiently flexible. Clearly, if a composer has entitled a piece with a particular genre designation he must have had a definite conception of this genre, and, furthermore, he must have assumed that the musical community for whom the composition was intended shared his conception to a certain extent. If such a conception did not exist the designation would have served little purpose.

Even today most people familiar with the music of the period have no difficulty distinguishing a toccata from a canzone or a ricercare. It is my contention that a composition is recognized as being in a specific genre by the presence of a number of features that form a complex of defining characteristics.

These characteristics may include a fund of stereotyped opening formulas, rhythmic patterns, ornamental figures, a predilection for a certain type of voice leading and dissonance treatment, and options on how the sections of the composition are to be differentiated and articulated. In most cases such features unambiguously define the genre of a composition, even when not all are present. Needless to say, some of these characteristics vary from period to period, from region to region, or even within the works of a single composer.

A fixed structural scheme, so important if not crucial for the definition of later instrumental forms, does not appear to form part of the conception of genre during this period (with the exception of the "strophic" variation forms); for this reason the term "form" when used with reference to these genres is misleading. In fact the structural scheme may form as much a part of the individuality of a composition as the choice of motivic material and its treatment. As a result of some of the other defining characteristics, similar types of structures do occasionally arise for certain genres (see, for example, the discussion of the canzone below), although even these structures are much more flexible than the harmonically and thematically defined forms of the 18th century.

One can divide the genres into five categories depending on their use of pre-existing compositional materials:

(1) *The abstract genres.* These genres, the most important of which are the toccata, the ricercare, and the canzone, do not depend for their structure on pre-existing materials, although they may quote and develop pre-existing "soggetti" (e.g., formulas such as la, sol, fa, re, mi).[1] The earliest canzoni were, of course, adaptations of vocal chansons—examples can still be found in Naples 48—but for the 17th-century canzoni this was generally no longer the case.

(2) *Intabulations of polyphonic vocal compositions.* Such intabulations are comparatively rare in 17th-century Italian sources; almost all of the surviving examples are based on a small group of famous 16th-century chansons and madrigals.

(3) *Settings of liturgical plain-chant melodies.* The melody may be set as a cantus firmus, or, more often, successive portions may be freely paraphrased. In either case the structure of the composition is to a certain extent determined by the given melody.

(4) *Settings of traditional arie, balli and tenori.* These settings comprise a large segment of the manuscript repertory and therefore will be treated at some length, the more so since the exact nature of some of the models has in the past been the subject of much discussion. The arie and balli may appear in single settings or may be subject to a series of variations (partite).

(5) *Independent dance compositions.* In addition to the dances that are settings of popular ballo-models, the manuscripts contain a number of dances for which no such models have been found. The number of different dance-genres is surprisingly small, the corrente being by far the most common.

In surveying the principal genres encountered in the manuscript repertory my comments will be brief. It is beyond the scope of this study to review the complex historical development of each genre; I shall merely provide some brief comments on their appearance in the manuscript repertory.

THE ABSTRACT GENRES

Table 5 summarizes the appearance of these genres in the principal sources.[2] Untitled compositions have not been included, even when the character of these compositions clearly corresponds to one of the genres.

Toccata. In defining the toccata Praetorius notes three important aspects: it is improvised, it serves as an introduction—for example, to a fugue or motet—and it is performed on organ or harpsichord (*Syntagma* III, 25). That in Italy the toccata was likewise regarded primarily as a keyboard genre—in fact, as perhaps the most characteristic keyboard genre—is evident: it is the only one among the genres to be found almost exclusively in keyboard sources. Whether the toccate preserved in the sources of the period are in fact written-down improvisations (or perhaps compositions which allow the performer to give the illusion that he is improvising[3]) is of course impossible to determine, since we do not know what improvisations of the time sounded like.[4] The idea of the toccata as prelude apparently remained part of the conception of the genre; this is evident from its position as opening piece in organ Masses (e.g., in Naples 73, f. 79), in toccata-ricercare and toccata-canzone pairs and in proto-suites (see pp. 46-47). The placement of toccate at the beginning of printed and manuscript collections is also suggestive of this role (see Chapter VIII).

One feature having possible bearing on the issue of improvisation is the similarity of many early toccate to keyboard intabulations of madrigals and of other vocal compositions. An examination of intabulations, say, by Andrea Gabrieli or by Claudio Merulo (see, for example the former's "Canzon Francese deta Le prens en gre" in his CANZONI VI, Sa. 1605g, and the latter's "La Zambeccara" in his CANZONI I, Sa. 1592c) reveals many resemblances to these composers' toccate. Similarly, the "collective" intabulation of Ferrabosco's "Io mi son giovinetta" by Montella, Mayone, and Stella (published in Mayone's CAPRICCI II, Sa. 1609f) shows many resemblances to the toccate of Mayone and of other Neapolitan composers. Frescobaldi was evidently conscious of a close relation between the two genres: in his TOCCATE II he includes only eleven toccate instead of the more usual set of twelve (as found, for instance, in his TOCCATE I); in the place of the twelfth toccata he offers an intabulation of Arcadelt's madrigal "Ancidetemi pur."[5] This intabulation is almost indistinguishable from the toccate and includes many of the devices also found in those compositions. Among these devices are brief points of imitation—usually in stretto. Such passages do not correspond to imitative sections in the madrigal but are merely a form of ornamentation of the polyphonic background texture. It seems quite conceivable that the frequent resemblances between toccate and intabulations in general might result, in part at least, from the composers' drawing upon a common fund of improvisational techniques and strategies at the surface level.

The defining characteristics of the toccata include a repertory of opening formulas. A common opening consists of a tone sustained in the bass over which the upper voices either hold a chord or move slowly (usually in minims) through interlocking suspensions; this texture may be overlaid by a series of ornamental figures ("colorature"), which often follow each other in quasi-imitation. Some form of imitation is also frequently present within the slower-moving background texture. The characteristic toccata colorature in use at the beginning of the century (for example, in the anonymous toccate in Trent) appear to have been largely derived from the toccate of Andrea Gabrieli. An entirely new vocabulary of colorature was introduced by Frescobaldi; these latter figures remained part of the toccata manner during most of the century and are found in practically all the manuscript toccate from after c. 1630.

Similarly, one can recognize a repertory of formulas commonly used towards the close of a composition (or of a section); characteristic for Frescobaldi and later composers are scale figures in contrary motion and sixteenth-note passages accompanied in another voice by extended (written-out) trills. In addition to opening and closing formulas, there are devices that may be introduced anywhere during the course of a composition—for example, the development of a point of imitation. These points of imitation are usually quite different from those found in genres such as the ricercare and the canzone: the initial entries are not restricted to the final and co-final of the mode, and may follow each other in close stretti, while the subjects themselves tend not to conform to the stereotyped patterns found in the other genres—they are sometimes in 12/8 meter or include colorature. Evidently, such points of imitation also constitute part of the toccata vocabulary.[6]

A prescribed structure, on the other hand, does not figure among the defining characteristics of the toccata. The longer toccate generally divide into sections, but this is also true of extended compositions in other genres. The number of sections, their length, the amount of contrast between one section and the next, and the smoothness or abruptness of the transition are all factors subject to much variation; indeed, they contribute to the individuality of each toccata.

Two trends can be observed in the toccate appearing in the manuscripts from the second half of the century (e.g., in Vat. mus. 569 and in Bologna 53): the individual sections become longer and fewer in number, and the rhythmic motion tends to become more regular and uniform (often consisting of continuous sixteenth-note passages).

A special type of toccata is the "Toccata per l'elevatione." Compositions designated for this purpose usually sustain during their entire length a texture found in other toccate only at the opening or intermittently: a full-voiced setting

Table 5

The Abstract Genres in The Manuscript Sources

Manuscripts	Toccata	Intrata	Preludio	Ricercare	Canzone	Capriccio	Fantasia	Sonata
Spello	2	—	—	3	1	1	—	—
Trent	5	7	—	5	6	—	—	—
Naples 48	6	7	—	1	8	—	—	—
London 30491	2	—	—	—	8	2	—	—
Ravenna 545	5	—	—	7	12	4	—	—
Chigi 24	3	—	—	4	3	—	—	—
Chigi 25	8	—	—	2	3	2	—	—
Chigi 27	6	—	—	—	1	—	—	—
Chigi 29	5	—	—	3	3	—	—	—
Chigi 205–206	7	—	—	1	2	1	1	—
Doria 250 A	3	—	—	1	2	—	—	—
Doria 250 B	2	—	—	—	—	1	—	—
Vall. 121	3	—	—	—	—	—	1	—
Vat. mus. 569	3	—	—	—	1	1	—	—
Bologna 360	2	—	—	—	—	—	—	—
Naples 73	7	—	4	4	17	—	1	—
Florence 2358	2	—	8	—	—	—	—	—
Bologna 53	11	—	—	2	—	—	—	19
London 40080	1	—	—	—	11	—	—	—

moving primarily in half-notes, with many chromatic passing tones and dissonant suspensions. The calm, contemplative mood of these toccate presumably reflects the special liturgical function that they fulfill. Examples are found in Chigi 25 (f. 37), Chigi 29 (f. 11), Ravenna 545 (f. 21'), and in Doria 250 A (f. 41). Similar in character are the "Durezze" (examples in Naples 73: ff. 119, 121, 134, 137') and the "Stravaganze" (examples in London 30491: ff. 19, 33).

Two other genres related to the toccata are found in the manuscript sources: the *entrata* or *intrada*, and the *preludio*. The entrata appears in two early manuscripts: Trent and Naples 48; the examples in Trent are brief preludes (each is followed by a ricercare in the same key) while those in Naples 48 are of a more varied character (see p. 108). The preludio appears in two late sources, Bologna 53 and Florence 2358, and serves to introduce a sonata (in Bologna 53) or a proto-suite (in Florence 2358).

Ricercare. The manner of the 17th-century ricercare is that of the stile antico. In his 1615 publication, RECERCARI, Frescobaldi took the final step towards purification of the genre and eliminated the sixteenth-note passaggi and contrasting sections in triple meter that are still found in the ricercari of the Gabrielis and Trabaci. Nevertheless, within the framework of the stile antico the genre allows a great variety of forms and techniques: variety in the number of subjects, in the manner in which these are introduced, in the number and length of the sections, and in the employment of various traditional contrapuntal devices such as diminution, augmentation, inversion, and ostinato cantus firmi.

In Trent and in Naples 48 one still encounters examples of the earlier type of ricercare with sixteenth-note passaggi, but in all the later manuscripts (and printed editions) the pure version of the genre as defined by Frescobaldi's works is adhered to. The manuscript ricercari, however, are almost without exception much more limited in conception than those of Frescobaldi. They tend to be brief and not to divide into sections, and almost all are monothematic.

The melodic language of the ricercari remains mostly within the bounds of the traditional church modes; usually the mode is clearly defined by the soggetti. Printed sets of ricercari, for instance those by A. Gabrieli (Sa. 1595b), Trabaci (Sa. 1603c), and Frescobaldi (1615), usually contain an example in every mode, but in the manuscripts ricercari in the first and second mode far outnumber those in all other modes. The soggetti of ricercari in a given mode often fall into certain stock patterns (see Ex. 2).

Canzoni. Most 17th-century keyboard canzoni can be immediately recognized as such from their openings. The canzone character usually is apparent from the initial subject, which often falls into one of a series of traditional types.[7] The rhythmic pattern associated with the canzone (♩ ♫ ♩) frequently is present.

Generally the canzone consists of a series of clearly articulated sections with alternating duple and triple meter. Since the opening and closing sections are mostly in duple meter, the total number of sections tends to be odd; Frescobaldi's canzoni usually have at least five sections, the manuscript canzoni (including those attributed to Ercole Pasquini) rarely more than three. These sections are brief and rarely contain much contrapuntal development beyond their exposition; often they end in toccata-like flourishes. The first sections are almost always monothematic, with the voices entering successively. The subsequent sections may be polythematic and often introduce several voices simultaneously. The subjects of the various sections are not infrequently motivically related.

In the canzone, perhaps more than in any other genre, one begins to recognize some common types of structure, i.e., forms consisting of three or five sections. As we have seen, however, such forms are the consequence of other defining characteristics (the alternation of sections with duple and triple meter, opening and closing with the former), and hence they cannot really be regarded as prescriptive principles of the genre.

Within the canzone repertory some regional practices can be recognized. The subjects in the Roman and Neapolitan canzoni are generally brief and succinct, but the later Northern composers such as Tarquinio Merula favored more extended and internally repetitive subjects, employing either series of repeated notes or sequences. Several examples of such subjects can be found in Ravenna 545 (see Ex. 3a). The *Sonate* in Bologna 53, which in many ways still follow the canzone tradition (e.g., imitative expositions, sections in contrasting meter) also tend to use this type of subject (see Ex. 3b).

In the Neapolitan sources one finds some canzoni which follow a rather different tradition. These compositions open with a full-voiced chordal section in triple meter (see Ex. 4); the subsequent sections may continue in triple meter or may switch to duple meter. London 30491 contains three canzoni of this type (f. 12, by Ippolito; f. 14, by Stella; f. 27, by Rinaldo) along with canzoni of the more conventional type.[8] The Canzona Quinta in Frescobaldi's TOCCATE II also appears to fall within this tradition, as do some of his ensemble canzoni. No examples of this type of canzone are found in any of the later manuscript sources.

Capriccio. The term capriccio was used frequently by Frescobaldi and by the Neapolitan composers (de Macque, Mayone, Trabaci, and Strozzi); its appearance elsewhere in the Italian sources is rare. The term is usually applied to a sectional composition somewhat similar to a canzone but much more extended and less standardized, both in their choice of subjects and in their overall structures. A capriccio is almost always based on a single soggetto—usually a well-known motif—and frequently has a title reading "capriccio sopra . . ."[9]

Fantasia. The term fantasia also appears only sporadically in Italian keyboard music, although it was in common use in most other European countries. The only printed collection of keyboard fantasie was Frescobaldi's publication of 1608; since it was published shortly after Frescobaldi's sojourn in Belgium the title may have been inspired by foreign models, such as those by Sweelinck and by John Bull.

Only three fantasie appear in the 17th-century keyboard manuscripts: Chigi

Example 2

Frescobaldi
RECERCARI (1615), p. 7
Recercar Secondo (mm. 1-2)

Chigi 24, f. 15
Recercare (mm. 1-2)

Chigi 29, f. 13
Recercare (mm. 1-2)

Example 3a

Ravenna 545, f. 42
Canzon di
Cesare Argentino (mm. 1-3)

Ravenna 545, f. 49'
Canzon (mm. 1-3)

Ravenna 545, f. 71
Canzon di
Tarquinio Merula (mm. 1-3)

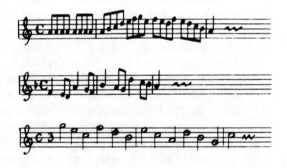

Example 3b

Bologna 53, f. 58
Sonata p$^{\underline{a}}$, p$^{\underline{o}}$ Tuono
Pollaroli (mm. 1-2)

Bologna 53, f. 60′
Sonata 2$^{\underline{a}}$, 2$^{\underline{o}}$ Tuono
Pollaroli (mm. 1-2)

Example 4

London 30491, F. 11
Canzon d'Ippolito
(mm. 1-3)

London 30491, f. 14
Canzon di Stella
(mm. 1-2)

London 30491, f. 27′
Canzon di Rinaldo
(mm. 1-3)

205-206, f. 32, Naples 73, f. 9′, and Vall. 121, f. 17′. The first two are brief ricercare-type compositions; the *Fantasia* in Vall. 121 is also imitative, but it is more extended, consisting of three sections with contrasting meter.

INTABULATIONS OF POLYPHONIC VOCAL COMPOSITIONS

Intabulations, which in the 16th century formed an important part of the repertory, rarely appear in Italian sources after c. 1610. Virtually the only examples found in the printed collections are settings of Arcadelt's "Ancidetemi pur" (Mayone, Sa. 1603b; Trabaci, Sa. 1615c; Frescobaldi, TOCCATE II, 1627; Strozzi, Sa. 1687h). The few examples in the manuscript sources also appear to date from the beginning of the century: settings of Lasso's "Susanne" (Trent, London 30491), de Rore's "Anchor, che col partire" (Trent), and of some French chansons (Naples 48). Trent also includes intabulations of sections from Palestrina's *Missa O magnum mysterium*. Most of these settings are for all practical purposes new compositions which use the model merely to provide a structural framework.[10] Simple keyboard settings of 16th- and 17th-century vocal polyphony, still found in large numbers in German sources, no longer appear in the 17th-century Italian collections. Possibly there was no need for these since much polyphony had become available in score—for example, madrigals by de Rore (Sa. 1577c) and by Gesualdo (*Partitura . . .*, Genoa: 1613); another explanation may be that Italian keyboard players no longer had any interest in such arrangements.

SETTINGS OF LITURGICAL PLAIN-CHANT MELODIES AND OTHER LITURGICAL COMPOSITIONS[11]

A large number of Italian publications contain organ Masses, hymn and Magnificat versets and other compositions intended for liturgical usage (see Bonta, *Sonata da chiesa*). Surprisingly, not many works of this type are found in the manuscripts. The most extensive collection appears in Naples 73, including pieces for virtually every movement of the Mass (these include, though not all within the same Mass: Introito, Kyrie, Gloria, per l'Epistola, Alleluia, per l'Offertorio, Sanctus, per l'Elevatione, Agnus Dei, Benedicamus Domino); less comprehensive sets of pieces are found in Spello and Trent. The Trent manuscript also contains a series of Magnificat verses, possibly by Ercole Pasquini.[12] Chigi 24 contains a *Kyrie delli Apostoli* and versetti on *Ave Maris stella* and *Iste confessor*; Chigi 27 contains a brief organ Mass (de Doppio) consisting of an Introito, a Kyrie, a Gloria and a Credo, and Chigi 205-206 contains a series of hymn settings attributed to Frescobaldi as well as some anonymous Kyrie and Gloria settings. Furthermore, several manuscripts contain brief pieces with titles such as "Verso del primo tono," or just "Primo tono."

Many of the Mass and hymn versets are based on plain-chant melodies. The chants usually are freely paraphrased; strict old-fashioned cantus-firmus settings rarely appear in the manuscripts.

SETTINGS OF TRADITIONAL ARIE, BALLI, AND TENORI

A large segment of the manuscript repertory consists of pieces that I will refer to, for want of a better name, as aria, ballo and tenore settings.[13] These pieces are based on a collection of models that provide, first and foremost, some sort of structural framework. What else they provide varies with the model; with some it has in fact been the subject of considerable controversy. I will soon comment further on this problem.

The terms aria, ballo and tenore do not necessarily imply distinct genres; in fact, in some cases these terms are used interchangeably. One of the earliest surviving collections of these settings is found in Ortiz, *Tratado* (Rome, 1553). Ortiz states that in Italy the models are commonly called "tenores" (*Tratado*, f. 85), and in his table of contents (f. 70) he refers to the settings as "Recercada sobre tenores Italianos." He does not name the individual models, but several familiar ones can be identified (for instance, the Passamezzo antico, la Gamba, and the Ruggiero).

A manuscript dated 1613, Bologna Q 34 (see discussion on p. 99), is of special interest in that it includes a collection of these models in more or less skeletal, unornamented form. Some appear as unfigured basses and some in soprano/bass settings; several are given in both versions. In the Tavola they are listed as "Arie alla Romana" but in the text they are called "Balletti alla Romana." Many of the well-known arie—such as the Romanesca, the Ruggiero, the Monaca, the Aria di Firenze, the Follia, and the Pavaniglia—appear, along with less familiar ones.

A most comprehensive collection of arie is included in Matteo Coferati, *Corona di Sacre Canzoni o Laude Spirituali*, published in 1675, 1689, and 1710 in three successively enlarged editions.[14] In this collection the arie are given devotional texts, but for the benefit of those unable to read music the traditional name of the aria is provided. For many arie several alternative titles are given, e.g., "Aria dell'Ortolano, o Ruggieri, ovvero Donne, mi chiamano il maturo"; "Ballo, ovvero arie [N.B.!] di Mantova, o Amor fals'ingrato." The collection is of great value for identifying some of the arie and for providing unadorned versions of the melodies. The 1710 edition includes an "Indice dell'arie antiche, e moderne, descritte sotto i nomi noti al volgo." The index is reprinted in Alaleona, *Laudi*, 8-10; it includes 154 entries among which can be found practically all the arie of the 17th-century repertory.

The musical sources are only partially consistent as to which of the three terms—aria, ballo, or tenore—is associated with a particular model. "Tenor di Napoli" and "Ballo di Mantova" (or just "Ballo") appear consistently; on the other hand, Frescobaldi, in TOCCATE I, uses "Partite sopra L'aria della

Romanesca," but Mayone, in CAPRICCI II (Sa. 1609f) calls his set on the same model "Partite sopra il Tenore antico, ò Romanesca." Similarly one finds "Aria di Fiorenza" and "Ballo del Granduca" used interchangeably.

Evidently no clear distinction existed between models that were primarily songs, those that were primarily dances, and those that were primarily "tenori" (i.e., ostinato basses). Of course some may have had their origin as dance songs (we know this to have been the case with la Fiorenza—see Kirkendale, *Fiorenza*); others may have been songs turned into instrumental dances or vice versa.

The aria and ballo settings appear to have been conceived as a distinct genre; they often are grouped together in the sources and they form the sole content of some collections. Nevertheless, among them are rather diverse types of compositions. Some are nothing but keyboard settings of popular songs, with the unadorned melody played by the right hand, and a simple chordal accompaniment provided by the left. Others are in the form of variations on a somewhat loosely defined harmonic scheme (e.g., the passamezzi), an ostinato bass pattern (e.g., the ciaccona), or an even less firmly prescribed framework (e.g., the passacaglia). Indeed the passacaglia might be thought of as belonging only marginally to this genre; it is interesting to note, however, that Frescobaldi in his ARIE MUSICALI (1630) uses the designation "Aria di Passacaglie" along with "Aria di Ruggeri" and "Aria di Romanesca."

There has been much discussion about the exact nature of some of these models—whether they are melodies, basses, or harmonic progressions. I believe that these disagreements stem from a faulty premise—that a composer constructs one of these settings by deliberately writing a variation on a given harmonic or melodic scheme. It seems more likely that he had a general conception of the particular aria abstracted from all the settings with which he was familiar. This conception may indeed include a melodic-harmonic scheme (more or less loosely defined, depending on the particular aria as well as on the period and region in which he was working), but also other features, such as the type of setting, opening formulas, phrasing schemes, rhythmic patterns, stereotyped figurations, tempo, key, and other characteristic elements. This notion of the aria setting is of course analogous to that presented above for "genre" in general, although the conception is much more specifically defined and extends to the structural scheme.

Modern commentators have often pointed to similarities among several of the well-known arie, for example, the Romanesca and the Passamezzo antico.[15] The impression of similarity is the result of concentrating almost exclusively on the harmonic progressions when viewing these arie. These progressions, sharing the harmonic idiom of the period, are indeed very similar. But upon listening to some Passamezzo and Romanesca settings it becomes readily apparent that the two are altogether different types of composition. In the passamezzi—whether antico or moderno—a strong binary rhythm is always maintained, usually by a short-short-long metrical pattern. The rhythmic and phrase structure reflects this binary character on all levels. The passage work tends to be similarly straightforward; for the most part it consists of scale segments traversed in equal note values. The Romanesca, on the other hand, thrives on ambiguity and asymmetry. The 17th-century examples are usually noted in duple meter, but different metrical groupings suggest themselves during parts of these compositions. The diminutions generally are irregular in rhythm as well as in contour, and the texture tends to be thick and rich in suspensions. It is not likely that these two types of compositions will easily be confused, even if only a few measures are heard.[16] Furthermore, it follows that, since an aria is not determined merely by its bass or harmonic progression, these do not offer sufficient criteria for classifying an otherwise unidentified composition as a setting of a specific aria if none of the other characteristics commonly associated with this aria are present.[17]

Table 6 lists the number of settings of the more common arie in the manuscripts (a set of variations has been counted as a single setting).[18] In the two bottom rows the total number of settings in the manuscripts and the total number of settings in the 17th-century printed keyboard collections are given. It is clear that these settings are quantitatively much more significant for the manuscript repertory, and, furthermore, that a greater variety of models is used.

The origin of most of the common arie can be traced to the 16th century, although a few models (the passacaglia, the ciaccona, and the Ballo di Mantua) did not appear on the scene until later in the 17th century. The popularity of the older types shows no marked chronological trends, except perhaps for the passamezzi, which seem to have lost some of the favor they enjoyed during the preceding period. In addition to these common types, there are a number of arie that appear only once or twice in the manuscripts; most of these can, however, also be found in other repertories, such as in the music for ensemble and for lute.

It is not likely that we will be able to determine the exact circumstances that gave birth to most of these arie, but it should be possible to establish where and when they begin appearing in musical (or literary) sources. Of course, for such an undertaking we cannot confine ourselves to the keyboard repertory but must also examine settings for instrumental ensemble and for voice, as well as the large number of versions for lute, guitar, and other plucked instruments. Perhaps of even greater interest than the first appearances of these arie are the transformations to which they are gradually subjected as they make their way through the musical world. Such further study of the aria settings will no doubt add much insight into musical practices during the period; it may also provide helpful information for dating some of the anonymous sources.

INDEPENDENT DANCE COMPOSITIONS

Table 7 tabulates the dance-types found in the manuscripts; dances based on a traditional "ballo" model (such as the Corrente lavignonne and the Ballo del

Table 6
Settings of Traditional Arie and Balli in The Manuscript Sources

	Fiorenza	Romanesca	Ruggiero	Spagnoletta	Passacaglia	Monaca	Ciaccona	Passamezzo antico	Passamezzo moderno	Pavaniglia	Follia	Abate, Napoli	Gagliarda	Ballo di Mantova	Bergamasca	Barriera	O Clorida
Trent	—	—	—	—	—	—	—	1	—	—	—	1	—	—	—	—	—
Naples 48	—	—	—	—	—	—	—	—	—	—	—	1	—	—	—	—	—
London 30491	—	1	1	—	—	—	—	—	—	—	—	—	—	—	—	—	—
Florence 106 b	—	1	—	—	—	—	—	—	—	—	—	—	—	—	—	—	—
Florence 115	—	1	—	1	—	1	—	—	—	1	—	—	—	—	—	—	—
Florence 138	1	1	—	1	—	1	—	1	1	—	—	—	—	—	—	—	—
Barb. lat. 4288	—	1	—	1	—	—	—	—	—	—	—	1	—	—	—	—	1
Ravenna 545	1	2	—	—	—	1	1	1	—	1	—	—	—	—	1	—	—
Chigi 24	1	—	1	—	—	—	—	—	—	—	—	—	—	—	—	—	—
Chigi 25	1	—	—	—	—	—	—	—	—	—	—	—	—	—	—	—	—
Chigi 26	1	—	—	—	3	—	1	—	—	—	—	—	—	—	—	—	—
Chigi 28	—	—	—	—	12	—	3	—	—	—	—	—	—	1	—	1	1
Chigi 205-206	3	2	4	1	1	—	—	—	—	2	—	—	—	—	—	—	—
Doria 250 A	—	—	—	—	1	—	—	—	—	—	—	1	—	—	—	—	—
Doria 250 B	2	3	2	2	1	2	—	—	—	1	1	2	2	—	—	1	—
Vall. 121	2	1	—	1	1	1	—	—	—	—	—	—	2	1	—	—	—
Vat. mus. 569	1	—	—	1	—	—	—	—	—	—	—	—	1	1	—	—	1
Nuremberg 33748-V	1	—	1	1	—	—	—	—	—	—	—	—	—	2	—	—	—
UCLA 51/1	1	—	2	1	—	—	—	—	1	—	—	—	—	—	1	—	—
Bologna 360	2	1	2	2	2	1	—	—	1	1	1	—	2	—	—	1	—
Venice 1299	2	—	—	3	—	—	1	—	—	—	1	—	—	1	—	—	—
Venice 1727	—	—	—	—	—	—	—	—	—	—	—	—	—	1	—	—	—
Total in Mss.	19	14	12	15	21	7	6	3	3	6	3	6	8	5	2	3	3
Total in Prints	0	3	5	2	8	2	4	2	1	0	2	0	0	1	1	0	0

Note: A set of successively appearing variations was counted as a single setting. Settings duplicated in the printed collections were not included in the tabulation of the manuscript entries; furthermore, only keyboard settings were counted.

Table 7
Dances in The Manuscript Sources

Manuscripts	Corrente	Ballo, Balletto	Gagliarda	Allemano, Allemanda	Sarabanda	Brando, Branle
Naples 48	3	—	—	—	—	—
London 30491	—	—	5	—	—	—
Florence 115	—	1	1	1	—	—
Ravenna 545	5	—	3	—	—	—
Barb. lat. 4288	2	3	—	—	—	—
Chigi 24	4	—	—	—	—	—
Chigi 26	2	1	2	—	—	—
Chigi 27	6	—	1	—	—	—
Chigi 28	2	3	2	—	—	—
Chigi 29	1	—	—	—	—	—
Chigi 205-206	3	3	—	—	—	1
Doria 250 B	4	—	—	—	—	—
Vall. 121	2	3	—	—	—	—
Vat. mus. 569	6	—	1	—	1	—
Nuremberg 33748-V	4	—	2	—	—	1
UCLA 51/1	6	—	—	—	—	—
Bologna 360	2	—	—	—	—	—
Naples 73	2	—	—	—	—	—
Florence 2358	—	—	—	1	—	—
Venice 1299*	15	3	10	—	—	—

*Not including copies from Frescobaldi prints.

Granduca) are not included in this tabulation. Of course, one can determine that a dance is a setting of such a ballo rather than an independent composition only if another setting of the same ballo is known. A large number of anonymous dances from the 16th and 17th century have turned out to be settings of these balli, and undoubtedly many others also belong in this category even if they have not been recognized as such. Indeed, the distinction between settings of traditional models and concordances of independent compositions cannot always be clearly made; for example, some of Frescobaldi's dances appear anonymously in several sources with substantial variants, and such versions could well be regarded as settings of popular balli (the models being Frescobaldi's compositions).

Compared with the large variety of dances found in Northern keyboard collections, the number of different types appearing in Italian manuscripts is very small. Even types that are encountered in Italian ensemble music, such as the volta, the sarabanda, and the brando, rarely or never appear in the keyboard collections. One also misses the old pavana, still very popular in the North during the earlier decades of the century.

The *correnti* are generally in some form of triple meter, with a quarter-note or half-note pulse. Most have two repeated strains, although some examples are found with one or three strains; no fixed metric or phrase groupings are discernible. As is the case with most non-dance genres no normative structural scheme can be defined; again, the most important identifying features appear to be the use of stereotyped rhythmic and melodic formulas (e.g., ♩|♩. ♪♪|♩ or ♩|♩. ♫♩|♩).

The *balli* and *balletti* are usually but not always in duple meter, with a quarter-note up-beat; they rarely use note values shorter than eighth notes, suggesting that they were performed at a brisk tempo.

The gagliarda is always in triple time, without up-beat, and usually with a half-note pulse.[19]

VIII

Organization of
the Contents

In Italy the contents of the printed collections traditionally were organized according to genre (except, of course, in collections of organ Masses). This arrangement persisted throughout the 17th century. The genres frequently follow each other in a more or less standard "pecking order," i.e., toccate, ricercari, canzoni, and "gallanterie" (dances and aria settings). Within each genre group the pieces may be ordered according to the modal system; such is the case, for example, with the set of ricercari in Frescobaldi's RECERCARI (1615) and the set of toccate in his TOCCATE I (1615).[1]

In most French organ and harpsichord collections (for example, in the Bauyn and Parville manuscripts, and in the various *Livre d'orgue and Livre de clavecin* publications) a very different principle of organization is observed: the pieces are grouped according to mode or key, and within each group follow some standard scheme or genre progression. These sets of pieces in a common key can be seen as precursors of multi-movement compositions, i.e., of suites, sonatas, and prelude-and-fugue pairs. In fact, the point at which the dance sequences in the French harpsichord collections began to be regarded as integral suites is not easy to determine. In the Italian publications, on the other hand, the appearance of groups or pairs of compositions tied together by a common key is exceptional; among the few examples are the dance sequences in Frescobaldi's AGGIUNTA (1637) (e.g., the *Balletto-Corrente del Balletto-Passachagli* sets in E minor, f. 67, and in B-flat major/G minor, f. 71), and the *Toccata-Ricercare* pairs in his FIORI (1635).

The Italian manuscripts are not nearly so systematically organized as the printed collections. Often one gets the impression that the compiler of a manuscript started out with the intention of following a traditional plan, but for one reason or another did not follow through with this idea. Many collections open with a toccata in the first mode, for example, Ravenna 545, Bologna 360, Vat. mus. 569, Naples 73, Doria 250 A (transposed); but as the collections progress the succession of genres tends to become more and more haphazard. Sometimes rudiments of a plan are still discernible; for example, in Ravenna 545 one can clearly detect the following succession:

ff. 1-11':	Toccate
ff. 12-21:	Ricercari
ff. 22'-42:	Capricci
ff. 42'-76':	Canzoni
ff. 86'-89:	Correnti
ff. 93-116':	Arie and balli, some with partite,

even though within some of these groups there are one or two pieces belonging to a different genre. Similarly, in London 30491 one finds several pieces in the same genre—but by different composers—grouped together: the collection opens with partite on the Romanesca by Stella, on the Ruggiero by de Macque, and on *Zefiro* by Rinaldo (ff. 3-8); on ff. 12-18' appear canzoni by Ippolito, Stella, Fillimarino and de Macque; on ff. 20'-22' are found Gagliarde by de Macque, Trabaci and Lambardo. In this manuscript, however, the "standard order" is not adhered to.

On the other hand, pairs or groups of pieces in the same mode or key are much more common in the manuscripts than in the printed collections. Most frequent are pairs that might be regarded as proto-preludes-and-fugues. Trent contains five such pairs, each consisting of an *Entrata* (or *Intrada*) followed by a *Ricercare* (or *Ricercata*): in "re grave" (f. 13'), in "mi grave" (f. 16), in "ut" (f. 30'), in "sol per B mol" (f. 33), and in "la B quadro" (f. 34'). Toccata-canzone pairs are found in Chigi 25, f. 5' and f. 31 (in the former the Canzona is marked "Canzona che seque alla Toccata," in the latter "Canzona doppo la Toccata"), in Vat. mus. 569: p. 71, and in Doria 250 A: f. 31. A toccata-ricercare pair appears in Bologna 360A (f. 1); there is a clear thematic connection between the two members of the pair. A later form of the toccata-canzone pairing is represented by the *Preludio-Sonata* pairs in Bologna 53: ff. 57'-68' (probably by Pollaroli, see p. 97); in fact, the compositions called *Preludio* and *Sonata* in Bologna 53 still follow closely the traditions of the toccata and the canzone, respectively.

The pairing of a toccata with a canzone or a ricercare must not be confused with the inclusion of fugal sections within toccate, although a dividing line cannot always be sharply drawn. Several toccate conclude with extensive imitative sections, which could be regarded as independent canzoni—see, for example Naples 73: f. 59, Chigi 24; f. 1, Chigi 25: f. 37.

Although the separation of the genres in the printed sources has given rise to the impression that "the combination of a free and fugal form . . . rarely occurs in Italy" (Apel, *Keyboard Music*, p. 482), the manuscripts are seen to provide evidence to the contrary. The fact that such couplings already appear in the earliest sources, Trent and Naples 48,[2] suggests that they represent a common practice throughout the period.

A somewhat less common pairing is that of a ricercare with a canzone. Several examples of such pairings are found in Chigi 24[3] and in Chigi 29; in all of these pairs the subjects are closely related, the canzone subject usually being merely a diminution of the ricercare subject. In Doria 250 A (f. 1′) a group appears which in a sense contains both types of pairs: it consists of a *Toccata*, followed by a *Ricercare*, which in turn is followed by a *Canzona*.

In two manuscripts, Vall. 121 and Florence 2358, grouping according to key becomes the organizing principle of the entire collection. The groups include as many as four or even five compositions, and in some cases take on the appearance of proto-suites or proto-sonatas. Vall. 121 consists of nine such groups; several of these open with a toccata, which is followed by various dances. In Florence 2358 the division into suites, respectively in A major, A minor, G minor and D minor, is still clearer, even though in the manuscript the groups are not set apart in any manner. Each group commences with a *Preludio*, which is followed by miscellaneous movements (*Aria alla Francese, Passagagli, Allemanda, Tochata,* etc.). We see that the manuscripts are able to provide evidence—missing in the printed collection—that the keyboard suite, which played such an important role in 17th-century French, German and English keyboard music, also existed in Italy.

IX
Concordances

Concordances among Italian manuscripts and concordances between these manuscripts and Italian prints are not very numerous. This very fact, however, lessens the likelihood that those concordances that do exist are merely the result of coincidence, and increases their value as potential evidence for a common tradition among the corresponding sources. No concordances to foreign publications have been found,[1] and concordances to foreign manuscripts are confined to a few exceptional cases to be discussed below. Table 8 lists the Italian prints to which concordances have been found in the manuscripts. The list is not long, and it becomes even shorter if one disregards the late, mostly 18th-century copies of entire publications. This situation is entirely different from that found, say, in German sources of the period in which copies from prints, many of them Italian, make up an appreciable part of the repertory. Perhaps printed editions were more easily and inexpensively available in Italy and hence there was less need for manuscript copies.

The list shows that of the immense number of collections published in Italy during the 17th century, only a few served as sources for manuscript copies (assuming that this is what such concordances imply, see below). The anthology appended to Diruta's treatise TRANSILVANO served as a source to some of the early collections, and the Neapolitan manuscripts occasionally drew upon some local publications. However, Frescobaldi's printed collections, especially the two books of TOCCATE, account for the large majority of the concordances.[2]

In most concordances the composer is named in the manuscript version; the main exceptions to this are some Frescobaldi dances, which occasionally turn up anonymously in the manuscripts (see p. 44). When attributions are present they invariably agree with the attributions in the prints, except in one case in Vat. mus. 569 (see p. 152). In the majority of these concordances the texts agree very closely, even with respect to notational details, such as beaming and placement of accidentals. When such is the case the manuscript versions probably were copied directly from the publications. For a number of pieces the manuscript versions deviate from the printed versions. These deviations range from trivial details, such as the addition or omission of trills and slightly different voicings of chords, to variants so substantial that the two versions can barely be regarded as the same composition. When such variants are present the historical relation

Table 8
Concordances to 17th-Century Italian Publications

Publication	Date of First and Last Edition	Manuscripts With Concordances[a]	Manuscripts Containing a Complete Copy Or a Substantial Segment of The Publication
TRANSILVANO I (Sa. 1593b)	1593-1625	Naples 48 (1) Ravenna 545 (1) Trent (1)	Bagnacavallo
Merulo, TOCCATE I (Sa. 1598b)	1598		Bagnacavallo
Trabaci, RICERCATE II (Sa. 1615c)	1615	London 30491 (1) Naples 48 (1)	
Frescobaldi, TOCCATE I (1615)	1615-1637	Bologna 360 (1) Chigi 24 (1) Chigi 27 (2) Chigi 205-206 (1) Ravenna 545 (3)	Milan 53 Venice 1727 Venice 1299
Frescobaldi, RECERCARI (1615)	1615-1642	Chigi 29 (1)	Bologna 270 Cologny T.II.1 Venice 1299 Vicenza 17
Frescobaldi, CAPRICCI (1624, 1626)	1624-1642	Chigi 25 (1, partial) Ravenna 545 (2)	Verona MCXXIX

Frescobaldi, TOCCATE II (1627)	1627-1637	Chigi 27 (4) Chigi 205-206 (3) Ravenna 545 (1)	Cologny T.II.1 Milan 53 Venice 1727 Venice 1299
Frescobaldi, FIORI (Sa. 1635)	1635	Naples 73 (2)	Assisi Bologna 270 Venice 1299 Verona MCXXIX Vicenza 17
Frescobaldi, AGGIUNTA (1637)	1637	Cecilia 400 (3) Chigi 24 (6) Chigi 205-206 (1) Nuremberg 33748-V (6) Vat. mus. 569 (2)	Venice 1299
Frescobaldi, CANZONI IV (1645)	1645		Verona MCXXIX
Cifra, RICERCARI I (Sa. 1619b)	1619	Ravenna 545 (1)	
Salvatore, RICERCARI (Sa. 1641c)	1641	Naples 73 (1)	
Storace, SELVA (Sa. 1664b)	1664		London 14246
SONATE DI VARII AUTORI (Sa. 1697?m)	1697?	Bologna 53 (3)	
Merula, CANZONI IV (Sa. 1651a) (part books)	1651	Assisi (1, partial)	

[a]The number in parentheses gives the number of concordances found in the manuscripts.

Table 9
Concordances Among The Manuscripts

Manuscript	Concordances[a]
Trent	Ravenna 545 (1)
Ravenna 545	Trent (1) Chigi 205-206 (1) Naples 73 (1) Chigi 205-206 (1) = Doria 250 B (1)
Chigi 26	Vat. mus. 569 (1) Oxford 1113 (1)
Chigi 28	Vat. mus. 569 (1)
Chigi 205-206	Ravenna 545 (1) Ravenna 545 (1) = Doria 250 B (1) Naples 48 (1) = Naples 73 (1) = Cecilia 400 (1) = Berlin 40615 (1)
Vall. 121	Vat. mus. 569 (2)
Vat. mus. 569	Chigi 26 (1) Chigi 28 (1) Vall. 121 (2) Modena 491 (1)

Doria 250 A   Oxford 1113 (4)

Doria 250 B   Chigi 205-206 (1)
                 Ravenna 545 (1) = Chigi 205-206 (1)

Modena 491   Vat. mus. 569 (1)

Oxford 1113[b]   Doria 250 A (4)
                 Chigi 26 (1)

Naples 48   Chigi 205-206 (1) = Naples 73 (1) = Cecilia 400 (1) = Berlin 40615 (1)

Naples 73   Ravenna 545 (1)
                 Chigi 205-206 (1) = Naples 48 (1) = Cecilia 400 (1) = Berlin 40615 (1)

Cecilia 400   Naples 48 (1) = Naples 73 (1) = Chigi 205-206 (1) = Berlin 40615 (1)

Berlin 40615[c] Naples 48 (1) = Naples 73 (1) = Chigi 205-206 (1) = Cecilia 400 (1)

---

[a]The number between parentheses indicates the number of concordances; multiple concordances are shown by means of an equal sign.
[b]Of English provenance.
[c]Of German provenance.

Table 10
Concordances Among Variation Sets
(Concordant versions are connected by arrows)

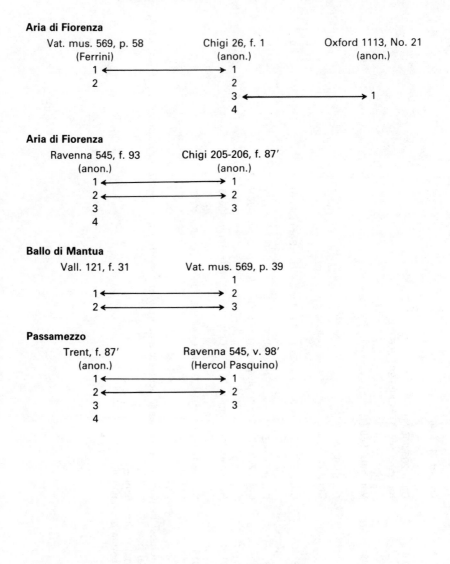

Aria di Fiorenza

Vat. mus. 569, p. 58 (Ferrini)	Chigi 26, f. 1 (anon.)	Oxford 1113, No. 21 (anon.)
1 ←——————→ 1		
2	2	
	3 ←——————————→ 1	
	4	

Aria di Fiorenza

Ravenna 545, f. 93 (anon.)	Chigi 205-206, f. 87' (anon.)
1 ←——————→ 1	
2 ←——————→ 2	
3	3
4	

Ballo di Mantua

Vall. 121, f. 31	Vat. mus. 569, p. 39
	1
1 ←——————→ 2	
2 ←——————→ 3	

Passamezzo

Trent, f. 87' (anon.)	Ravenna 545, v. 98' (Hercol Pasquino)
1 ←——————→ 1	
2 ←——————→ 2	
3	3
4	

between the printed and the manuscript version is more problematic. I shall return to this issue in Chapter XI, where some examples of variant versions will be examined. It will be shown that, even in these cases, the assumption that the published version served as primary source probably remains valid.

A few compositions are found in several manuscripts as well as in printed collections. The manuscript versions do not show any consistent variants that distinguish them as a group from the printed ones; hence there is no evidence that an independent manuscript tradition existed for these compositions.

Concordances exclusively among manuscripts are even more sporadic than those between manuscripts and prints (see Table 9). Only two compositions are found in more than two manuscripts: one of these, a canzone attributed to Ercole Pasquini, appears in six different sources (see Table 16b); the other, a corrente attributed to both Ercole Pasquini and Frescobaldi, appears in three sources (see Table 16a). These last two compositions and a *Toccata* attributed to Ferrini in both Modena 491 and Vat. mus. 569 are the only ones for which more than one of the concordant versions includes an attribution; hence the infrequency of conflicting attributions can scarcely be taken as an indication that the attributions in the manuscript repertory are reliable.

A curious aspect of the manuscript concordances is that, when a concordance involves a variation set, as is frequently the case, this concordance does not extend over all the variations in the set (see Table 10). In view of these "wandering variations" it appears unwarranted to extrapolate an attribution given in one source to variations appearing only in another source, as was done by Kirkendale (*Fiorenza*, 73) for the partite on *la Fiorenza* in Chigi 26.

The versions of these compositions usually are not wholly identical, even though the variants tend to involve only minor details. An exceptional case is a Gagliarda found in Vall. 121 and in Vat. mus. 569 (see p. 140). Not only do these two versions correspond closely, but they are in the same handwriting— one of the rare instances among these manuscripts of a scribal concordance (the only other one being between Chigi 26 and Chigi 28). The small number of concordances among these manuscripts suggests that most of the compositions had an extremely limited circulation, and, hence, a concordance can be taken as an indication that a fairly close relation must have existed between the sources in question, even when literal copies are not involved.

Only two foreign manuscripts contain compositions from the Italian manuscript repertory: Oxford 1113 and Berlin 40615. Oxford 1113 is a somewhat enigmatic manuscript in the hand of an Englishman (possibly William Ellis), dating probably from c. 1650.[3] The opening portion contains a complete copy of the pieces in Frescobaldi's TOCCATE I (1615), interspersed with a group of anonymous pieces almost certainly of Italian provenance. Among the latter are the four concordances in question. Berlin 40615 is a large South-German anthology from the middle of the 17th century. It contains a fair amount of Italian repertory, mostly from Venetian publications; however, it includes one canzone by Ercole Pasquini found in a number of Italian manuscripts but not in any publication.

I have not included among the concordances a number of settings of French tunes and dances appearing in Barb. lat. 4182 and 4288, Chigi 24, Vat mus. 569, and Cecilia 400. Almost all involve melodies and pieces that were popular throughout Europe and that are found in a large number of sources, in some cases in a variety of vocal and instrumental settings. When the common element is merely a popular melody, treated in unique fashion in the source, one clearly is dealing with an aria or ballo setting. The situation is more ambiguous in the case of a dance with an attribution to a composer that appears in several other sources (for example, the Courante by La Barre in Chigi 24). However, for the French dances in these manuscripts, the variants are so substantial that the correspondences probably should be looked upon as independent settings of the same popular models rather than as concordances among art compositions, although, as we noted earlier, the dividing line cannot always be clearly drawn (see p. 44).

These French pieces, or rather, Italian settings of French tunes, constitute virtually the only "foreign element" in our manuscripts. What is surprising is not their appearance, but rather their scarcity, considering how common they are in keyboard anthologies from other countries. We might note that in Italy they are found only in Roman manuscripts.

X
Attributions

The evaluation of an attribution has to be based on considerations of probability or plausibility unless an authoritative source (such as an autograph or composer's edition) can provide an absolute basis for its acceptance. Factors entering into such considerations are:

(1) *Proximity of the source to the time and place of the composer's activity.* What connections could have existed between the copyist and the composer? Was the copyist likely to have had access to reliable sources of the composer's work?

(2) *Form of the attributions in the source.* Were they included systematically by the copyist, or were they inserted sporadically at a later date?

(3) *Reliability of the copyist, judged on the basis of other compositions in the same source.* Are there other attributions in the source that conflict with those in authoritative sources? Do the texts of other compositions agree with the texts of concordances in authoritative sources?

(4) *Stylistic criteria.* Is the composition acceptable within the context of the composer's work as we know it from authoritative sources?

Here follow some comments on these four factors in reference to the Italian keyboard manuscripts.

PROXIMITY OF THE SOURCE TO THE TIME AND PLACE OF THE COMPOSER'S ACTIVITY

Von Dadelsen, in an article on the role of style criticism in authenticity problems, groups sources according to three levels of transmission ("Überlieferungsstufen"):[1]

(1) *Substantiated transmission:* To this level belong autographs, authorized editions and other material stemming from the composer; with these there ordinarily is no need to question authorship. None of the Italian manuscripts show any evidence of being autographs; the earliest surviving autographs appear to be those of Bernardo Pasquini (c. 1700). A so-called Frescobaldi autograph has proven to be spurious (see p. 84).

(2) *Plausible transmission:* To this level are assigned sources for which it can be ascertained that they came from circles closely associated with the author.

The attributions in these sources may generally be taken at face value unless a strong case can be made against them on the basis of stylistic considerations. The manuscript London 30491, which contains music of de Macque and his circle, belongs to this category, since it is in the hand of Luigi Rossi, a one-time student of de Macque. The only other manuscript that might qualify is Vat. mus. 569, as far as the attributions to Giovanni Battista Ferrini, Bernardo Pasquini, and Fabritio Fontana are concerned. The manuscript belonged to Virginio Mutij, a pupil of Fontana; furthermore, there are many ties connecting Pasquini and Ferrini to Fontana.

(3) *Unsubstantiated transmission:* To this level von Dadelsen assigns all sources for which no unambiguous indication of a connection with the author can be found, regardless of their geographical or chronological proximity. For these sources the burden of proof falls to the other side: the attributions cannot even be accepted as probable unless a convincing case can be made in their favor on the basis of stylistic analysis. With the exceptions noted above, all of the Italian manuscripts belong to this level.

It must be remembered that von Dadelsen's criteria, which may appear excessively stringent—especially the rejection of spatial and temporal proximity as significant considerations—were drawn up primarily for dealing with well-known composers with established reputations. Such composers traditionally become the victims of numerous misattributions, and the appearance of their names must be countered with a great deal more skepticism than is necessary with attributions to minor figures. It is for this reason that, in dealing with attributions to Frescobaldi in the Italian manuscripts, more so than with any other composer, the guilty-until-proven-innocent rule must be insisted upon (see the discussion below).

As is typical of many early repertories, most of the attributions in these sources appear in manuscripts dating from the composer's last years or from the generation following his death. Generally I shall regard such dating as supportive of the attributions (except for the attributions to Frescobaldi) and will regard sources chronologically more remote with reservation. In the case of Ercole Pasquini and de Macque it will be seen that such reservation is warranted.

FORM OF THE ATTRIBUTION IN THE SOURCE

The systematic and accurate crediting of authorship does not form part of the tradition of Italian keyboard-music manuscripts. A number of manuscripts contain no attributions whatsoever; when attributions are given there often is no regular pattern of how, when, and where they appear. They show up in almost haphazard fashion, as if they were an afterthought; and, in fact, they often were clearly a later insertion. I shall try to categorize the manuscripts according to the manner in which the attributions are given.

(1) *Manuscripts with systematic attributions.* In these manuscripts the

copyist systematically included the name of the composer with almost every composition he copied. Many Northern anthologies are of this type, for example, the Fitzwilliam Virginal Book, the Bauyn Manuscript, the Lübbenau Manuscripts Ly A1 and Ly A2. Only one Italian manuscript, London 30491, can be included in this category.

(2) *Manuscripts with a blanket attribution*. In these manuscripts the name of the composer appears only once, usually on a flyleaf, but the attribution presumably was intended to apply to all the pieces in the manuscript. Examples are Chigi 25, Venice 1299, London 40080 and London 30491 (the blanket attribution in the latter is contradicted by the internal attributions). Another form of blanket attribution is a table in which portions of the manuscripts are assigned to various composers, for instance, in Naples 73, f, [i]: "Cimino-f. 1 a f. 56/Boerio, Francesco-f. 57 a f. 59, . . ."

(3) *Manuscripts with unsystematic attributions*. In these the attributions appear with some compositions but not with others—on the average perhaps with about half of the compositions. Examples are Trent, Ravenna 545, Chigi 27, Vat. mus. 569, and Naples 73. Often the attributions appear in "bunches," in a specific segment of the manuscript. These bunches are usually not distinguished by a different hand, and, hence, their presence cannot be explained as representing the habit of a different copyist. Generally the attributions appear to be in the hand of the music copyist; in Vat. mus. 569 there is evidence that the copyist added them after several compositions had been entered (see p. 152).

(4) *Manuscripts with sporadic attributions*. In this type of manuscript a composer's name appears only sporadically. The exact number of attributions varies from one (e.g., in Doria 250 B, Bologna 360) to half a dozen or more in some large collections (Bologna 53, Naples 48). What distinguishes this category from the preceding one is that the attributions do not appear in bunches, but are scattered, apparently at random, throughout the manuscript, and they usually are not in the hand of the music copyist (or in the hand responsible for the titles of the pieces).

(5) *Manuscripts containing no attributions*. This category includes principally the aria and ballo manuscripts, such as Florence 115 and 138, Barb. lat. 4288, Nuremberg 33748-V, and UCLA 51/1.

The absence of systematic attributions in the Italian manuscripts probably is related to the fact that they appear to have been compiled for the practical use of performers rather than for collectors (see Chapter XII). Of course, even if a copyist did want to include attributions, he could do so only if this information was available to him, for example, if it was provided in the sources from which he made his copies. The fact that not all his sources may have provided this information would account for the unsystematic attributions; when a succession of pieces was copied from a source that did include attributions, the "bunching" phenomenon noted before would arise. Ravenna 545, for example, may have been copied by someone who worked this way; in fact, the copyist was evidently concerned about not having an attribution available for one of the pieces (f. 57) and wrote above it "d'Incerto."

I believe the sporadic attributions to have been the result of a different process. In such manuscripts the original copyist did not include any attributions. However, someone at some later date recognized—or thought he recognized—a piece, and inserted the presumed composer's name. In Bologna 53, for example, attributions were added by a later hand to several individual pieces. In the manuscript these pieces appear within larger groups of compositions (for example, a group of *Preludio-Sonata* pairs in six modes, probably by Pollaroli) that had been copied in their entirety. The pieces selected from such a group to receive attributions happen to be pieces that were included individually—i.e., not as part of the entire set—in some published collection (in Pollaroli's case, in the SONATE, Sa. 1697?m). Evidently a later owner of the manuscript or a librarian noticed the concordances to the publications and took it upon himself to insert the composers' names into the manuscript.

Attributions inserted by later hands can usually be spotted by examining handwriting and ink color. It is not always easy to tell during what period they were added. I suspect that in many cases they are of comparatively recent origin, i.e., from the 19th or 20th century. For example, Naples 73 has an attribution to Donato Cimino, which has been identified by the current librarian of the Naples Conservatory as being in the hand of her predecessor, Rondinella; according to her, this attribution was based on a mistaken assumption (see pp. 109-10).

The blanket attributions on the flyleaves of Chigi 25, London 40080 and Florence 2358 are all in hands not appearing in the manuscripts; the attribution in Florence 2358 is in pencil and is definitely of recent origin.

Blanket attributions and attributions above the first piece in a manuscript (e.g., the attribution in Naples 73, and the one to Frescobaldi in Bologna 53—also known to be incorrect) should be regarded with skepticism. Anonymous manuscripts present a cataloguing problem to librarians, especially when the manuscripts are catalogued alphabetically by author, as is often the case in Italy; a librarian may be tempted to insert an attribution based on his presumed recognition of a composition or style. I believe that the blanket attribution of Chigi 25 to Frescobaldi, for example, may have been based on the "recognition" of the *Capriccio sopra il Cucho* (see p. 66), or perhaps on a mistaken association of Frescobaldi with the *Aria di Fioranza*, which opens the manuscript (see pp. 164-65).

It seems clear that sporadic attributions and blanket attributions, unless supported by concordances to reliable sources, must be treated with extreme suspicion. Attributions that appear systematically in an entire manuscript or portion thereof, and that are in the hand of the copyist, can be given more weight. In either case, however, the form of the attributions in the manuscript is only one of several factors to be taken into account when evaluating their credibility.

RELIABILITY OF THE COPYIST OR SOURCE

In Chapter IX it was observed that when concordances to printed works exist attributions are usually given, and that in practically all such cases the attributions agree—presumably because the compositions in question were copied directly from the published versions. As we saw, however, the situation is rather different for concordances between the manuscripts. In particular, we might recall that for only three compositions with concordances are attributions found in more than one version; in one of these, moreover, the attributions conflict (see p. 55).

It is clear that when a copyist (or whoever inserted the attribution) had a source available which gave an attribution he reproduced this attribution correctly. For most of the repertory, however, the copyist was probably not working from sources that supplied this information, and the attributions were made on the basis of other, perhaps less reliable, considerations, such as recognition or hearsay.

Concordances to printed sources can also provide a measure of the reliability of the text of a manuscript. Comparison of manuscript versions and printed versions of compositions reveals an entire spectrum of relationships, ranging from exact copies to variants that are so substantial that it becomes questionable whether one can still speak of concordances. The implications of such variant versions, which I will call partial concordances, are discussed in the following chapter.

STYLISTIC CRITERIA

Two issues are usually lumped together under stylistic comparative analysis: (1) Does the idiom resemble that of the composer, as evidenced in his authenticated works? (2) Is the quality of craftsmanship or artistry on a level with that displayed by the composer's authenticated works? Failure to meet the first criterion might suggest that the composition originated in a different period (e.g., the music attributed to Frescobaldi in Florence 2358) or in a different place (for example, the Frescobaldi attributions in German manuscripts such as Berlin 40316 and Munich 1581). Failure to meet the second criterion might suggest that the composition is the work of a pupil or emulator (or perhaps someone's clumsy parody of a genuine lost work by the composer). In the Italian manuscripts the latter situation seems to be more common.

The evaluation of the attributions in these manuscripts by means of stylistic analysis will be a large task—one that can be accomplished only within the context of a detailed stylistic study of the repertory. However, I do not believe that it is a hopeless task. In the discussion of the Frescobaldi attributions in Part Three, I will present a "pilot study" on a specific composition, showing how even on the basis of fairly simple considerations a reasonably secure conclusion can be drawn with respect to authorship.

Needless to say, stylistic analysis presupposes the availability of a group of authenticated works to serve as a control group. When such a group is not available (as in the case of Ercole Pasquini) one will have to follow less reliable procedures, such as taking into account the stylistic ambience of the composer or the internal stylistic consistency within the attributed repertory.

XI

Parody, Pasticcio, and Partial Concordance

The types of variants encountered in manuscript and printed versions of the same composition can best be illustrated by a series of examples.

(1) Chigi 27, f. 63': Corrente, [anon.]
Frescobaldi, TOCCATE II, p. 83: Corrente Prima

The differences are slight but interesting (see Example 5). The manuscript version undoubtedly would give an inexperienced player fewer problems: some awkward skips are eliminated (as in the left hand of mm. 4-5 and 6-7), and the difficult left hand cadence in m. 7 (presumably a trill would grace the dotted quarter before the turn) is transferred to the right hand.

Unfortunately, the gain in ease of playing of the manuscript version is offset by a loss in musical interest. The anticipation of the F-harmony in the last beat of m. 6 weakens the climactic downbeat of the following measure, and mm. 7-8 suffer from an excess of parallel downward motion. Furthermore, the most charming aspect of this entire passage in the printed version is missing here: the tenor, which emerges from the bass in m. 6, follows the soprano in parallel tenths, making in its course occasional dissonant clashes.

The manuscript version also includes a number of trills not found in the printed edition; presumably trills of this type were added as a matter of course by the experienced player.

(2) Venice 1299, p. 50: Toccata
Frescobaldi, TOCCATE II, p. 7: Toccata Terza

The alterations in the manuscript version consist chiefly of a simplification of the rhythms of the ornamental figurations (see Example 6).

(3) Chigi 205, f. 114: Corrente, [anon.]
Frescobaldi, TOCCATI I, p. 66: Corrente Prima

The differences are more extensive than in the preceding examples; they include transposition, simplification of the bass, and elimination of two entire measures (see Example 7).[1] Again, pedagogical considerations could account for the variants in the manuscript version. The transposition may have had the purpose of limiting the downward range of the left hand. As a result of this transposition the right hand would have extended to B-flat; this is now avoided by the changes in m. 4 and the elimination of m. 5. Another difficult skip, in mm. 7-8 (left hand), is also avoided by the expedient of omitting a measure. It is also possible that the reading in the manuscript is the result of an altogether different process: the recording on paper of a composition remembered in general outline, but not in specific detail.

The elimination of entire measures is, of course, a much more radical editorial change than the simplification of the texture; it attacks the basic fabric of a composition. When the process is extended to the point of omission, substitution and rearrangement of entire sections, it is perhaps no longer appropriate to speak of a concordance with variants. The term "pasticcio" has been suggested for such adaptations in distinction to parodies, that is, recompositions affecting principally the surface texture.[2] Since, however, the sections of the original that have been retained usually have been subjected to some modifications, the division between pasticcios and parodies is not clear-cut. Perhaps the term "partial concordance" can serve both categories; furthermore, it avoids prejudging precisely what functioned as model.

(4) Chigi 24, f. 38': [no title], [anon.]
      Frescobaldi, TOCCATE I, p. 67: Corrente Terza

The differences (not illustrated here) consist of a downward transposition by a fourth, the elimination of seven measures towards the end of the second section, and a complete revision of the upper voice, mainly in the direction of simplification.[3]

(5) Chigi 205-206, f. 95: Passagalli (fragment), [anon.]
      Frescobaldi, AGGIUNTA (1637): Partite cento Sopra il
      Passachagli

Only six partite correspond:

Manuscript version:	1	2	3	5	6	13
Printed version:	1	2	3	4	27	21

This type of correspondence is similar to that found among variation sets with concordances between manuscripts (see Table 10). The corresponding partite are

Example 5

(a) Chigi 27, f. 63′: Corrente (mm. 1-3)

(b) Frescobaldi, TOCCATE II (1627), p. 83: Corrente Prima (mm. 1-8)

Example 6

(a) Venice 1299, p. 50: [Frescobaldi], Toccata (mm. 1-4)

(b) Frescobaldi, TOCCATE I (1615), p. 7: Toccata Terza (mm. 1-2)

essentially identical, except that in the manuscript version the note values are doubled.

The *Passagalli* in Chigi 205-206 also share a partita (beginning m. 144) with the *Passachagli* in Frescobaldi's AGGIUNTA, p. 74 (16th partita).

(6) Chigi 27, f. 70′: Toc. del Signor Gierolamo Frescobaldi
   Frescobaldi, TOCCATE I (1615): Toccata Quinta

The correspondence is restricted to two passages:

Manuscript version:	mm. 6-12	19-20
	↕	↕
Printed version:	mm. 27-29	7

For a discussion of the relation of these two versions in view of the chronology of the sources, see p. 161.

> (7) Chigi 25, f. 24: Capriccio fatto sopra il Cucchù (blanket
>   attribution to Frescobaldi)
>   Frescobaldi, CAPRICCI (1624): Capriccio Terzo sopra il
>   Cucho, p. 23

The first three measures are identical; for the remainder the two pieces share no more than the "cuckoo" bird-call ostinato on the notes D-G, and a similar structural plan (i.e., a succession of imitative sections with contrasting mensurations).

The final example involves a partial concordance among three compositions appearing only in manuscripts.

> (8) London 40080, f. 14: Canzona Sesta (blanket attribution to Frescobaldi)
>   London 40080, f. 25': Canzona Nona (same)
>   London 36661, f. 28': Del Sigl. Freses Baldi. Toccata

The three compositions share a lengthy closing section; in the two *Canzoni* there is, furthermore, a similar earlier section (not immediately preceding this closing section), but beyond this the compositions contain no common material. None of the versions appear in authoritative sources; in fact, both manuscripts are of questionable reliability (see pp. 156-58). Example 8 presents a comparative score of the closing sections of the three compositions. Arrows have been inserted to draw attention to variants and to apparent errors (the latter are indicated by an encircled question mark).

The quoted passages start with cadential transition sections similar in character but different in content. The section that follows, however, is almost identical in all three versions; most of the discrepancies involve errors or omissions. Substantial differences do not appear until the last measure of version A (see Example 8). While A at this point comes rather suddenly, and not too convincingly, to a halt, versions B and C continue with cadenza-like passages. Initially these progress in similar fashion—although a beat appears to be missing from C—but eventually they, too, part ways. The conclusion of the B version is clearly incorrect; the conclusion of C, on the other hand, is quite satisfactory. It is evident that none of the versions provides a text that is entirely superior to the others; each includes passages for which the other versions provide better readings. Clearly, we cannot rely upon any of the three sources to give us a satisfactory representation of these compositions; by extension the trustworthiness of their readings of other compositions is brought into question. Whether or not the passage discussed here is based on a genuine Frescobaldi composition is a further problem, distinct from the issue of textual corruption.

Example 7

(a) Chigi 205, f. 114: Corrente (mm. 1-7)

(b) Frescobaldi, TOCCATE I (1615), p. 66: Corrente Prima (mm. 1-11)

Example 8

London 40080, f. 14
[Frescobaldi?]
Canzon Sesta (mm. 53-74)   A

London 40080, f. 25'
[Frescobaldi?]
Canzon Nona (mm. 53-78)   B

London 36661, f. 28'
Del Sigl. Freses Baldi
Toccata (mm. 58-80)   C

Example 8—Continued.

Example 8—Continued.

My examples have been chosen from works attributed to Frescobaldi; however, similar partial concordances can be found among the works attributed to de Macque (see p. 165) and to Ercole Pasquini (see p. 178). Nor is the phenomenon restricted to Italian manuscripts;[4] similar variants were observed by John Ward in 16th-century Spanish tablatures and by Margarete Reimann in the 17th-century German keyboard repertory.[5] Reimann, in fact, holds that in 16th- and 17th-century instrumental sources extensive editorial revisions were the rule rather than the exception, and that unless the texts can be authenticated by some other means, we should not assume them to be representative of the composer's intentions. She takes the point of view that deviations from the versions in reliable sources do not represent revisions (or earlier versions) by the composer, but, rather, are the result of such editorial adaptations—a process to which a text that has come down to us may have been repeatedly subjected.

By and large I believe that Reimann's conclusions are applicable to the Italian repertory, although it must be kept in mind that the Italian manuscripts do contain many faithful copies from the printed publications—sometimes in the same manuscripts that include these pasticcios. In addition, one cannot dismiss the possibility that a variant version represents a revision stemming from the composer; a few examples of such revisions are known from the Frescobaldi publications, the authenticity of which appears to be above question.[6]

The question remains: what was the reason behind the apparently widespread practice of editorial revision? Are the variant versions simplifications for the convenience of students, adaptations to someone else's taste, or compositions imperfectly preserved in a player's memory? These questions will be explored in the following chapter.

XII

Provenance
and Function

The Italian keyboard manuscripts have emerged as a remarkably homogeneous group of sources with respect to physical characteristics as well as to musical contents. It has also become apparent that they cannot be regarded in any sense as unpublished equivalents of the contemporary printed collections; indeed, they follow a quite distinct tradition.

The background of the keyboard publications is fairly clear. Most appear to have been prepared by a musician active as a composer who wished to present the musical community with a collection of his own works. Generally the collection consisted of systematically arranged sets of compositions in a few related genres. An eloquent dedication and a preface "Al lettore" stated the two-fold aim of the publication: to honor a patron (probably in gratitude for past favors or, perhaps, in the hope of future ones), and to meet performers' needs for musical materials.

The manuscripts, on the other hand, contain neither dedications nor instructions to performers. Their content tends to be much more varied than that of the publications, and usually shows few signs of planned organization. Because many compositions do not have attributions—only London 30491 provides them with each entry—it is difficult to establish how many composers are represented in each manuscript. A few manuscripts contain no attributions whatsoever, but the majority furnish names with some compositions; when such is the case, several composers' names will appear within the manuscript. A few collections have a blanket attribution to a single composer; in all the manuscripts for which this is the case the attribution is to Frescobaldi. I have shown in Chapter X that each of these blanket attributions (except for those on manuscript copies of his printed works) is problematical for one reason or another; furthermore, most of the collections in question do not date from our period.

It appears that, in general, the manuscripts were not compiled with the intention of making available a representative collection of a single composer's works. This is not really surprising; not many surviving manuscript anthologies of any type from the 17th century or earlier are exclusively devoted to the works of a single composer. Apparently, compilers of manuscripts had no particular interest in restricting themselves to the works of one composer. Collections prepared by composers themselves of their own works have come down to us only rarely.

Were the manuscripts then compiled with the intent of providing a collection of representative works by different composers? There exist a number of Northern manuscripts that clearly were put together with that purpose in mind. Some notable examples are the Turin manuscripts—apparently compiled for the Fugger family—the Fitzwilliam Virginal Book, and the Bauyn Manuscript. Such collections are carefully and neatly copied and often are quite elegant in appearance. Most, if not all, compositions are provided with an attribution; major works by noted composers of the period as well as from previous eras are included; and not infrequently music from several different countries can be found. The intent of the copyist appears not to have been primarily to furnish material for use in performance, but rather to provide an anthology for study and reference. In fact, the main interest of the person for whom the manuscript was prepared may have been to possess a collection of music by great masters of the past and present, a collection that would afford him a pleasure and prestige comparable to that of owning a collection of beautiful paintings or fine books.

Several Italian manuscripts of the period containing material other than keyboard music appear to be of a similar type; such is the case with a number of aria and cantata collections. These are often beautifully bound in tooled leather showing the coat of arms of the owner; lavish initials and at times rather extravagant decoration are not uncommon.[1] Generally the names of the composers, and sometimes also those of the poets, are noted with the compositions.

Only one of the Italian keyboard manuscripts (London 30491) corresponds to this type (or, at least was begun with this intention). The other collections have an appearance that is best described as utilitarian. No effort was wasted on making them attractive to the eye; speed usually appears to have been the copyist's prime concern. Neither does their musical content, consisting in large part of modest compositions of unknown but probably local authorship, suggest the eclectic taste of a collector.

That these manuscripts, unlike the collectors' anthologies, were copied mainly for practical and private use seems evident. Nevertheless, this conclusion leaves much about their content unexplained. No doubt most of the printed collections were also published for practical use (at least such tends to be their stated purpose), yet the type of music they present is quite different; in fact, the repertory of these collections, far from duplicating the manuscript repertory, could be said to complement it. Of the many traditional arie and balli found in the manuscripts, only a few of the most popular ones appear in the publications; those that do appear are usually subject to lengthy sets of variations, which is rarely the case in the manuscripts. On the other hand the manuscripts contain few of the long, artfully constructed toccate, ricercari and canzoni found in the prints; the abstract genres are represented mainly by works comparatively slight in scope.

At first glance this difference might suggest that the two types of sources were used by different groups of performers: the prints by sophisticated professionals, the manuscripts by dilettantes with more simple tastes. But this explanation does not seem altogether adequate. Why would no collections be published for amateur musicians (a group, one assumes, at least as affluent as the professionals), and why would professionals not also rely on manuscripts?

Before attempting to give a satisfactory explanation for the special character of the two types of sources I wish to consider another matter: why have these manuscripts survived at all—or, rather, what kinds of manuscripts are most likely to have survived? Musical materials in the hands of the average private individual or family are not likely to be preserved for more than a generation; they are too subject to fashion and too fragile. At best they may be kept in an attic for a while, but sooner or later the demand for space and the lack of interest will cause them to be discarded. The best—perhaps only—chance for survival exists for those manuscripts which belong to persons or institutions that maintain collections of other materials considered worth preserving, and that have appropriate facilities for their care and storage. Most of the surviving Italian sources probably belonged at one time to religious institutions or to noble or wealthy families and thus were preserved for posterity in their libraries and archives.

Several of the keyboard manuscripts can with certainty or with high probability be associated with a prominent family: Barb. lat. 4181, 4182, and 4288 with the Barberini; the Chigi manuscripts with the Chigi; Doria 250 A and B with the Doria-Pamphilj; and Florence 115, 138 and 2358 with the Medici. On the other hand, few manuscripts offer positive indications to associate them with any religious institution. One might have expected that churches and monasteries still would possess manuscripts from the period with liturgical organ music, but, with the exception of the Assisi and Spello manuscripts, no collections of this type have thus far been found in their libraries and archives. It is possible that manuscripts such as Naples 73 and Trent, whose contents consist mainly of serious material (i.e., abstract genres and liturgical music), belonged at one time to religious institutions, although they may just as likely have been prepared for use in private chapels.

Of course, the fact that a manuscript found its way into the library of a noble family does not tell us why and for whom it was compiled, since, as we have already seen, it was not likely to have been prepared by professional copyists for the purpose of becoming part of this library. Was the original user a musician who was a member of the family or perhaps a professional in their service? In order to give a tentative and perhaps somewhat speculative answer to this question we must go back a bit further into the history of keyboard playing.

Our knowledge of the early practices of keyboard players is limited, since comparatively little music survives from before c. 1550. Furthermore, much of what has survived from before this time is artistically and technically on a rather low level; only a few collections—for example, those by Marc'Antonio and Girolamo Cavazzoni—show that organ music did exist which attained the same high standards found in vocal music of the period. Yet one would like to believe that in the many great churches and sophisticated courts keyboard music was heard of a more artistic quality than is suggested by most of the preserved materials. The reason that almost none of this music is preserved is probably that it never was written down; professional keyboard players mostly played music of their own creation and had no need to record this music on paper (or, if they did, it would have been against their professional interests to let copies get out of their hands). They were trained in a tradition that did not rely on performing written music; improvising on a plain-chant, on popular songs and dances, on well-known madrigals, or even without any model, formed part of their basic skills. Much of the time they probably were not so much actually improvising as performing a version of a composition that existed in a semi-permanent state in their memory—such is the case in many non-written traditions. Needless to say, many of the organists were well-rounded musicians, quite familiar with musical notation, but they would be more likely to use that knowledge when composing music for choirs or other ensembles than for their own solo performances.

Amateur musicians may also have possessed some compositional skills, but to a more rudimentary degree, and it is probably from their ranks that the first interest in written-down music arose. Such notated compositions when mastered would allow them to some extent to sound like professionals; in addition the written examples could serve as models for study and emulation.[2]

In the 17th century the tradition of improvising, or at least of performing one's own music from memory, was still very much alive (in fact, to some extent, it has never died out altogether), but at the same time reading from notated music· was becoming a more and more widespread practice. One imagines that especially in amateur circles compositional skills were becoming rare, and that there was an increasing reliance on the written or printed page. One important reason for this no doubt was a rising interest in the extended instrumental genres; the composition of these required considerably more skill than the adaptation of vocal compositions and dances that had formed the standard keyboard fare of the previous generation.

When keyboard players had need or desire for these extended compositions they could turn to the increasing number of printed collections of toccate, ricercari and canzoni that the leading composers were making available. For popular-song settings and brief versets most players were probably still capable of relying on their own devices. However, many apparently began to feel the need to write these down or have a teacher provide them with a notated setting.

It is my hypothesis that most of the keyboard manuscripts are repertory books for the use of players of modest attainment, amateurs or beginners. In these books a player would enter simple settings of the songs and dances popular in his day; most of these settings were his own adaptations (hence they would usually be unique to the manuscript), although on occasion he may have had the opportunity to copy out someone else's setting (i.e., the "wandering variation" —see p. 55). In addition to these settings he might write down some short instrumental pieces of his own composition. When, however, the need arose for works requiring more sophisticated compositional skills he would turn to the printed collections, either playing directly from these editions, or, if he did not have them permanently available, copying some compositions into his book. To suit his needs he might in this process shorten or simplify those pieces. In many cases the manuscript may actually have been prepared by a teacher for the use of his pupil; collections of adaptations of popular songs and simplified excerpts from works by the masters are still much used for musical instruction.

The above theory about the origin of the manuscript collections explains several of their special characteristics. It shows why concordances are fairly rare, and also explains why the existing concordances often are to printed collections: the latter were the most easily available sources of music by other composers. Finally, the theory accounts for the fact that attributions are often found with compositions that also have concordances. Since the copyist did not expect anyone else to use his book he tended to be casual about inserting attributions. But it is possible that some writers were more conscientious and included an attribution with the pieces copied from other sources (i.e., not of their own composition)—provided, of course, that the name of the author was known to them (see also p. 60).

If the above theory is correct we should not expect to find many unpublished compositions—or authentic alternate versions of published compositions—by prominent composers in the Italian manuscripts. Such compositions are more likely to be found in the Northern collectors' anthologies and in the few Italian collections of a similar type, e.g., London 30491 and Bologna 53 (the latter in spite of the scarcity of attributions corresponds in other ways to this genre; note, however, that it is of 18th-century origin). In Italy keyboard music was disseminated primarily through publication; circulation in manuscript played a subordinate role. Some exceptions to this rule did exist. There were two composers whose keyboard music, in spite of its importance, was not available in print: Giovanni de Macque and Ercole Pasquini. It is probably no coincidence that their works appear in appreciable number in several manuscripts. Evidently there was sufficient interest in their music for some musicians to take the trouble of copying the pieces by these two composers into their books. One suspects that in most cases the sources of these copies did not stem directly from the composer; the process of transmission may have included several intermediary sources (i.e., other people's repertory books) and may even have involved versions taken down by ear from live performances, or learned by rote and put into notation at a much later date. This could account for the frequent corruptions in the texts and the many variants among concordant versions.[3]

PROVENANCE OF THE INDIVIDUAL MANUSCRIPTS

In the second part of this study the provenance of the individual manuscripts will be considered. In general I have not attempted to associate the manuscripts with well-known musicians; for most manuscripts it is not likely that such associations existed. Rather I have tried to ascertain from what city or region the manuscripts derive, what family they may have belonged to, and during what period they were compiled. In forming my conclusions I used certain assumptions that deserve some comment.

Regional origin. Rarely do the manuscripts give any explicit indication of the region of origin. A valuable clue is offered, however, by the present location of a manuscript. In general, European manuscripts are known to have travelled much, and one does not necessarily assume that they reside today in the place where they originated. However, for the Italian keyboard sources, this is often a fairly safe assumption. As I have postulated above, these manuscripts early in their history were deposited in institutional or family libraries, and there is no reason they would ever have been separated from these libraries. Even if part or the entire library was put up for sale, these rather plain manuscripts were not likely to have attracted the interest of an out-of-town collector. The collection of which they formed part may have changed hands; perhaps it was taken over by some other religious or public institution, but even when that happened it rarely travelled far. For many keyboard manuscripts there is other evidence confirming that they remained in their place of origin (for example, Naples 48 and 73), and for none are there any indications to the contrary.[4]

The presence of attributions to composers whose reputations appear to have been primarily local and whose works were not disseminated much outside their region is another factor taken into account in determining the regional origin, as is some evidence provided by physical appearance, notation, and musical contents of the manuscripts. These factors will be evaluated in the sections on the individual manuscripts.

Dating. In estimating the period of origin of the manuscripts I have assumed that a majority were copied over a comparatively brief time-span, within approximately a decade (usually, I suspect, even within a few years). I believe this to be true in general with most unified music manuscripts; when several dates are found (as in Vat. mus. 569, in Naples 73, and in the Pasquini autographs) these tend to confirm this assumption. It is also in line with the idea that the keyboard manuscripts were prepared for the use of players during their learning stages. Hence, when a manuscript contains a date I shall assume that this date roughly represents the time during which the entire collection was copied. Of course, this assumption does not necessarily apply when a manuscript was put together from originally independent segments, when it includes sections in different handwriting, or when there is a marked change in the writing style of an individual hand (see, for example, the discussion of London 30491).

Secondly, I will assume, in accordance with the conclusions reached earlier, that when a concordance exists to a printed edition, the composition in question was in fact copied from this edition (conceivably, though not usually, through intermediary copies) and hence that the date of publication of the edition provides a terminus post quem for the manuscript. Sometimes the close resemblance between the written and the printed text leaves little doubt about this; in other cases, when the manuscript text deviates substantially from the printed versions, this assumption may seem less secure. In general, however, I believe it to be valid, in view of the theory presented above about the genesis of the manuscript sources.

Again, there are a number of further factors that are taken into consideration, such as the composer and the type of repertory included in the collection. Each of these factors by itself might be regarded as somewhat speculative; it is only when all appear to point towards the same conclusion with respect to the origin of a manuscript that one feels that one's estimates have a good chance of being not too far off the mark.

PART TWO

ANNOTATED CATALOGUE OF THE MANUSCRIPTS

Introductory Note

The following annotated catalogue lists all known Italian manuscripts compiled between c. 1500 and c. 1700 as well as a few later collections containing 17th-century materials.[1] The manuscripts are listed in alphabetical order by country, city, library, and collection, and alphabetically or numerically according to call number within each collection.[2] For most manuscripts the following information is provided:

(1) The manuscript short title.

(2) The location and name of the library or collection, followed by the call number or other identifying signature. This entry is preceded by the library siglum (in parentheses) as given in Benton, *Research Libraries* (usually based on the RISM siglum).

(3) Titles or other identifying inscriptions, when such appear on cover, spine, or flyleaf.

(4) Physical data: height x width in cm (rounded to the nearest cm), and number of pages.[3]

(5) The form(s) of notation (e.g., four-staff score, two-staff keyboard score) and staff ruling employed in the manuscript.[4]

(6) The attribution(s) found within the manuscript. In listing these attributions the composers' names generally are standardized (variant spellings are not listed individually).

(7) The provenance of the manuscript. In most cases the given time and place of origin are conjectural; the bases for the estimates are discussed in the annotations.

(8) A selective bibliography, usually including only sources giving the most detailed and recent information.

(9) A list of modern editions that include a substantial segment of the contents of the manuscript.[5]

The discussion following each listing is oriented primarily towards establishing the provenance, although it usually includes a consideration of other noteworthy aspects of the manuscript.

Most of the information presented in the catalogue was obtained from first-hand examination of the manuscripts, or, in a few cases, of microfilms. For a few sources of marginal importance to this study (e.g., 18th- and 19th-century copies of 17th-century publications) I have relied on secondary sources or on information provided me by other scholars. For such sources only a summary description is given. No full discussion is generally included here for 16th-century sources, although some are dealt with in Part One, Chapter II.

Table of Manuscripts

COLOGNY T.II.1

(CH-no siglum) Cologny/Geneva, Biblioteca Bodmeriana, Musik T.II.1

Title:	Girolamo Frescobaldi Toccate, Canzoni e Correnti Autografo (on board case containing the manuscript).
Physical data:	16 × 24 cm; 94ff.
Notation:	Two-staff keyboard score (2 × 6/8).
Attributions:	See title; no further attributions.
Provenance:	North-Italian, c. 1650-70.
Literature:	Abbiati, *Storia* II, 345, 350-54.
	Darbellay, *Manuscrit frescobaldien*.

This manuscript contains an almost complete copy of Frescobaldi's TOCCATE II (1627), two toccate from TOCCATE I (1615), and four compositions not known from other sources (see Table 14).

The volume was first described in 1943 by Abbiati (*Storia* II, 345). At the time it was owned by Natale Gallini of Milan; in 1949 it was sold in New York by Parke-Bernet to the firm of W.S. Kundy (Lucerne, Switzerland). It now forms part of the Bodmer Collection.

Abbiati believed Cologny T.II.1 to be a Frescobaldi autograph;[6] its autograph status was questioned, however, by the present author in a paper presented at the 1974 Annual Meeting of the American Musicological Society. Etienne Darbellay has since established that the manuscript definitely is not in the hand of Frescobaldi. According to Darbellay the watermarks belong to a paper used in Northern Italy between c. 1640 and 1670, from which he concludes that the manuscript originated in this region. This conclusion is supported by the character of the opening subject of one of the pieces not known from other Frescobaldi sources (f. 83'). This subject begins with the four-fold repetition of the note e; as we point out elsewhere (p. 159), such reiteration in imitative subjects is uncharacteristic for Frescobaldi, but common in North-Italian compositions. Darbellay, furthermore, notes some harmonic features in the third and fourth of these additional pieces that point to an origin several decades after Frescobaldi's death.

NUREMBERG 33748-V

(D-Ngm) Nuremberg, Germanisches Nationalmuseum, Ms. 33748-V (formerly 271-V)

Physical data:	16 × 21 cm; 12 ff.
Notation:	Two-staff keyboard score (2 × 5/8).
Attributions:	None.
Provenance:	Probably North-Italian, c. 1640-1660.
Literature:	None.

Nuremberg 33748 is a collection of eight separately bound manuscripts. Vols. I, II, III, IV, and VI contain lute tablatures (Vol. I also includes a page in mensural notation: an altus part "Unam petij a domino," and Vol. IV includes music for voice and basso continuo), Vol. V contains keyboard music, Vol. VII contains violin tablatures, and Vol. VIII (actually a set of individual pages) contains lute tablatures and keyboard music. There is no indication of any relation between these volumes, although all appear to date from the early-middle 17th century (except for the page of mensural notation, possibly of 16th-century origin). The keyboard music in Vol. VIII contains no titles or attributions; although the staff system is 2 × 5/8, the upright format and the musical style suggest a South-German provenance; it will therefore not be discussed here.

Nuremberg 33748-V has the characteristic appearance of the oblong Italian keyboard booklets; its contents also appear to be exclusively Italian. Conceivably the collection belonged to an Italian working in Southern Germany, or to a German trained in Italian traditions. There are no attributions, but six pieces are concordant with dances in Frescobaldi's TOCCATE I (1615), TOCCATE II (1627) and AGGIUNTA (1637). The manuscript versions of these dances have been simplified and some of the cadences have been slightly altered. The remaining pieces are almost all standard arie; among them are settings of Ruggiero, la Fiorenza, Spagnoletta, and *Fuggi, fuggi* (= Ballo di Mantua). Most of these settings have simple melody-chord textures; frequently the left hand consists merely of bare octaves—or at least is notated as such. Concordances and repertory suggest that the manuscript originated sometime between 1640 and 1660.

LONDON 14246

(GB-Lbm) London, British Library, Ms. Add. 14246

Physical data:	21 × 28 cm; 41 ff.
Notation:	Two-staff keyboard score (2 × 6/7).
Attributions:	None.
Provenance:	Italian (Mantua?), probably between 1664 and 1685.
Literature:	Hudson, *Development*, 436.
	Hughes-Hughes, *Catalogue* III, 108.

A note on f. 1 appears to connect this manuscript with Mantua and dates it to before 1685 (Hughes-Hughes III, 108). The entire content corresponds to compositions included in Storace, SELVA (Sa. 1664b).

LONDON 30491

(GB-Lbm) London, British Library, Ms. Add. 30491

Title:	Libro di canzone franzese del Signor Gio[v]anni de Macque . . . (on front cover).
Physical Data:	Upright format, 36 × 24 cm, except for ff. 23-26, which are oblong; 53 ff. (including front and back cover).
Notation:	Four-staff score, two-staff keyboard score (2 × 6/8), vocal monodies (5/5), and passaggi for viola bastarda (single five-line staff).
Attributions:	In keyboard segment: de Macque, Ippolito, Stella, Fillimarino, Trabaci, Lambardo, "il principe" [Gesualdo?]. In viola bastarda segment: de Macque, Orazio della Viola, Lambardo, Effrem (in Tavola only—music missing). In monody segment: Monteverdi, Peri.
Provenance:	In the hand of Luigi Rossi. Keyboard and viola bastarda segments: Naples, c. 1610-1620. Monody segment: probably Rome, after 1620.
Literature:	Ghislanzoni, *Rossi*, 18-20. Apel, *Keyboard Music*, 424-428. Caluori, *Rossi*, ix.
Editions:	Watelet, Macque. Jackson, *Neapolitan Composers*.

London 30491 is undoubtedly one of the most important of the manuscript collections. It is the principal source for the keyboard works of Giovanni de Macque; furthermore, it contains perhaps the only surviving keyboard composition attributable to Gesualdo, an assortment of keyboard compositions by a group of Neapolitan composers associated with de Macque and Gesualdo, monodies by Peri and Monteverdi—including the latter's *Lamento d'Arianna* and a unique copy of his *Lamento d'Olimpia*[7]—and, finally, a group of divisions on madrigals for the viola bastarda.[8] It is also one of the most complex of the sources; to fit the many data it provides into a consistent picture is no easy task. The manuscript has been drawn upon for several modern editions, but no detailed description or critical study has appeared. On the basis of information provided on f. 1 (front cover) and f. 2 it has been described as being in the hand of the composer Luigi Rossi. Before dealing with Rossi's relation to the manuscript I shall discuss the physical and musical contents.

The manuscript has a foliation as well as a pagination. As we shall see shortly, the pagination was probably entered during the manuscript's first phase, the foliation after the manuscript had acquired its present form. The foliation includes the front and back cover (f. 1 and f. 53) as well as the inserted oblong gathering (ff. 23-26). The pagination stops at f. 33 (p. 55); it is not found in the oblong gathering, which intervenes between p. 41 and p. 43 (there is no paginated p. 42).

The manuscript contains four kinds of repertory (see also Table 12, p. 91):

(1) Music notated in four-staff score probably for keyboard,[9] attributed to Stella,[10] Giovanni de Macque,[11] Rinaldo,[12] Francesco Lambardo,[3] Ippolito,[14] Fabritio Fillimarino,[15] Trabaci,[16] and "il principe"[17] (ff. 3-38', 51-51').

(2) A single composition, "Capriccio di Gio. de Macque sopra rè, fà, mi, sol" in two-staff keyboard notation (ff. 23-26').

(3) Vocal monodies by Monteverdi and Peri in two-staff score (texted soprano and figured bass) (ff. 39-45, 50).

(4) Passaggi for the viola bastarda attributed to Oratio della Viola,[18] Francesco Lambardo, Giovanni de Macque, and, in the *Tavola* only (see below), Muzio Effrem (ff. 45-50).[19]

With the exception of the segment ff. 23-26' the pages are in upright format, and are uniform with respect to paper and size; the staff-ruling is also uniform except for ff. 47-48', which have a narrower ruling. The first part of the manuscript, ff. 3-44, consists of five gatherings of different size; the remaining folios are single pages, bound individually. The segment ff. 23-26' (in two-staff keyboard notation) is a single gathering in oblong format.

The handwriting in the instrumental compositions has, at first sight, a strikingly different appearance from that found in the monodies; this is true for the music as well as for the text and captions. The writing in the instrumental portions more nearly resembles that of 16th-century than that of most 17th-century manuscripts. It does not have the flowing "cursive" character common in the latter, but is careful and deliberate; it has tear-drop note shapes, and shows use of a thick pen. The writing of the monodies is more characteristic of later, 17th-century hands (of course, some are known to date from after 1600 in any case); it gives the impression of being the work of a copyist more concerned with speed than with appearance.[20] Careful examination shows, however, that in spite of marked internal differences in clef, note shapes, etc., the writing is in all likelihood the work of a single person. The establishment of the connection between the two styles of writing is facilitated by the "Canzon francese del principe," f. 74', the notation of which shows a more or less transitional stage. Its appearance is closest to that of the monodies, but it contains some features similar to those found in the instrumental pieces. Evidently the two styles of writing do not represent two different scribes, but rather two stages in the development of a single hand—most likely separated by some span of time. Indeed, the instrumental segments convey the impression of being the work of a young copyist working hard at producing an elegant score, the monodies of being the product of a mature musician trying to complete a usable copy in the shortest amount of time. That the monodies and the "canzon del principe" were entered at a later date is also apparent from the fact that they are not included in a *Tavola* that appears on f. 52.

The handwriting of the *Tavola* is the same as that of the captions and the page numbers in the earlier segment. It lists in alphabetical order all the keyboard pieces on the paginated leaves (pp. 1-55) and includes page references for these. It also lists the keyboard piece appearing on f. 51, the *Partite sopra Fidele* by Francesco Lambardo.[21] For this piece the *Tavola* gives as page reference "p. 97." As the manuscript now stands f. 51 corresponds to p. 91; hence, if the page reference was correct at one time, three folios must have been lost. The viola-bastarda divisions are also listed in the *Tavola*, but without page references; this accords with the fact that the pagination does not extend to the pages on which these divisions appear. While there is complete correspondence between the *Tavola* and the keyboard pieces, there are some discrepancies with respect to the viola-bastarda divisions—see Table 11. Apparently some of the divisions have been lost (possibly they appeared on the three missing folios mentioned above); furthermore, the *Tavola* makes no mention of the fact that the madrigals appear twice: as unornamented tenor lines and in passaggiato form. It is also evident that this section has been rebound: "Nasce la pena" continues from f. 48' to f. 45', and the plain version of "Cara la vita mia" has been separated from the ornamented version. This is probably due to the fact that the reverse sides of "Nasce la pena mia" (f. 45) and of "Cara la vita mia" (f. 49) both were used for the continuation of Monteverdi's "Voglio morire."

In summary, the manuscript must have evolved through the following stages (see Table 12):

(Ia)	The keyboard music in four-staff score ff. 3-22', 27-33'
(Ib)	The oblong gathering, ff. 23-26'
(IIa)	The *Partite sopra Fidele*, ff. 51-51'
(IIb)	The divisions for viola bastarda
(III)	The *Tavola*
(IV)	The *canzon del principe*
(V)	The monodies

Stage I corresponds to the paginated segment, stages I and II to the segments included in the *Tavola*. There remains to be discussed how the writing found on ff. 1 and 2 fits into this history. This writing is partly in a cipher code, partly in ordinary script. A typewritten page, "Key to Cypher," has been inserted into the manuscript, providing a key to the code as well a transcription of the coded statement. The full text of all the material found on these pages is given in Ghislanzoni, *Rossi*, pp. 18-19.

On f. 1 appears a poem that in the "Key to Cypher" is transcribed as follows:

Libro di canzone franzese del signor Gio[v]anni Demacque
Che fù maestro di Luigi Rossi sfortunato
E sfortunato fù da quando nacque
Poiche 14 anni in (?) corte è stato
Nepur un mezzo (?) grosso mai a alquistato

Table 11
Passaggi For The Viola Bastarda in London 30491

Foliation	Manuscript	*Tavola*
45'	[continuation of Nasce . . . from 48' below]	[see below, f. 48']
46	Cara la vita mia [unornamented tenor line]	Cara la vita mia per la viola bastarda passaggiato da Oratio della Viola
46'	Susanna un giorno [unornamented tenor line]	[not in *Tavola*]
47	blank	
47'-48	Susanna di Oratio: per la Viola bastarda [divisions]	[not in *Tavola*]
48'	Nasce la pena mia di Gio: Macque [divisions], cont. on f. 45'	Nasce la pena mia, passaggiato Fran[ces]co Lambardo
49-50	Cara la vita mia di Oratio [divisions]	[see above, f. 46]
	[not in manuscript]	Io mi son giovanetto passaggiato di Mutio Effrem
	[not in manuscript]	Non ch'io no voglia mai, passaggiato da Gio: de macque

On f. 2 appears in code the statement:

"Questo libro lo fece fare il duca di Traetta,[22] per me Luigi Rossi"

and further down on the same page in ordinary script:

"Ce libro es de Don Luis Rossi."

These statements have formed the basis for identifying Rossi as the copyist of this manuscript, although it is not entirely clear that the coded inscription on f. 2

means that Rossi (about whose relations with the Duke nothing further is known) was the scribe of this volume rather than its recipient. Caluori (*Rossi*, ix) observes, however, that the hand of the monodies in London 30491 is similar to that of other alleged Rossi autographs—i.e., Vatican, Barb. lat. 4175, ff. 59'-96' and 102'-105, and the composer's will of 1646. She believes that the earlier instrumental portion is in a different hand, but we have seen that, in spite of the different character of the notation, it appears to stem from the same scribe. Hence there is a high probability that the entire manuscript is a Rossi autograph. It is also evident from the second inscription on f. 2 that, even if the volume was originally prepared for the Duke of Traietto, it subsequently came into the composer's possession. We shall see that apparently Rossi later took it with him to Rome.

Nevertheless, several problems remain with respect to Rossi's relation to this collection:

(1) Why did Rossi use cipher code and why is the uncoded statement in Spanish? Was the employment of code merely the prank of an adolescent (on Rossi's age, see below), perhaps to hide the dissatisfaction expressed in the poem? The use of Spanish is less puzzling; Naples was under Spanish rule, and Spanish influence extended to every aspect of cultural life.

(2) The first line of the poem refers to a "Libro de canzone franzese del signor Giovanni Demacque." However, the manuscript opens neither with canzoni francese, nor with compositions of de Macque; the only canzoni attributed to de Macque appear on f. 17, f. 29, and f. 30'. The latter two are entitled, respectively, *P[rima] Canzon* and *S[econda] Canzon*, and hence may form part of the originally projected *Libro*. Since the first line suggests that the intention was to copy only compositions by de Macque, the poem must have been written before any keyboard music was entered.

(3) It is curious that Rossi did not include any of his own compositions among either the vocal pieces or the keyboard music. Only a single keyboard composition attributed to him has survived, a "Passacaille du Seigneur de Louigi," which appears in the French Bauyn and Parville manuscripts and in two English sources.[23]

(4) What is the meaning of the line "14 anni in corte è stato"? Presumably it was Rossi who spent fourteen years in court, not de Macque. Does "da quando naque/poiche 14 anni . . ." imply that he had been there since birth? Since he was born in 1598 this would imply that the poem was written in 1612. This is not an implausible date so far as the repertory and handwriting style are concerned, but it raises one problem. According to the poem, de Macque *had been* his teacher. In 1612 de Macque was still alive (he died two years later). Are we to believe that at the age of fourteen Rossi's studies with de Macque were already over? Besides, how can we account for his being born at a court? More likely he entered a court chapel as a choir boy, say at age seven. In that case the date of the

Table 12
Summary of the Contents of London 30491[a]

Foliation	Pagination	Contents	Stage
1-2		front cover and title page	before I?
3-22'	1-41	four-staff keyboard score, de Macque, et al.	I
23-26'		two-staff keyboard notation, de Macque, Capriccio . . .	I
27-33'	43-55	four-staff keyboard score, de Macque, et al.	I
34'-38'		four-staff keyboard score, Gesualdo, Canzon . . .	IV
39-45		monodies, Monteverdi, Peri	V
45'-46', 48'-49		viola-bastarda divisions	II
50		monody, cont. from f. 45	V
51'-51'	97?	four-staff keyboard score, Stella	II
52-52'		*Tavola*	III

[a]Not included in this table are ff. 2', 47 and 50', which are blank, and f. 34, which contains a brief, unidentified fragment in four-staff score.

poem would be c. 1619 (i.e., 1598 + 7 + 14), and the use of the past tense in reference to de Macque would make more sense.

Scribbled on the final page of the manuscript is a date that is rather difficult to read. Jackson (*Neapolitan Composers*, ix) believes it to be in Rossi's hand and thinks it can be interpreted as either 1612 or 1617, though he considered the latter date more likely. The earlier date would agree with the "since birth" theory, the later date with the "choir boy" theory—that is, if we are willing to accept that Rossi entered the court at the age of five. However, since Jackson's reading of the date itself remains a conjecture, it may not be possible to resolve the whole matter until further biographical information on Rossi's early years comes to light.

In 1620 Rossi moved to Rome to enter the service of the Borghese family. Probably he took the manuscript with him since apparently it formed at one time part of the Borghese family library[24] It appears likely that the monodies were not entered until after he had come to Rome, i.e., after his twenty-second year; this would account for the transformation in the script described above.

It appears then that stages I and III (see p. 88) were completed in Naples before 1620, stage IV (the *Canzon del principe*) probably also in Naples (the handwriting suggests an interval of some years after the earlier stages), and stage V in Rome after 1620.

LONDON 40080

(GB-Lbm) London, British Library, Ms. Add. 40080

Title:	Fioretti d[e]l Frescobaldi (f. 1).
Physical data:	16 × 22 cm; 51 ff.
Notation:	Two-staff keyboard score (3 × 5/5).
Attributions:	See title; no further attributions.
Provenance:	Italian or English, late 17th or 18th century.
Literature:	Willetts, *Manuscripts*, 11 (catalogue entry only).

In spite of a blanket attribution to Frescobaldi, London 40080 seems to have remained entirely unknown; it is not mentioned in the literature and none of its contents has been published. A note on the flyleaf states that it was purchased from a Signore Vincenzo de Giorgio on 11 June 1921. The manuscript contains eleven canzoni (entitled *Canzoni Prima*, etc.) and one toccata. In spite of the title on the opening flyleaf no compositions are entitled "Fiorette" (this is not unusual—none of the pieces in Frescobaldi's *Fiori musicali* are called "Fiore"). There are reasons for questioning whether this manuscript is of 17th-century and of Italian provenance. This matter as well as the validity of the attribution (which is in a hand not appearing elsewhere in the manuscript) will be discussed in Part Three, pp. 156-58.

LONDON 2088

(GB-Lcm) London, Royal College of Music, Ms. 2088

Title:	Laus Deus MDLXXXVI Libro di Intavoladura di arpicordo. F.A.P. (on f. [1]).
Physical data:	Oblong format; 22 ff.
Notation:	Two-staff keyboard score (2 × 5/8).
Attributions:	Marco Facoli.
Provenance:	Venice, late 16th century (?).
Literature:	Brown, *Instrumental Music*, 343 ([1586]₂) (includes complete inventory).

The manuscript includes dances (some probably from the lost *Primo Libro d'Intavolatura* of Marco Facoli) and settings of vocal compositions; it is discussed at greater length in Chapter II, pp. 13-14.

ASSISI

(I-Af) Assisi, Archivio musicale del Sacro convento (no call no.).

Physical data:	Upright format; 24 ff.
Notation:	Four-staff score.
Attributions:	Frescobaldi, Tarquinio Merula.
Provenance:	North-central-Italian, second half of the 17th century.
Literature:	Curtis, *L'opera*, 142.
	Curtis, *Merula*, xi.
Edition:	Curtis, *Merula*, 18 (of *Canzone*, f. 23).

This manuscript contains compositions from Frescobaldi's FIORI (1635) and, in another hand, a canzone attributed to Tarquinio Merula (see p. 171). According to Curtis the manuscript dates from the middle (*Merula*, xi) or from the second half (*L'opera*, 142) of the 17th century.

BAGNACAVALLO

(No siglum) Bagnacavallo, Biblioteca comunale Giuseppe Taroni, Codice C.M.B.1

Physical data:	34 × 23 cm; 96 ff.
Notation:	Two-staff keyboard score (5 × 5/8)
Attributions:	Diruta, Merulo, Tomaso Fabri.
Provenance:	Probably early 17th century.
Literature:	None.
Edition:	Varotti, *Fabri* (of *Toccata del P^O Tuono*, f. 32)

This manuscript is presently located in the Biblioteca communale in Bagna-cavallo, a small town about mid-way between Ravenna and Faenza; an inscription on the opening page indicates that at one time it belonged to a Franciscan monastery.[25] It consists for the most part of copies from Diruta's TRANSILVANO I (Sa. 1593b), Merulo's TOCCATE I (Sa. 1598b). On ff. 32-32' appears a "Toccata del P$\underline{o}$ Tuono del Sig$\underline{r}$ Tomaso Fabri." In the tavola at the end of the volume this author is identified as "Tomaso Fabri Faentio," i.e. from Faenza; nothing further is known about him. His composition falls entirely within the Venetian toccata tradition of the Gabrielis.

BOLOGNA 360

(I-Bc) Bologna, Civico museo bibliografico musicale, Ms. AA/360

Physical data:	16 × 24 cm; 192 ff.
Notation:	Two-staff keyboard score (2 × 5/8); tablatures for various instruments.
Attributions (in keyboard segments):	Frescobaldi
Provenance:	North-Italian, c. 1640-1680.
Literature:	Kirkendale, *Fiorenza*, 71-72.
	Pacchioni, *Balli*, 2.
Editions:	Casimiri, *Frescobaldi*, 13-14 (of f. 20, *Ducale*).

This unusually diversified collection apparently belonged at one time to Gaetano Gaspari (1807-1881), librarian of the Liceo musicale; his name appears on the second flyleaf.

Except for the flyleaves all pages are uniformly ruled for Italian keyboard notation; however, only a fraction of the contents consists of keyboard music. In the remainder the ruling is used (or adapted) to notate music for a variety of instruments. The following instrumentations can be identified:

> *Keyboard:* ff. 1-4', 14-38', 40-51', 54'-56, 90
> *Violin*[26] (some in tablature): ff. 11'-12, 57'-59', 64-72, 75'-80, 84, 85, 105-108', 112-145, 147-155, 156 (with bass), 157-179, 183-188, 189-190, 191'-192
> *Two violins and organ* (bass): 94'-100
> *Guitar* (number tablature and letter tablature): 9', 53-53', 84', 108'-110', 145'-146'
> *Lute:* 86'-89', 102'-103, 111', 180-181'
> *Tromba marina:* ff. 5-8 (possibly the only surviving example of notated music for this instrument)
> *Texted keyboard, voice and keyboard* (realized bass): 39-39', 52-52', 30'-83', 107-107'.

Many of these materials clearly were intended to serve a pedagogical function; they include instructions for tuning the various instruments,[27] for reading the tablatures and for realizing a ·bass on various instruments. There are also elementary exercises (e.g., f. 75': "Tremulo in Scale per il violino a 2: corde") and pieces of a presumably didactic nature, consisting principally of simple and often rather clumsy settings of arie and balli. Of some interest are a set of instructions "per cantare l'ottave sopra il leuto," for which the first line of Tasso's "Gerusalemme liberata" is used as model.

The recto of the second flyleaf contains what is apparently the last page of a table of contents (the pieces are listed in order of appearance). On the verso of the flyleaf begins a *Tavola Alfabetico*, which is continued on the back flyleaves; it only covers the letters A to F. This table is useful in that in many cases it specifies the instrumentation of pieces whose captions in the body of the manuscript lack such indications (e.g., "nel spineto," "nel leuto"; these spellings are used consistently).

The only composers named in the manuscript are Frescobaldi (f. 57'), Monsu la Barra (f. 67')[28] and Fr. Ludvico (f. 155). Various other names are mentioned in the titles of some of the pieces, but it is not clear whether these names refer to composers or—more likely—to people who have some other association with the pieces in question: "Lo Balletto del Sig. Marche[se] Fran-[ces]co Gonzaga: (f. 120); "Corrento del Sig. March[ese] Agnelli" (f. 123); "Corrente di Monsū Tragola" (f. 130-131); "Ballo della Contessa di Monterei" (f. 153'); "Gagliarda di Monsū Gioachino" (f. 161'); "Partita insegnata mi da Se. Anibale Medici" (f. 169-170); "Balletto del Sig. Duca di Parma" (f. 176).

Another aspect of the heterogeneity of this manuscript is the large variety of handwriting styles. There appears to be one principal hand, although its characteristics fluctuate rather drastically, making identification not always certain. This hand is responsible for many of the keyboard pieces as well as for some of the music for other instruments, including the instructional materials. In addition there are a large number of entries—many of them brief fragments—in other hands; some of these clearly are the work of persons inexperienced with music copying.

The changes in the writing style of the principal hand suggest that this manuscript—unlike most of the Italian keyboard collections—was compiled over a considerable period of time. This is confirmed, at least in the second half of the manuscript, by three dates separated by successive intervals of ten years:

> f. 119: "Le tre di novembra 1661 in Ricciana [= Riccione?]"
> f. 169': "10 novembra 1671"
> f. 176': "finis 1681, 16 agosta."

The notation and the musical style of the earlier portion, in particular of the opening keyboard segment ff. 1-4', seem to indicate that the beginning of the manuscript dates back to several decades earlier. Hence I propose an overall dating of c. 1640-1680. The inscription on f. 119 evidently was entered while the scribe resided in Riccione, south of Rimini; reference to towns such as Bologna, Parma, Turin, Florence and Venice, and to families such as Medici and Gonzaga in the titles of some of the dances suggest a North-central-Italian origin for the entire manuscript.

While the musical quality of much of the content of this manuscript is slight, the collection is of unusual interest for its documentation of pedagogical methods of the period.

BOLOGNA 258

(I-Bc) Bologna, Civico museo bibliografico musicale, Ms. BB/258 (Manuscript addendum to a copy of Michel'Angelo Rossi, TOCCATE, Sa. 1657a).

Physical data:	Same (upright) format as the printed edition; 12 pp.
Notation:	Two-staff keyboard notation (5 × 5/8).
Attributions:	Michel'Angelo Rossi.
Provenance:	c. 1700 (copyist's dates: 1700-1701).
Literature:	White, *Rossi*, vii-viii.
	Apel, *Keyboard Music*, 486-489.
Edition:	White, *Rossi* (complete).

This manuscript addendum to Rossi's only surviving keyboard publication contains seven compositions not found in the publication: four toccate, two versetti, and a set of partite on la Romanesca. The question of Rossi's authorship of these works is discussed in Part Three, p. 186.

When I reexamined this volume in 1979 the manuscript supplement had been removed because of its fragile condition and replaced by a photocopy. The original is now kept in a separate container and is catalogued as AA.CSI (cassetto 1).

BOLOGNA 53

(I-Bc) Bologna, Civico museo bibliografico musicale, Ms. DD/53

Title:	Sonate d'autori diversi (on cover); Varj Autori/Toccate/e Sonate/per/Cembalo (on spine).
Physical data:	22 × 30 cm; 103 ff.
Notation:	Two-staff keyboard score (3 × 5/8).
Attributions:	Frescobaldi, Kerll, Bernardo Pasquini, Pollaroli, and Tarquinio Merula.
Provenance:	Bologna (?), second decade of the 18th century or later.
Literature:	Tagliavini, *Kerll* (includes complete inventory).

This manuscript is the subject of an article by Luigi Ferdinando Tagliavini, who discusses its importance as a source for the works of Johann Kaspar Kerll (Tagliavini, *Kerll*). The article provides a complete table of contents as well as concordances with early prints and modern editions.

Tagliavini believes that the collection was compiled before the end of the 17th century. This estimate appears to be supported by the notation (5/8 staff-line system, rare after 1700) and by the repertory: all the attributions are to composers who lived most if not all of their lives in the 17th century. However, the last two compositions in the manuscript (ff. 102, 103), both untitled and anonymous, almost certainly belong to the 18th century. I would place them at the earliest in the 1720s—see Example 9. Since these pieces are copied in the same hand as the rest of the manuscript, and in all probability during approximately the same period (there is no discernible change in writing style), the entire manuscript is most likely of 18th-century provenance. The copyist may have worked, however, from 17th-century sources and simply reproduced their old-fashioned staff systems.

Bologna 53 differs from typical 17th-century manuscripts in other ways as well. It is a neat and methodical copy; the pieces are mostly ordered in a systematic fashion, suggesting that, contrary to 17th-century habits, compositions were generally copied in the order in which they appeared in the model sources.

Unfortunately these systematic procedures were not extended to the attributions. Composers' names appear sporadically throughout the manuscript; the majority were clearly added at a later time—and may have been based on sources other than those used by the copyist for his musical text.

Tagliavini has established that the opening segment, ff. 1-48', contains the first twenty-three pieces listed in Kerll's thematic index of his own works. This list was appended by the composer to his *Modulatio organica* (1686); the pieces appear there in the same order as in our manuscript. There is hence no question about Kerll's authorship of these compositions; yet in the manuscript the first of these works is attributed to "Sig. Frescobaldi." Several others are indeed attributed to Kerll (the name appears in several different spellings: Cherll, Cherl, Kerl, Kerll); the remainder of the pieces in this group have no attribution. Since in this case a systematically ordered group of pieces (i.e., eight *Toccate* in the eight tones, six *Canzoni*, etc.) proves to be the work of a single composer even though his name does not appear with every composition, it is tempting to account in similar fashion for other organized blocks of pieces in the manuscript. For example, from f. 57' to f. 88' there appears a set of *Preludio-Sonata* pairs in the first six tones. The *Sonata* of the first pair has an attribution in a later hand to Pollaroli. This same work appears singly, i.e., without the preceding *Preludio* (or any of the other pieces in this set) under Pollaroli's name in Arresti's anthology, SONATE, Sa. 1697(?)m. It seems likely that the entire set of six pairs was taken from a collection of Pollaroli's works and that the attribution was inserted by a later owner of the manuscript (or by a librarian) who noticed the identity of the first Sonata with the

Example 9

(a) Bologna 53, f. 102, [untitled composition] (mm. 1-14)

(b) Bologna 53, f. 103', [untitled composition] (mm. 1-8)

Sonata in Arresti's collection (cf. p. 60)[29] A similar situation may exist with respect to other blocks of pieces—for example, those including Bernardo Pasquini attributions.

This manuscript appears to be centered around some of the same composers represented in Arresti's anthology. It furnishes, however, a much more comprehensive sample of their works than is provided in the printed collection. In fact Bologna 53 probably should be regarded as the most important surviving anthology of Italian keyboard music composed during the last decades of the 17th century.

BOLOGNA Q 34

(I-Bc) Bologna, Civico museo bibliografico musicale, Ms. Q 34

Title:	Spartitura Generale & Particulare di diversi Motetti, et Madrigali, con altre Opere belle, & di molto studio. Joanus Amigonus Mantuanus scribebat Roma Anno Domine 1613 (f. 1).
Physical Data:	Upright format; 161 ff.
Notation:	Five-line ruling, single-staff and two- to five-staff scores.
Attributions:	None for the instrumental compositions; some composers are named for the vocal models (e.g., Palestrina).
Provenance:	Rome, 1613.

This collection contains two- to five-staff scores of vocal music (mostly untexted) and instrumental pieces. Among the former are many of the madrigals and chansons commonly used for intabulations, such as "Susanne un jour," "Vestiva i colli," and "Anchor che col partire"—although the settings generally do not include any passaggi.

Several pieces are notated in two-staff (5/5) score; however, these are probably intended for melody instrument (or in the case of texted lines, for voice) and continuo rather than for solo keyboard. In some of them the instrumentation is in fact specified as such, for example, f. 66: "Sinfonia prima per violino solo." All of these compositions consist of a single treble and a single bass line, without any chordal filling; occasionally the basses are figured. Folios 99-108' contain a series of traditional arie and balli, called "Balletti alla Romana," notated in this fashion; they are of considerable interest since they provide unornamented "skeletal" soprano-bass settings.

BOLOGNA 270

(I-Bc) Bologna, Civico museo bibliografico musicale, Ms. Z.270

A copy of Frescobaldi's RECERCARI (1615) and FIORI (1635), probably of 18th-century origin.

CASTELL 'ARQUATO

(I-CARc) Castell'Arquato, Chiesa Collegiata, Archivio, ten fascicles of keyboard music numbered I to X, no call numbers.

Literature and Editions:	Benevuti, *Cavazzoni* (partial edition of fascs. I, II and III).
	Jeppesen, *Orgelmusik* (including inventory and partial edition of fasc. I)
	Slim, *Ricercar.*
	Slim, *Keyboard Music (1960)* (including inventory fasc. 2).
	Slim, *Keyboard Music (1975)* (including complete edition of fascs. III and IV).

The reader is referred to Colin H. Slim's published and forthcoming studies for a detailed description of this complex and heterogeneous collection. Most materials date approximately from the middle of the 16th century. The two latest fascicles appear to be fasc. X, containing some pieces in Italian lute tablature followed by copies of fifteen compositions from Maschera's CANZONI (Sa. 1584a), and fasc. IV, a bifolio (notation: 2 × 8/5) containing anonymous organ versets for a Credo Apostolorum and the beginning of a Credo Dominicalis. Judging by the character of the handwriting this last fascicle is the only one in the collection that probably dates from after 1600.

COMO 820/40 and 820/55

(I-COd) Como, Archivio Musicale del Duomo, Mss. 820/40 and 820/55

Physical data:	Ms. 820/40: 21 × 28 cm; 16 ff.
	Ms. 820/55: 22 × 29 cm; 16 ff.
Notation:	Two-staff keyboard notation (3 × 5/8).
Attributions:	None.
Provenance:	Late 17th century.
Literature:	None.

Ms. 820/40 contains a *Gagliarda*, five pieces entitled *Toccata*, and three *Versetti*. Judged by style and notation this collection appears to date from the end of the 17th century. Ms. 820/55 is similar with respect to format and notation; it is entitled "Versetti per li tuoni," but also contains a few untitled dances.

FLORENCE 641

(I-Fl) Florence, Biblioteca Medicea-Laurenziana, Ms. Acquisti e Doni 641.

Title:	Intavolatura di M. Alamanno Aiolli (on cover).
Physical Data:	23 × 17 cm; 62 ff.
Notation:	Two-staff keyboard score (2 × 6/8).
Attributions:	Aiolli.
Provenance:	Florence, c. 1565-1600.
Literature:	D'Accone, *Aiolli* (includes inventory).

This collection is discussed in Part One, p. 13.

FLORENCE 106b

(I-Fn) Florence, Biblioteca Nazionale Centrale, Ms. Magl. XIX. 106 bis.

Physical data:	25 × 23 cm; 42 ff.
Notation:	Four-staff score.
Attributions:	de Macque, Nenna.
Provenance:	Naples (?), c. 1600-1620.
Literature:	Becherini, *Catalogo*, 40-41 (includes inventory).
	Lowinsky, *Early Scores*, 136.
	Watkins, *Gesualdo*, 215.
Editions:	None.

The manuscript Florence 106b is briefly described by Becherini (*Catalogo*, 40-41), and—somewhat inaccurately—by Lowinsky (*Early Scores*, 136).[30] An inscription on the opening flyleaf "di Carlo del Rio fiamengho" presumably does not represent an attribution but refers to the one-time owner of the manuscript.[31] The manuscript is notated in four-staff score, which continues across both pages of each opening. It consists of three sections, each of which is in a different hand:

(1) ff. 1'-9: A *Romanescha* and two *Ricercari* without attributions.

(2) ff. 9'-34: Twelve untitled pieces in the twelve tones attributed to de Macque (see below).

(3) ff. 34'-42: Eight madrigals by Pomponio Nenna (from the *Primo libro a 4*—see below), partially texted.

These compositions may be adaptions of ensemble music, but in their present form they were probably intended for keyboard performance (possibly as accompaniment). Indicative of this is, for example, the octave doubling of the last note in the bass line of the Romanescha. The twelve pieces making up the second segment are entitled "P[rim]o," "secondo," "3°," etc.; they clearly form a set of *Ricercari* in the twelve tones similar to those by Frescobaldi and Trabaci.

The attributions to de Macque appear only at the beginning (f. 9': del Macque) and at the end of the set (f. 34: "Joannis de Macques Psalmodiare Finis").

The presence of compositions by de Macque and by Nenna suggests that the manuscript, if not of Neapolitan origin, was at least derived from Neapolitan sources. The title "ricercare con 3 fughe, e rovesci" is characteristically Neapolitan (compare, for example, Trabaci, RICERCATE II, Sa. 1615c, f. 10: "Con tre fughe, e suoi riversi"); Northern composers generally do not add such a description to the titles of their ricercari (Frescobaldi, in his FANTASIE, 1608, does specify the number of subjects, but calls them "soggetti").

Lowinsky assigns this collection, on the basis of handwriting and content, to the beginning of the 17th century; he thinks it probably originated during the first years of the second decade—a dating that to me appears entirely plausible. He suggests the first portion may be written by a later or younger hand than the rest of the manuscript. The handwriting of the first portion does indeed have more pronounced 17th century characteristics but is unlikely to be of later date than the subsequent sections. The music is notated "a libro aperto" (i.e., the score continues from a system on the verso side of an opening to the adjacent system on the recto side before proceeding to the next lower system), and the compositions are entered continuously on both sides of each page, even when a new hand appears (e.g., the second hand begins on the verso side, f. 9', of the last entry of the previous hand, f. 9); hence in all probability the contents were entered in the order in which they now appear. Becherini (*Catalogo*, 40), believes the manuscript to be considerably older; she places it in the second half of the 16th century, but without giving her reasons.

The dating of this manuscript is of more than ordinary interest, since it plays a crucial role in Watkins's theory of the influence of Nenna on Gesualdo (Watkins, *Gesualdo*, 214-215). Watkins observes a number of stylistic connections between settings of identical texts of madrigals in Nenna's *Primo libro a 4* and in Gesualdo's *Libro V*. The latter collection was first published in 1611, but its contents were apparently composed as early at 1596 (Watkins, *Gesualdo*, 166). If we are to assume that Nenna's madrigals provided models for Gesualdo's, we have to establish that the former were composed prior to 1596. Unfortunately the only surviving copy of Nenna's *Primo libro a 4* dates from 1621; a copy of a 1613 edition existed earlier in this century.[32]

The ten Nenna madrigals in Florence 106b are identical to the first ten in the 1621 collection, and appear in the same order. The possibility that they were in fact copied from the 1621, or even from the 1613 edition would of course not seriously contradict Lowinsky's dating. However, Watkins, apparently unaware of Lowinsky's discussion,[33] uses Becherini's dating to support his hypothesis that Nenna's collection was composed during the years 1582-1603, and hence may antedate Gesualdo's collection. He believes, furthermore, that Becherini's dating is confirmed by the fact that de Macque and Nenna were publishing in the

1570s and 1580s. However, we have no evidence that de Macque's *Ricercari* were composed during these years; all the surviving sources of de Macque's keyboard music date from after 1600.[34] Watkins's hypothesis concerning Nenna's primacy may well be correct, but it cannot be supported by the concordances in Florence 106b since there is no compelling reason to date the manuscript before 1600.

FLORENCE 115

(I-Fn) Florence, Biblioteca Nazionale Centrale, Ms. Magl. XIX. 115.

Physical data:	21 × 27 cm; 50 ff. (ff. 15'-50 blank).
Notation:	Two-staff keyboard score (2 × 5/8).
Attributions:	None, except for an "Aria di Santino da Parma" (f. 4).
Provenance:	From the Mediceo Palatina collection; most likely Florentine, c. 1600-1620.
Literature:	Porter, *Solo Song*, 82, 320 (includes inventory).
	Becherini, *Catalogo*, 50-51 (includes inventory).
	Apel, *Keyboard Music*, 235.

This manuscript is discussed jointly with Florence 138 under the entry of the latter manuscript.

FLORENCE 138

(I-Fn) Florence, Biblioteca Nazionale Centrale, Ms. Magl. XIX. 138.

Physical data:	17 × 13 cm; 48 ff. (ff. 11'-46 blank).
Notation:	Two-staff keyboard score (2 × 6/8).
Attributions:	None, except for a "Gagliarda di S[antino] da Parma" (f. 47).
Provenance:	From the Mediceo Palatina collection; most likely Florentine, c. 1600-1620.
Literature:	Porter, *Solo Song*, 82, 322-323 (includes inventory).
	Becherini, *Catalogo*, 59-60 (includes inventory).
	Apel, *Keyboard Music*, 245.

In Willi Apel's *Keyboard Music* (p. 245) Florence 115 and 138 are dated "around 1570." A study of their contents shows, however, that they are not likely to have originated until several decades later at the earliest. Both of these volumes contain keyboard settings of vocal compositions, some with partial text underlay. Florence 115 includes seven settings of songs that appear in monody sources from the first two decades of the 17th century (see Porter, *Solo Song*,

320-21). It is therefore improbable that this keyboard manuscript was compiled much before 1600; more likely it was approximately contemporaneous with the vocal collections. Florence 138 includes only one composition with a concordance to a monody source. Nevertheless, it probably should be assigned to the same period as Florence 115, that is, the years 1600-1620. Its repertory is very similar: both manuscripts contain settings of the Monica, the Romanesca, the Spagnoletta, the Terza rima, and of the aria "La violetta." Furthermore, each contains a composition attributed to Santino [Garsi] da Parma (d. 1604).

Each of the two volumes is in a single hand and has a regular collation.

FLORENCE 2358

(I-Fc) Florence, Biblioteca del Conservatorio di musica Luigi Cherubini, Ms. D. 2358.

Physical data:	22 × 28 cm; 20 ff.
Notation:	Two-staff keyboard score (3 × 6/8).
Attributions:	Pencilled attribution to Frescobaldi on flyleaf; otherwise without indications of authorship.
Provenance:	Medici (Florence), last decades of the 17th century.
Literature:	Gandolfi, *Catalogo*, 260.

This is a virtually unknown collection from the late 17th century. A pencilled attribution to Frescobaldi appears on one of the flyleaves; his attribution almost certainly is mistaken (see discussion on pp. 158-59).[35]

Unlike most 17th-century keyboard manuscripts this volume has an elegant appearance. It is bound in leather with a gold-tooled design showing the Medici coat of arms (six balls topped by a crown) and a floral design. The handwriting is neat in appearance and clearly is the work of a single copyist; the collation is regular (quaternions).

The compositions in this collection are grouped according to key and effectively form three suites. Each suite opens with a *Preludio*; among the remaining pieces one finds *Toccate, Passacaglie*, an *Allemanda*, and several *Arie alla Francese*. The latter do not appear to be particularly French; however, they do have a binary structure with the typically French "petite reprise."

The compositions show an overall consistency that suggests they are the work of a single composer. None of the works have known concordances; stylistically they are hard to place. One recognizes traits from the North-central-Italian school as represented in Bologna 53, such as thick acciaccatura chords and violinistic textures; other passages suggest familiarity with the works of the French clavecinistes of the generation of Louis Couperin.

The presently available evidence suggests that the contents date from the last decades of the 17th century. The compositions included in this manuscript deserve to be better known; they possess an elegance and individuality that set them apart from much Italian keyboard music of the period.

MILAN 53

(I-Mc) Milan, Biblioteca del Conservatorio di musica Giuseppe Verdi, Riserva mus. 53.

Physical data:	Oblong format; 290 pp.
Notation:	Two-staff keyboard score.
Attributions:	Frescobaldi.
Provenance:	First half of the 19th century (?).
Literature:	None.

This manuscript includes the complete contents of Frescobaldi's TOCCATE I with the AGGIUNTA (1637) and of his TOCCATE II (1627) and apparently is a 19th-century copy of these publications. The compositions have not been copied in the order in which they appear in the prints; compositions from both publications are interspersed.[36]

MODENA 491

(I-MOe) Biblioteca Estense, Ms. App. Campori 491 (formerly Y .K.7.8)

Title:	Cantate diverse, sec. XVI-XVII (on front cover).
Physical data:	10×26 cm; 53 ff.
Attributions:	In aria segment: Carissimi, Mario [Savioni], Stefano Landi (only in tavola). In keyboard segment: Ferrini.
Provenance:	Probably Rome, c. 1650-1670.
Literature:	Lodi, *Catalogo*, p. 83.
Editions:	None.

Modena 491 is a mid-17th-century aria anthology with a characteristic extended oblong format. Most arias are anonymous, but there are a few attributions to Roman composers. The last nine pages contain keyboard music, a single composition with three independent movements entitled *Toccata, 2ª p[art]e* and *3ª p[art]e,* respectively. The first two parts are in the traditional toccata manner, the third is imitative. At the beginning of this composition appears the inscription "Sig. Gio: Batt Ferrini." The first of the three parts is also found, with an attribution to Ferrini, in Vat. mus. 569, there entitled: *Toccata 2ª per Organo.* The 2ª and 3ª parte do not appear in the Vatican manuscript, where the first part is followed by a canzona in the same key (C major). This type of partial concordance is similar to the phenomenon of the wandering variation (see p. 55); as usual we do not know whether the composer or the copyists were responsible for the discrepancy.

Although the keyboard segment appears in an independent fascicle, continuity of paper and staff ruling show that this fascicle formed part of the original manuscript. The aria segment is ruled 2 × 5/5; in the keyboard segment lines clearly have been added to obtain the 6/7 ruling. The keyboard music appears to have been copied by the same hand that was responsible for the arias. The attribution, concordance, and notation suggest a Roman provenance for this volume.

The manuscript formerly belonged to the 19th-century collector Marchese Giuseppe Campori, whose library was acquired by the Biblioteca Estense.

NAPLES 48

(I-Nc) Naples, Conservatorio di musica San Piètro a Majella, Ms. Mus. str. 48 (formerly 61.4.11).

Physical data:	16 × 23 cm; 65 ff.
Notation:	Two-staff keyboard notation (2 × 6/8).
Attributions:	G. B. Castello, Converso, Gaetano, Gallucio, de Macque, Merulo, E. Pasquini, Sansone, Trabaci, and Vandalem.
Provenance:	Naples, earliest layer from c. 1600, second layer from the first decades of the 17th century.
Literature:	Debes, *Merulo*, 78-79 (inventory, with some inaccuracies—see discussion below).

Naples 48 is an anthology of keyboard music from the late 16th and early 17th centuries, mainly of Neapolitan origin. Its contents apparently are not widely known. The collection includes an *Intrata* attributed to Giovanni de Macque that is not found in the *Monumenta Musica Belgica* edition of de Macque's keyboard works (Watelet, *Macque*)[37] and a version of a canzone by Ercole Pasquini not listed among the sources of this work in Shindle, *Pasquini*.

There can be little doubt about the Neapolitan provenance of this collection. Several of the composers named in the attributions are known to have worked in Naples: Pietro Vandalem,[38] Trabaci,[39] Gaetano,[40] Giov. de Macque, and Galluccio.[41] Two others, Merulo and Ercole Pasquini, have no known associations with Naples, but the works attributed to them here are known to have gained wide dissemination; the *Toccata* attributed to Merulo is included in TRANSILVANO I, Sa. 1593b, and the *Canzona* attributed to Ercole Pasquini appears in several other manuscripts—see p. 183. Three composers have not been identified, although one of these was also evidently a Neapolitan: Battista Converso Napoli, Fra Giovanni-Battista Castello, and Sansone.

Debes states that the manuscript is dated 1600 (*Merulo*, 78). The date "1600" does in fact appear twice in the manuscript: in the captions on f. 10, "Canzon a francese d'Ercole Pasquini. 1600," and on f. 39, "Toccata del 3: tono di Claudio Merulo (1600)." Nonetheless, I believe we must question its precise significance. First, to judge from their appearance, the captions may well have been entered at a much later time by someone who noticed the above-mentioned concordances of these pieces to other sources, and who was eager to establish, for catalogue description or for other purposes, the date of the manuscript. Second, "1600" does not necessarily imply an assertion that the pieces date precisely from the year 1600, but might mean merely that they originated during the 1600s, i.e., in the 17th century. On one of the flyleaves another apparently still more recent hand notes that the Merulo *Toccata* is "del 500 e non del 600," that is, from the 16th and not from the 17th century. Strictly speaking, this is correct, since it was first published in 1593 (it was reprinted in 17th-century editions of TRANSILVANO which might explain the original dating in the 1600s); this appears at least partially to confirm my interpretation.

The manuscript consists of several independent segments bound together in rather disorderly fashion. One section, ff. 30-33, is bound upside down, and a page f. 9, is inserted out of place between f. 11 and f. 12 (see p. 184). The various segments can be distinguished by paper, ink, and, in one case, handwriting:

Hand	Foliation[42]
(1) A	ff. 1-25
(2) A	ff. 26-29
(3) A	ff. 30-33 (bound upside down)
(4) A	ff. 34-37
(5) B	ff. 38-52
(6) A	ff. 53-64

The segment in hand B probably is the oldest.[43] Its notation has a rather 16th-century appearance and includes such old-fashioned features as the use of dots for accidentals (see p. 24). The repertory also reflects late 16th-century taste; it includes two intabulations of French chansons:

f. 47, "Ce mois de Mai a 4" (Godard; other settings in Merulo, CANZONI, Sa. 1592c, f. 13, "La gratiosa" and in Verona MCXXVIII, p. 7).[44]

f. 51, "La lanza," intabulation of Crecquillon, "Ung gay bergier" (other settings in Sperindio Bertoldo, CANZONI, Sa. 159lb, f. 1, and Andrea Gabrieli, CANZONI, Sa. 1601g, f. 4).

The other canzoni alla francese in this segment also have the appearance of being intabulations of vocal chansons rather than independent instrumental canzoni. Nevertheless, because of the presence of a *Toccata* by Merulo first published in 1593 (in TRANSILVANO I), this segment presumably cannot be dated before the last years of the century.[45]

The contributions by hand A have a more modern, 17th-century appearance. They include works attributed to several composers still active during the first decade of the 17th century—Ercole Pasquini, de Macque, and Vandalem—as

Example 10

Naples 48, f. 30': Pastorale

well as a *Verso* attributed to Trabaci that also appears in Trabaci's RICERCATE
II, Sa. 1615.[46] A's segments were probably completed by the 1620s—at least,
nothing in their content suggests a later date.

Copyist A employs some unorthodox practices with respect to genre
designation. A number of pieces of diverse character are all entitled "Intrata."
For example, the "Intrata del Galluccio in C sol fa ut" on f. 1 appears to be a
typical sectional canzone; the following "Intrata in G sol re ut," f. 3', consists
of a section with a toccata character followed by an extended imitative movement; and the third "Intrata in G sol re ut," f. 7', is a kind of gagliarda whose
strains all conclude with a toccata-like flourish in duple time. A composition
attributed to de Macque (f. 55) is also entitled "Intrata"; this designation does
not appear elsewhere among his works.

There is a similar situation among the five compositions entitled "Toccata"
that appear towards the end of the manuscript. These also include several
different types of pieces, none of them, however, with the usual toccata
characteristics. The first two (ff. 52', 54) are brief, imitative versetti, moving
predominantly in half-notes. The other three have imitative openings with

canzone-like subjects; the part-writing suggests that they are adaptations of ensemble music. They have a formal scheme that is uncommon among instrumental canzoni: two repeated sections in duple time. In all likelihood they are intabulations of vocal part songs.

The manuscript contains one curiosity, a composition entitled *Pastorale* (f. 30)—perhaps the oldest preserved example of this keyboard genre—in which all rules and traditions of 17th-century art music are abandoned in order to achieve a realistic imitation of a Neapolitan zampogna (see Example 10).[47]

NAPLES 73

(I-Nc) Naples, Conservatorio di musica San Pie̔tro a Majella, Ms. Mus. str. 73 (formerly 34.5.28).

Title:	Toccate per Organo di varj Autori/anno 1675/
	Miscellanea del Sig^e/Donato Cimino (on flyleaf;
	19th-century inscription).
Physical data:	17 × 24 cm; 142ff.
Notation:	Two-staff keyboard score.
Attributions:	Frescobaldi, Salvatore, de Macque, E. Pasquini,
	Giacinto Ansalone, Francesco Boerio.
Provenance:	Naples, c. 1675.
Literature:	Apel, *Clavierschule*, 131.
	Apel, *Keyboard Music*, 496.
	Oncley, *Conservatorio* (contains inventory).
Editions:	Oncley, *Conservatorio*.
	Watelet, *Macque*.
	Shindle, *Pasquini*.
	Hudson, *Salvatore*.

This manuscript has been subjected to a detailed study by Oncley (*Conservatorio*). On the title page a 19th-century hand has attributed successive portions of the manuscript to Cimino (ff. 1-56), Francesco Boerio[48] (ff. 57-59), Cimino (ff. 69-104), Giovanni Salvatore[49] (ff. 105-112, 119, 129), Frescobaldi (ff. 113-118), Giovanni de Macque (ff. 120-128), Giacinto Ansalone[50] (f. 131), and Ercole Pasquino (ff. 135-142). According to Anna Mondolfi, present librarian of the Naples Conservatorio, these entries are in the hand of one of her 19th-century predecessors, Rondinella.[51] In the manuscript proper appear attributions to Boerio (ff. 56′, 59), Giacinto Ansalone (f. 131), Salvatore (ff. 105, 108, 110′, 129, 130), Frescobaldi (ff. 113, 115′), de Macque (ff. 120, 121, 122′, 125, 127), and Ercole Pasquino (ff. 135, 137′). The name Donato Cimino appears in two inscriptions on ff. 112′ and 118′, but in them Cimino is identified only as copyist.[52] These inscriptions appear at the end of compositions attributed, respectively, to Salvatore and to Frescobaldi: both entries include the date 1675. The only other appearance of Cimino's name is on f. 1: "Donato Cimino fine del secolo XVI [sic]''; however, this attribution has also been identified by Mondolfi as being in Rondinella's hand. Hence there appears to be no basis for regarding Cimino as the composer of any of the compositions in this manuscript; he can be considered only as its principal copyist (the entire manuscript is in one hand except for the segment ff. 105-110—containing a series of compositions attributed to Salvatore—which shows a different style of writing).

The contents of Naples 73 can be summarized as follows:

(1) ff. 1-32: Anonymous compositions; mostly toccate and canzoni.

(2) ff. 32'-55': Short pieces with curious titles such as "Pace," "Verità," "Gelosia," "Farfalla," and "Breve Diletto"; some compositions are accompanied by proverbs. Titles of this type are not found elsewhere in the 17th-century Italian keyboard repertory.

(3) ff. 56'-67': Compositions in various genres, some attributed to Boerio.

(4) ff. 69-99': Anonymous organ Masses.

(5) ff. 101-137': Compositions in various genres, almost all with attributions (to Giacinto Ansalone, Salvatore, Frescobaldi, de Macque, and Ercole Pasquini).

We see that manuscript provides an example of "bunching" of attributions (see p. 59); up to f. 101 hardly any are given, but from there on almost every composition is provided with one.

Oncley states that "there are several factors which tend to relate this manuscript to the keyboard music of Rome in preference to the music of Naples, the city of its origin" (*Conservatorio*, 39). He does not make clear what kind of relation he envisions; the factors to which he refers are principally differences between the manuscript and 17th-century Neapolitan prints, as well as some superficial similarities of its content to Frescobaldi's keyboard works. However, the differences in question are basically of the same degree and kind as those between Roman manuscripts and Roman prints. For example, Oncley points to the fact that the manuscript uses two-staff keyboard notation, whereas most (though not all) of the Neapolitan prints use four-staff score notation. This does not necessarily point to a different regional tradition: two-staff keyboard notation is found in other Neapolitan manuscripts (Naples 48 and in a segment of London 30491) and four-staff scores are frequently employed in Roman prints. An examination of the composers represented in the manuscript will remove any doubt about the local origin of most of its contents. The few works attributed to non-Neapolitan composers (two to Frescobaldi and one to Ercole Pasquini, in addition to one piece that is anonymous here but attributed to Pasquini in Chigi 205-206) are compositions widely disseminated in prints or in other manuscripts, and the composers were well known throughout Italy. A much larger number of compositions is attributed to Neapolitan composers; many of them are unica, and, with the exception of de Macque, the composers are represented almost exclusively in Neapolitan sources.

RAVENNA 545

(I-RAc) Ravenna, Biblioteca comunale Classense, Ms. Classense 545).

Title:	"Libro di fra Gioseffo da Ravenna. Opere di diversi Autori, di/Girolamo Frescobaldi, d'ErcolPasquino, Cesare Argentini, Incert' Autore" (on the flyleaf).
Physical data:	20 × 28 cm; 116 ff.
Notation:	Two-staff keyboard score (2 × 5/7).
Attributions:	Cifra, Frescobaldi, Merula, E. Pasquini, and Argentino.
Provenance:	Probably Ravenna, 1630-1640.
Literature:	Apel, *Keyboard Music*, 485.
	Curtis, *Merula*, ix.
Editions:	Shindle, *Frescobaldi*.
	Shindle, *Pasquini*.

Ravenna 545 receives brief descriptions in Apel, *Keyboard Music*, 496, and in Curtis, *Merula*, ix. Curtis states that the manuscript dates from the first half of the 17th century; Apel does not discuss its date or origin.

About a third of the compositions are provided with attributions, including eight to Frescobaldi, ten to Ercole Pasquini, and one each to Cifra, to Tarquinio Merula, and to Cesare Argentino. Furthermore, of the compositions appearing anonymously three (ff. 86', 87, 110) can be identified as being by Frescobaldi, and one (f. 8') as being by Andrea Gabrieli from concordances to printed editions.

The one-time owner named on the ornately decorated title page, Fra Gioseffo di Ravenna, can be tentatively identified. The manuscript Bologna Q 21, a collection of early 16th-century Italian songs for four voices, bears the inscription "Est S. Uitalis de Rau.[enn]a ad usum Reu.[erendissi]mi P.[atris] D. Josephi de Rau.[enn]a/Abbatis Cassin.[ensis]/2741." In his study on Bologna Q 21 Claudio Gallico reports that according to the records of the monastery of Montecassino a certain Giuseppe Rasino, also known as D. Giuseppe da Ravenna, was ordained in the order of S. Vitale on 17 September 1634. Furthermore, documents from S. Vitale in Ravenna show that D. Joseph Rasimus was in that city from 1669 to 1674.[53] The reference "da Ravenna" in the Montecassino records imply that Ravenna also was Rasino's native city. Although the handwriting of the inscription in Bologna Q 21 could not be identified with that on the title page of Ravenna 545, nor with that of the headings within the manuscript, it appears probable that Giuseppe was the owner or user of both collections. It is not clear, however, whether he was also the scribe of the keyboard manuscript or whether he acquired it after its completion. Neither does his connection with this volume necessarily imply that it originated in Ravenna. At any rate, even if both Bologna Q 21 and the keyboard manuscript were in his possession, they subsequently parted ways; the former ended up in Bologna, the latter in the Biblioteca Comunale of Ravenna—possibly after having resided in the Monastery of Classe (as is suggested by its signature "Classense").[54]

Ravenna 545 has a regular collation, being made up of a succession of quaternions. Most of the music writing is uniform in style; towards the latter part of the manuscript a few pieces are interspersed that show certain variant traits (principally, differences in the form of the C-clef and in pen thickness). Nevertheless, the prevailing identity of other features of the script leads me to assume that all of the writing is the work of a single copyist and that the pieces showing the scribal variants were entered somewhat later than the rest of the manuscript.

The scribe shows signs of working rather hastily. He frequently makes transposition errors of a third ("Terzverschiebung"). Sometimes the mistake is corrected by the placement of the number three over the passage; in other instances the passage is inserted correctly, sometimes without complete erasure of the erroneous one. Often the error was not noticed and hence was left standing.

The copyist evidently attempted to group the pieces according to genre, though he did not carry out his plan with complete consistency (see pp. 45-46).

Since the manuscript includes concordances to publications from the years 1619, 1624, and 1627 (see Table 8) it probably dates from the late 1620s or from the 1630s. Concerning the provenance of its repertory, the concordances suggest connections both with Rome (Frescobaldi, TOCCATE I and II; Cifra, RICERCARE, Sa. 1619b; the manuscripts Chigi 205-206, and Doria 250 B) and with Venice (TRANSILVANO I, Sa. 1593b; Frescobaldi, CAPRICCI, 1624). Much of the anonymous repertory seems to be stylistically closer to Northern than to Roman traditions. The ricercari are very unlike the purified Roman examples of the genre; they abound in eighth-note and sixteenth-note passages. Several of the canzoni and capricci show features often found in the works of Tarquinio Merula, such as extended chains of sequences, strings of repeated notes, large leaps, and chromatic-tetrachord clichés (cf. p. 35). These characteristics are also much in evidence in the *Toccata* on f. 5, described by Apel as "ungewöhnlich" (*Keyboard Music*, 496). Further stylistic analysis will be required to estimate the likelihood of whether these compositions might in fact be by Merula.

ANTONIANO

(I-R, no siglum) Rome, Biblioteca del Pontificio Ateneo Antoniano, Ms. di Musica c. 1650.

Title:	Ballata di Michel Angelo del Violino (M. A. Rossi), Prov. Biblioteca Marchesi Ricci, Feb. 1948 (on flyleaf, in recent hand).
Physical data:	Upright format; 56ff.
Notation:	Two-staff score (2 × 5/5); also some guitar tablature.
Attributions:	In addition to the attribution on the flyleaf an attribution to Michel Angelo del Violino appears on f. 31'.
Provenance:	Rome, middle of the 17th century (?).
Literature:	None.

This collection consists mainly of dances ("le corant," "Balet," "Sarabanda," etc.) in general sketchily notated (often, but not always, with soprano-bass texture), and in many cases incomplete. In addition it includes two compositions for voice and basso continuo (f. 24': "Ch'importa a me"; and f. 45: "Di qual orfeo"). The only attribution appears on f. 31': "Ballo di Michel Angelo del Violino"; the more recent title page presumably is based on this caption. The ballo is not known from any other Michelangelo Rossi source and has not been reported in the literature. In several pieces the soprano (which goes up to e''') and the bass are widely separated. This separation, the thin textures, and the use of a 5/5-staff leave some doubt as to whether any of the contents of this collection were intended for keyboard.

DORIA 250 A

(I-Rdp) Rome, Biblioteca Doria-Pamphilj, Ms. 250 A.

Physical data:	16 × 22 cm; 48 ff. (ff. 13'-30 blank).
Notation:	Two-staff keyboard score (2 × 6/7).
Attributions:	None.
Provenance:	Probably Rome, c. 1630-1650.
Literature:	None.

This manuscript is discussed jointly with Doria 250 B in the following entry of the latter manuscript.

DORIA 250 B

(I-Rdp) Rome, Biblioteca Doria-Pamphilj, Ms. 250 B.

Physical data:	16 × 22 cm; 50 ff.
Notation:	Two-staff keyboard score (2 × 6/7).
Attributions:	A Corrente is attributed to Sig. Girolamo
	[Frescobaldi?]; no further attributions.
Provenance:	Probably Rome, c. 1630-1650.
Literature:	None.

Scholars have had only very limited access to the music collection belonging to the Doria Pamphilj family.[55] As a result, the two volumes of 17th-century keyboard music catalogued as 250 A and 250 B have remained generally unknown.[56] In a rather cursory hand-written catalogue of recent origin in the Archivio Doria Pamphilj they are listed as "250A: Toccata per organo" and "250 B: Arie?" The two manuscripts contain no information about their provenance, but probably formed part of the Pamhilj collection in the 17th century, since such was the case with other musical materials of that period (for example the aria collection Ms 51, containing the Pamphilj coat of arms and including works by musicians known to have served the family).

The volumes are similar, with respect to appearance as well as to repertory, to other Roman manuscripts from the period c. 1630-1650, and probably date from those years. There is no direct connection between the two manuscripts; they are of slightly different dimensions and have no scribal concordances. The contents are entirely anonymous except for a *Corrente, del Sig. Girolamo* in Doria 250 B (see p. 156).

Doria 250 A is in a single hand and has a regular quaternion collation. It opens with a *Toccata-Ricercar-Canzona* sequence in G minor; the *Toccata* and the *Canzona* (but not the *Ricercar*) also appear in Oxford 1113 (Nos. 35 and 36—see p. 55). Another sequence of pieces in a common key begins on f. 31; it consists of a *Toccata* and a *Canzona* in D minor. These, too, appear in Oxford 1113 (Nos. 32-33 and 34). The manuscript contains, furthermore, a *Passacaglia*, a *Toccata* "per l'elevatione del Signor," three settings of the *Tenore di Napoli*, an *Aria p. sonetti* (figured bass only), and an *Aria p. Ottave* (bass partly realized).

Doria 250 B has a more complex collation and appears to be the work of several hands. It contains principally settings of traditional arie and balli; it is in fact one of the most comprehensive collections of such pieces. Several of the arie appear in two or three separate settings located in different parts of the manuscript.

BARB. LAT. 4181

(I-Rvat) Rome, Biblioteca Apostolica Vaticana, Ms. Barb. lat. 4181.

Physical data:	Oblong format; blank except for ff. 2-2'.
Notation:	Two-staff keyboard score (2 × 6/7).
Attributions:	None.
Provenance:	Rome, Barberini, first half of the 17th century.
Literature:	Celani, *Canzoni*, 133.

This manuscript is discussed in the entry for Barb. lat. 4288 below.

BARB. LAT. 4182

(I-Rvat) Rome, Biblioteca Apostolica Vaticana, Ms. Barb. lat. 4182.

Physical data:	Oblong format, decorated parchment cover; 41 ff. (ff. 4-39' are blank).
Notation:	Two-staff keyboard score (2 × 6/7).
Attributions:	None.
Provenance:	Rome, Barberini, first half of the 17th century.
Literature:	Celani, *Canzoni*, 133.

This manuscript is discussed in the entry for Barb. lat. 4288 below.

BARB. LAT. 4288

(I-Rvat) Rome, Biblioteca Apostolica Vaticana, Ms. Barb. lat. 4288.

Physical data:	22 × 15 cm; 41 ff. (ff. 28-41' blank).
Notation:	Two-staff keyboard score (3 × 6/7).
Attributions:	None.
Provenance:	Rome, Barberini (?), c. 1610-1630.
Literature:	Celani, *Canzoni*, 417.

The Fondo Barberini is as rich in 17th-century manuscripts as the Fondo Chigi (see p. 119), but keyboard music is by comparison poorly represented. The only volume of some interest is Barb. lat. 4288, a typical aria and ballo collection; in addition there are two volumes that contain a few pages of keyboard music: Barb. lat. 4181 and 4182.

During the reign of Maffeo Barberini as Pope Urban VIII (1623-44), the Barberini were among the leading patrons of music in Rome; Frescobaldi received a stipend from Urban's nephew, Cardinal Antonio Barberini, and honored the latter with the dedication of his FIORI MUSICALI (Sa. 1635).[57]

The three volumes containing keyboard music give the appearance of being the work of a noble dilettante rather than of a professional musician; Barb. lat. 4181 and 4182 can in fact be directly connected to the family.

Barb. lat. 4181 has the usual parchment binding; on the front cover a design has been stamped in gold: a frame, with a bee (the Barberini symbol) in each corner. The name Nicolo Barberini is inscribed on the back of the first page.[58] Folios 2-2' contain an untitled keyboard piece, perhaps a dance; the remainder of the volume consists of blank music paper ruled for two-staff keyboard notation.

Barb. lat. 4182 presents the same external appearance as Barb. lat. 4181, including the four bees stamped in gold on the front cover. Its musical content is only slightly larger. On the first few pages (ff. 2-3') appear three dances; the first, "Avignon Corrente," is a setting of the popular French song "la Vignon" (see p. 41); the second and the third are untitled. The remainder of the volume contains blank music paper except for the last pages, ff. 40' and 41, on which are entered keyboard harmonizations of the first and second psalm-tones.

The parchment cover of Barb. lat. 4288 contains no decoration. Its format is atypical, being upright rather than oblong, with six staves ($3 \times 6/7$) per page. Only the first 27 folios contain music.

The first three compositions have a complete text underlaid (see p. 26). Some of the other compositions have text incipits; most of the remaining pieces are settings of familiar arie and balli, such as the Spagnoletta, the Romanesca and the Tenor di Napoli. A few pieces deserve further comment:

f. 15: *Ballo Francese*. A setting of a French dance also found in Michael Praetorius' *Terpsichore* (1612) (No. 32, *La Bouree*).

f. 16: *Corrente*. Surprisingly, in view of its title, this composition is notated in duple time. It is a setting of "Est ce Mars," a melody popular with Northern composers, but not found, so far as I know, in any other Italian sources.

f. 21: *Corrente del Re*. This setting is also in duple time; versions in triple time can be found in Vat. mus. 569, f. 84, and in Praetorius' *Terpsichore*, No. 117.

f. 23: *La battaglia di Pavia*. A lengthy battle piece.

In some pieces dots are found, placed above nots. These dots do not appear to represent accidentals, but probably indicate ornaments.

The collection shows many resemblances to Florence 115 and 138; it contains a similar repertory of partially texted settings of secular and sacred songs along with traditional arie and balli. It probably dates from the same period, or perhaps slightly later: c. 1610-1630.

INTRODUCTION TO THE MANUSCRIPTS CHIGI 24-29 AND CHIGI 205-206

The manuscripts Chigi 24-29 and Chigi 205-206 form the largest surviving manuscript collection of 17th-century Italian keyboard music. Its importance is enhanced by the presence of a number of compositions attributed to Frescobaldi and to Ercole Pasquini that are not known from other sources. A large portion (though not all) of their contents has been published in Shindle, *Frescobaldi*, Shindle, *Ercole Pasquini*, and Lincoln, *Chigi*. Lincoln, *Manoscritti chigiani* provides a brief study and an inventory of the collection; unfortunately both this inventory and Lincoln's edition suffer from a large number of inaccuracies. Many discrepancies exist between the inventory and the edition, and between both and the manuscripts. I shall not attempt to correct every mistake found in these publications, but will point out some of the errors in the course of my discussion of the individual manuscripts.

The first questions that arise with regard to these manuscripts are: Is there any connection between them? Do they form in any sense an integral collection? I shall begin by discussing these questions with respect to Chigi 24-29, a set of six bound volumes which—unlike Chigi 205-206—contain only keyboard music. They are similar in appearance, their dimensions are nearly uniform and they all have a 2 × 6/7 staff ruling. These physical similarities are, however, not necessarily indicative of any relation between the volumes, since they are shared by other Roman keyboard manuscripts of the period. There are correspondences between the watermarks: Chigi 24, 28, and 29 have a star-and-crown design, Chigi 26 a three-mounts design, and Chigi 25 contains both types of watermarks. Nevertheless, the watermarks do not match exactly from one manuscript to the next; nor could an exact agreement be found with any of the watermarks shown in Heawood, *Watermarks*.[59] Each manuscript is in a single hand, but only one of these hands appears in more than one manuscript: the same hand is responsible for Chigi 26 and 28. The contents of the volumes are not in any way complementary—unlike, for example, the volumes of the Turin manuscripts, each of which is devoted to a different genre. Chigi 24, 25, 27, and 29 are typical general collections containing a variety of genres; Chigi 26 and 28 are aria and ballo collections. The fact that the manuscripts have consecutive library numbers is not significant, since these numbers were not assigned until the beginning of our own century. On the other hand, all six volumes appear to date from approximately the same period, c. 1630-1650, and contain a rather similar repertory, suggesting that they derive from the same circles. Chigi 205-206 consists of two folders containing independent fascicles and loose pages with music for various vocal and instrumental combinations. A large number of fascicles and pages contain keyboard music of 17th-century origin; in fact the latter materials clearly derive from the same milieu as the bound volumes, although there is no match between any of the papers nor any obvious match between scribal hands. Some of the fascicles in Chigi 205 and 206 are themselves connected through handwriting; the same hands appear in both collections. As a matter of fact, we shall see that the division of materials between the two folders was made arbitrarily; for this reason they will be discussed together, and will be referred to in this study as a single collection: Chigi 205-206.

Since the manuscripts contain no information indicating their original owners, we can only surmise their early history from their presence in the Fondo Chigi. The materials of this major collection at one time formed part of the private library of the Chigi family; they were acquired by the Italian Government in 1918 and donated to the Vatican in 1922. Within the Fondo Chigi are several handwritten catalogues and inventories, some dating back to the 17th century. However, with the exception of a 17th-century "Catalogo che comprende le Collezione delle Opere Musicali" (Chigi S.V. 13),[60] there exists no catalogue of the music-manuscript holdings earlier than the inventory of the entire collection prepared by Baronci during the first decades of the present century.[61] Hence it is impossible to determine precisely how long any of the music manuscripts have formed part of the collection. There are, however, reasons to believe that most of the earlier materials have been in the hands of the Chigi family since the 17th century.

The Chigi, a family of Sienese origin, can trace their history back to the 13th century.[64] Through banking they acquired a large fortune, which enabled them to become generous supporters of the arts—a tradition they have maintained to this day. In the 15th century the family split into two branches, one of which has remained in Siena, where its current representative, Prince Guido Chigi-Saracini, is still active as patron of music (and of musicology).[63] The other branch of the family, however, is of greater interest to us. This branch established close connections with Rome, beginning with Agostino "il Magnifico," who settled there in 1502 to establish a bank, and who, as financier of popes (Julius II, Leo X) and as patron of the arts (Rafael, Bembo, Aretino), became one of Rome's most influential citizens. A century-and-a-half later another member took up residence in the city, not as banker but as its Holy Father.

Fabio Chigi was born in Siena in 1599. After studies in law and in philosophy at the University of Siena he moved (in 1626) to Rome, where Urban VIII appointed him as Referendario della Segretaria di Grazia e di Giustizia. From 1629 he held various positions in the diplomatic service of the church, first in Ferrara, then in Malta (1635), and from 1639 as Papal Nuncio in Cologne. In 1651 he was called to Rome to serve as Secretary of State, and in 1655 he assumed his sacred Office as Pope Alexander VII.

Alexander VII reigned for twelve years, "senz'infamia e senza lode."[64] Artistically, however, his tenure was of considerable significance for Rome; it saw the construction of many architectural monuments, including Bernini's colonnade in front of St. Peter's and his Scala Regia.[65] Fabio also was an avid collector of books and of ancient manuscripts[66] and laid the foundations of the Biblioteca Chigi, incorporating within it some of the collections of his ancestors and predecessors, as well as materials acquired during his travels (Pastor, *Popes*, 274-275).

Although much information is available concerning Fabio's involvement with the arts and with various branches of learning, there has been no general study devoted to his interest in music and his patronage of musicians. Alexander VII had several musicians on his personal payroll, as is shown by accounts preserved in the Rome Archivio di Stato: Marco Marazzoli 1602-1662; composer, singer, and harpist), Pietro Paolo Capellini (composer and theorbo player), Lelio Colista (1627-1680; composer and virtuoso on the lute and related instruments), and Francesco Boccalini (active from c. 1641 until at least 1678; composer and instrumentalist).[67] Marazzoli in fact seems to have served as official court composer and set several texts honoring his patron;[68] Colista appears to have been in charge of performances at special occasions such as Christmas and Carnival.[69]

A direct association with the Chigi family can furthermore be established for Bernardo Pasquini. In 1664 Alexander VII sent his nephew Cardinal Flavio Chigi (1631-1693) on a mission to the French court; the delegation apparently included Colista and Pasquini.[70] During his later years Pasquini continued to serve Cardinal Flavio on special occasions, but, as far as I can tell, he never appeared regularly on the Chigi payroll.[71]

An indication of Fabio Chigi's personal interest in music has come to light in a study on Athanasius Kircher (Scharlau, *Kircher*, 347-48). Apparently Kircher and Chigi maintained a close friendship, and in a letter of 11 February 1651 in thanking the German scholar for a copy of the *Musurgia* Fabio mentions having been introduced by Kircher into the latter's method of mechanical composition during his stay in Malta (1638).[72]

We can learn more about the musical interests of the Chigi from an examination of their music collection. The music manuscripts are catalogued under the signatures Q.IV.1 to Q.VIII.206; the arabic numerals run continuously from 1 to 206, so that there are altogether 206 catalogued items.[73] In a very rough way Baronci has attempted to catalogue the manuscripts systematically, grouping together the works for the same performance medium (e.g., the keyboard volumes Q.IV.24-29), and following a vaguely chronological order, although often he did not strictly adhere to this plan. The manuscripts can be divided into several groups:

(1) Collections of 17th-century vocal chamber music. These form by far the largest group within the collection, numbering over fifty. Most consist of arias and cantatas for one or more voices and basso continuo. Among the composers appear virtually all the significant masters of these genres: Luigi Rossi, Carissimi, Cesti, Cavalli, Stradella, Bernardo Pasquini, and Alessandro Scarlatti; all worked in Rome at one time or another.

(2) 17th-century opera scores. These form the second largest group of items; the composers include most of those listed above. There are also some oratorios by Bernardo Pasquini and by Legrenzi.

(3) The keyboard manuscripts, to be discussed below.

(4) Operatic scores and performing materials from the second half of the 18th century, including works by Piccini, Sacchini, and Sarti.

(5) Operatic excerpts arranged for flute, dating from the early 19th century.

(6) A small number of items from the 17th to the 19th century that cannot be fitted into the above categories; among them are a collection of madrigals (Q.IV.4—see below) and two volumes of 17th-century sacred music (Q.IV.19 and 20).

(7) A miscellany of small fascicles and loose pages under the signatures Q.VIII.196 to 206 gathered together in a set of folders. The majority of these items date from the 18th and 19th centuries; the earlier materials are gathered principally in Q.VIII.205-206.

The core of the collection is formed by the 17th-century volumes presumably acquired by Alexander VII and by his nephew Cardinal Flavio Chigi (1631-1693); further volumes were added by other members of the family. Among the composers represented are several known to have served the Chigi family (Marazzoli, Pasquini, Pier Simone Agostini) or to have sung in the Sistine Chapel during the pontificate of Alexander VII (Matteo Simonelli, Isidoro Cerruti, Marc'Antonio Cesti).[74] Some volumes in the collection contain internal evidence of having belonged to the Chigi in the form of coat of arms (Q.IV.10, 11, and 17, and Q.V.82). The collection includes, furthermore, a set of Marazzoli autographs (Q.V.68 and 69, Q.VI.80 and 81, Q.VII.177 to 186) probably acquired shortly after the composer's death in 1662.[75] We noted earlier that Marazzoli was in the service of Alexander VII, and wrote cantatas (included among these autographs) honoring his patron.

For the keyboard manuscripts internal evidence supporting an association with the Chigi, in the form of coat of arms, texts, or attributions, is lacking. Nonetheless, since such an association can be established for other manuscripts, and since as far as I know none of the 17th-century items in the collection shows signs of having been acquired at a later time, it appears probable that the keyboard volumes were already in the possession of the Chigi family during the period in which they originated, or shortly thereafter.

Before proceeding to a discussion of the main keyboard manuscripts I shall briefly describe two items in the collection containing some fragmentary materials possibly intended for keyboard: Chigi 4 and Chigi 23. Chigi 4 is a manuscript dated 1633 whose contents consist for the most part of vocal scores of madrigals for from four to eight voices. The manuscript includes, however, a series of pieces and fragments or sketches notated in two-staff keyboard score (ff. 123-128'). Some of the pieces are in a two-voice soprano-bass setting; others have a fuller texture, suggesting that they are intended for keyboard. On f. 123 appears a "Basso ballo del delice alla lombarda," on f. 125 an "Aria di Ruggiero in tripla" (both are soprano-bass settings); most of the other entries are untitled or are called *Tenore* [= cantus-firmus setting]. Several pieces consist merely of sequential patterns and have the appearance of being compositional or keyboard exercises.

Chigi 23 consists of twenty folios ruled for two-staff keyboard notation

(2 × 6/7). It is similar in physical appearance to the manuscripts Chigi 24-29, but, except for some fragments on ff. 1-2, there are no musical entries.

CHIGI 24

(I-Rvat) Rome, Biblioteca Apostolica Vaticana, Ms. Chigi Q.IV.24.

Physical data:	16 × 22 cm; 56 ff.
Notation:	Two-staff keyboard score (2 × 6/7).
Attributions:	de la Barre, Fr[escobaldi?].
Provenance:	Probably Rome (Chigi?), c. 1640-1650.
Literature:	Apel, *Keyboard Music*, 497.
	Lincoln, *Manoscritti chigiani*, 66-68
	(includes inventory).
	Gustafson, *Sources*, 142-43, 542-46 (includes inventory).
Edition:	Lincoln, *Chigi*.

Chigi 24 is more homogeneous in appearance than in content. It is in a single hand; the writing generally is neat and careful; the collation is regular, consisting of seven quaternions. However, a wide variety of genres is represented, from dances and arie with partite to versets for liturgical use. Among these are several successions of related pieces; such groups probably reflect the sources from which the pieces derive rather than an attempt by the copyist to organize the contents of the collection. The following groups can be distinguished:

(1) ff. 8'-14': Six dances from Frescobaldi's AGGIUNTA (1637). Judging by the close correspondence of all notational details, the pieces were probably copied directly from the publication. The composer is not acknowledged.[76]

(2) ff. 15-25': A group of *Recercari* and *Canzoni*, probably taken from a set of ricercare-canzone pairs in the various modes, similar to the set in Cifra's RICERCARI II, Sa. 1619d (see p. 47). The group contains a pair in the second tone (f. 15-19) and a pair in the third tone (f. 22-25'): the subjects of the members of each pair are related (as is also the case in Cifra's publication)—see Example 11a. In addition the group includes a canzone in the first tone (f. 19'-22), which is not accompanied by a ricercare; a ricercare with a related subject appears, however, elsewhere in the manuscript (in fact it appears twice—on f. 7' and f. 39'—in virtually identical versions)—see Example 11b. Probably this ricercare belongs to the same set; a *Recercare* in the fourth tone (f. 35) may also form part of the set, although no companion *Canzona* is included in this manuscript.

(3) ff. 28'-31' and 37-38: Two groups of liturgical pieces. The first group consists of several versets on the hymns "Ave maris stella" and "Iste confessor," the second consists of a "Kyrie delli Apostoli" (Cunctipotens) and a "Toccata per l'elevatione."

(4) ff. 47-49': Two correnti (with "doubles") and a sarabanda, all

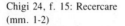

Chigi 24, f. 15: Recercare
(mm. 1-2)

Chigi 24, f. 16': Canzona
(mm. 1-2)

Chigi 24, f. 22: Recercare
(mm. 1-2)

Chigi 24, f. 23': Canzona
(mm. 1-2)

Example 11b

Chigi 24, f. 7' (= f. 39'):
Recercare (mm. 1-2)

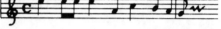

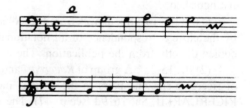

Chigi 24, f. 19': Canzona
(mm. 1-2)

apparently by LaBarre (the second corrente has the caption "Del Med[esi]mo" and the sarabanda is inscribed "Sarabanda del M[edisim]o.[77] The first of the correnti also appear with substantial variants in seven North-European manuscripts, and the melody of the sarabanda is found elsewhere in two different settings;[78] no concordances have been found for the second corrente.[79]

(5) ff. 51-56': Three compositions with attributions possibly referring to Frescobaldi. On f. 51 appears a composition entitled "Canzona D. Fr.," and on f. 52' a composition entitled "Fuga D. Fr." In Lincoln's edition these titles are given as *Canzona Francese* and *Fuga di Francese* (Lincoln, *Chigi* I, 35 and 37). In view of the abbreviation habits of the period the readings "Canzona d[i] Fr[escobaldi]" and "Fuga d[i] Fr[escobaldi]" would seem equally plausible if not

more so.[80] Following these two compositions is a "Toccata di G . . ."; the remainder of the name cannot be clearly read. Lincoln's inventory gives "Gio. Batt[ist]a"; his edition interprets it as "Giovanni." A reading of "Girolamo" would have as much or as little justification; it might receive some support from the attribution of the preceding two pieces (assuming that my reading of their titles is correct). I shall include these three pieces among the Frescobaldi attributions discussed in Part Three, p. 161.

The three compositions appearing on ff. 4, 5' and 6', described as "toccata del tipo dell' intonazione" in Lincoln, *Manoscritti chigiani, 67*, are three partite on the Ruggiero; they are identified as such in Lincoln, *Chigi* III, 12-14. In a reversal of this situation, the untitled pieces of ff. 32'-35 are correctly described in Lincoln's inventory as "[*3 partite sopra l'aria di Fiorenza*]"; in his (later) edition, however, Lincoln entitles them simply *Dance with variations* and does not group them together with the other Fiorenza settings.

The influence of Frescobaldi is evident in much of the repertory. Several of the anonymous pieces appear to be modelled on compositions from his TOCCATE II (1627): e.g., f. 1, *Toccata sopra li Pedali* (on *Toccata Quinta, sopra li pedali*); f. 28', *Ave maris stella* (on *Hinno Ave maris stella*); f. 43, *Balletto* (on *Aria del Balletto*).[81]

In view of the inclusion of copies from Frescobaldi's 1637 publication the manuscript should probably be dated from the late 1630s or from the 1640s.

CHIGI 25

(I-Rvat) Rome, Biblioteca Apostolica Vaticana, Ms. Chigi Q.IV.25.

Title:	Sonate d'Intavolatura del Sig. Girolamo Frescobaldi (on f. [i']).
Physical data:	16 × 22 cm; 69 ff.
Notation:	Two-staff keyboard score (2 × 6/7).
Attributions:	None, other than the one appearing on f. [i'].
Provenance:	Probably Rome (Chigi?), c. 1630-1650.
Literature:	Apel, *Keyboard Music*, 482, 497.
	Lincoln, *Manoscritti chigiani*, 69 (inventory).
Editions:	Shindle, *Frescobaldi* (complete).
	Santini, *Frescobaldi* (complete).

The cited title inscription appears on the verso of the flyleaf in a hand-writing different from that found in the rest of the manuscript. There are no attributions in the remainder of the volume, nor have concordances been found to any of the compositions it contains, with the exception of a partial concordance (extending only over the first three measures) to Frescobaldi's Capriccio sopra il Cucho (see p. 66).

Only one music hand appears in the entire manuscript, and superficially the volume gives an impression of being a unified collection. Nevertheless, closer

Table 13
Structure and Content of Chigi 25

Section	ff.	Size[a]	Watermark	f.	Title
flyleaf			human figure	[i]	blank
				[i']	Sonate d'Intavolatura del Sig. Girolamo Frescobaldi
I	1-8	4	three mounts	1	Partita p$^{\underline{a}}$ sopra l'aria di Fiorenza, 2$^{\underline{a}}$ Partita, 3$^{\underline{a}}$ Partita
				5'	Toccata Per organo
	9-12	2		8'	Canzona che segue alla Toccata
II	13-18	3	three mounts[b]	13	Toccata Per organo Capriccio sopra Vestiva i Colli (crossed out)
				14'	(untitled, second section of above work)
III	19-22	2	crown &	19	Capriccio
	23-26	2	star	24	Capriccio fatto sopra il Cucchù
	27-34	4		31	Toccata per organo con pedali
IV	35-42	4	crown & star	35	Toccata
				37	Toccata Per organo
				40'	Canzona
	43-50	4		42'	Recercare Recercare cromatico
V	51-54	2	crown &	51	Toccata p$^{\underline{a}}$
	55-62	4	star	56	Toccata 2$^{\underline{a}}$
	63-69	4		63	Toccata 3$^{\underline{a}}$
				69	(chord progression, in diff. hand)
flyleaf					blank

[a]Number of bifolios in each gathering.
[b]Not identical to the figure of Section II.

examination reveals that it consists of several independent sections, each containing one or more gatherings—see Table 13. The different sections are distinguished in some cases by different papers (different color, thickness, watermarks), in others by variations in width of staff-ruling, pen thickness and ink shade. Each section begins with a new piece on its opening page. The musical contents also confirm the independence of some of the sections; for example, the last section contains three toccate, entitled, respectively, *Toccata p^a*, *Toccata 2^a*, and *Toccata 3^a*, even though several toccate appear in earlier sections.

The musical contents of this manuscript will be discussed in Part Three. It is shown there that for several reasons the attribution to Frescobaldi appearing on the flyleaf must be questioned.

CHIGI 26

(I-Rvat) Rome, Biblioteca Apostolica Vaticana, Ms. Chigi Q.IV.26.

Physical data:	16 × 22 cm; 28 ff.
Notation:	Two-staff keyboard score (2 × 6/7).
Attributions:	None.
Provenance:	Probably Rome (Chigi?), c. 1640-1650.
Literature:	Lincoln, *Manoscritti chigiani*, 70 (inventory).
Editions:	Lincoln, *Chigi*.

This manuscript is discussed jointly with Chigi 28 in the entry of the latter manuscript.

CHIGI 27

(I-Rvat) Rome, Biblioteca Apostolica Vaticana, Ms. Chigi Q.IV.27.

Physical data:	16 × 22 cm; 107 ff. (ff. 100'-107' blank).
Notation:	Two-staff keyboard score (2 × 6/7).
Attributions:	Frescobaldi, Ercole Pasquini.
Provenance:	Probably Rome (Chigi?), c. 1640-1650.
Literature:	Lincoln, *Manoscritti chigiani*, 72-73 (inventory).
	Apel, *Keyboard Music*, 497.
Editions:	Lincoln, *Chigi*.
	Shindle, *Frescobaldi*.
	Shindle, *Ercole Pasquini*.

This manuscript has a homogeneous appearance insofar as physical characteristics and handwriting are concerned. Its musical contents, however, show a clear division into two segments of rather different character. The first part, extending from f. 1 to f. 61 consists of a set of 44 untitled pieces ordered according to key in the following sequence: C major, C minor, D major, D minor, E-flat major, E major, E minor, F major, G major, G minor, A minor, A major, B-flat major, B minor. The second part, f. 62' to f. 100, includes a variety of works, among which are a number of toccate and correnti, along with an organ Mass. The pieces in the first part are anonymous and have no con- cordances; those in the second part include works with attributions to Ercole Pasquini and to Frescobaldi, as well as anonymous compositions with con- cordances to Frescobaldi's TOCCATE I (1615) and TOCCATE II (1627).

The untitled pieces in the first segment are all based in one way or another on a descending scale pattern. They can be subdivided according to meter into two distinct types. Those in triple time are called by Lincoln—with every justification—passacaglie. They are very similar to the *Passagalli* in Chigi 26 and 28 (see pp. 128-29), and equally close to the *Passacaglie* in Frescobaldi's AGGIUNTA of 1637. Like most passacaglie of the period they are based on descending tetrachords, alternating occasionally with an ascending variant.[82] A favored device is an ostinato chord on the second beat, usually V_4^5, reiterated against the successive notes of the tetrachord (I-VII-VI-V) appearing in the bass—see Example 12. This device also was used by Luigi Rossi and by Storace, in SELVA (Sa. 1664b).

The pieces in duple time also generally use descending scale patterns, but these continue beyond the tetrachord and occasionally encompass two full octaves. In counterpoint against these descending scales are set a variety of figurations, often by several voices in imitation, resulting at times in toccata-like textures. Here, too, the ostinato V_4^5 chord makes an occasional appearance, at times being unusually persistent—see Example 13.

There is a striking resemblance between the beginning of the triple-time piece on f. 36' and the opening of a *Passacaille* in the *Pièces de Clavecin* (1689) of J. Henry d'Anglebert (p. 51)—see Example 14. The similarity probably does not imply a direct borrowing of this particular passage, which presents a version of a stock formula of the genre, but it does suggest a rather direct link between the Italian passacaglia genre and its French counterpart—a link that may very well have been forged by Luigi Rossi.[83]

About half of the pieces in the second part of the manuscript have some connection with Frescobaldi or with Ercole Pasquini, either through attributions or through concordances to Frescobaldi's publications. When such concordances exist, the versions in the manuscript often are found to deviate considerably from the printed versions—see pp. 63, 66. Some of the anonymous pieces in this section are rather old-fashioned compared with the contents of the first part of the manuscript; the *Toccata* on f. 84, for example, resembles the late 16th-century Venetian form of this genre.

The repertory of the first part of the manuscript suggests that the copyist was wroking in the 1630s or, more likely, in the 1640s (see the discussion of the

Example 12

Chigi 27, f. 37′: [untitled composition] (mm. 21-25)

Example 13

Chigi 27, f. 19′: [untitled composition] (mm. 1-4)

Example 14

(a) Chigi 27, f. 36′: [untitled composition] (mm. 1-5)

(b) D'Anglebert, Pièces de Clavecin (Paris, 1689), p. 51: Passacaille (mm. 1-5)

Passacaglia style, p. 128). The second part indicates, however, that he had at his disposal some older source or sources containing, in particular, the Ercole Pasquini compositions and at least a part of the anonymous repertory.

CHIGI 28

(I-Rvat) Rome, Biblioteca Apostolica Vaticana, Ms. Chigi Q.IV.28.

Physical data:	16 × 22 cm; 72 ff.
Notation:	Two-staff keyboard score (2 × 6/7).
Attributions:	None.
Provenance:	Probably Rome (Chigi?), c. 1640-1650.
Literature:	Lincoln, *Manoscritti chigiani*, 73-74 (inventory).
Edition:	Lincoln, *Chigi*.

Since Chigi 26 and Chigi 28 are in the same hand and have similar contents it will be expedient to discuss them jointly. They do have different paper, watermarks, and dimensions; hence they are independent manuscripts rather than separate segments of a single volume. Unlike the other manuscripts in the Chigi collection, Chigi 26 and 28 contain a strictly secular repertory of dances and variations. As is the case with other aria and ballo collections, there are no attributions and no concordances, the single exception being a *Battaglia* in Chigi 28, f. 59' of which a segment also appears in Vat. mus. 569.

A considerable portion of the repertory consists of ciaccona and passacaglia sets—a genre also prominently represented in Chigi 27. The three manuscripts together include a total of thirty-five such sets, each consisting of between four and twenty-six partite. This constitutes by far the largest body of such variations to be found in any of the keyboard sources. Neither Walker nor Hudson in their various studies on the passacaglia and the ciaccona has discussed the examples found here.

According to Walker (*Ciaccona*, 313-320) the first published ciaccona and passacaglia sets date from the 1620s; he dates the height of their popularity to the period from about 1630 to the early 1640s. Actually, the fame of Frescobaldi's contributions to these genres—in his TOCCATE II (1627) and in his AGGIUNTA (1637)—has obscured the fact that their appearance in printed keyboard collections is extremely rare. Except for the sets apparently included in the lost INTAVOLATURA of Scipione Giovanni (Sa. 1650d) the only other known examples are those in Storace's SELVA (Sa. 1664b). If the ciaccone and passacaglie in the three surviving publications are taken as representative of successive stages in the development of these genres, one can conclude that the examples in the Chigi manuscripts belong to the period following the appearance of Frescobaldi's publication in 1637. The sets published in 1627 are rather simple and do not yet contain many of the stereotyped patterns that pervade those of 1637, those of Storace and those in the Chigi manuscripts.[84] Another aspect that relates the passacaglie in the Chigi manuscripts to those in Frescobaldi's 1637 publication and to the later ones by Storace is the use of "remote" keys. Furthermore, some of the passacaglie in Chigi 26 change key several times (for instance, the set of *Passagalli* commencing on f. 15, which starts in C major, moves to A minor, and ends in G major)—a procedure not found in Frescobaldi's sets in 1627, but used in those of 1637 as well as in Storace's 1664 print.

Of course we do not know whether Frescobaldi's *Passacaglie* of 1637 reflect the fashionable figurations and practices of that time, or whether they form the models for the clichés of the next decade. I am inclined to believe the second alternative, and hence propose that Chigi 26 and 28 date at the earliest from the 1640s.

A few works contained in Chigi 28 merit individual discussion. A Bergamasca (f. 36') with 34 (!) partite is a virtual compendium of keyboard techniques. Its intent may very well have been didactic; it resembles a set of finger exercises for scales, trills, tone repetitions, octaves, parallel thirds, parallel sixths, etc. The technique that these exercises would develop is not the one required for the expressive colorature of the early Frescobaldi toccate but rather that needed for the brilliant passage work found in the later 17th-century repertory (for example, in the works of Bernardo Pasquini).

A *Colascione* (f. 41) is clearly named after the long-necked Sicilian lute of Middle-Eastern derivation. LIke the *Piva* (on f. 71) and the *Pastorale* in Naples 48 (cf. p. 109) this curious piece attempts to reproduce the sound of a folk instrument. The colascione often had only two strings, tuned to A and D (though the long neck and large number of frets allowed a considerable melodic range), and was played with a plectrum. A transcription of this piece is given in Example 15; the two-part texture, the melodic range, and the tone repetitions all accord with the description of the instrument and its technique.[85]

Example 15

Chigi 28, f. 41: Colascione

Chigi 28 contains a few sequences of pieces that probably belong together and may even form part of a single composition. One such sequence is formed by a *Romanesca* (f. 49), a *Favorita* (f. 55), and a *Saltarello* (f. 57). These three have been separated in Lincoln's edition (*Chigi* III, 1; III, 38; and II, 56); Lincoln evidently regarded them as belonging to different genres. The Favorita is an aria with a harmonic framework similar to that of the Romanesca, but with a different rhythmic scheme; it is represented here by three partite. The *Saltarello* is not a separate piece at all, but is simply the "ripresa" of the third partita on *la Favorita*; this is evident from the notation (the double repeat sign at the end of the *Favorita terza*) and from the musical continuity.

Probably the most interesting composition (or group of compositions) in this manuscript is an extended Battle sequence (ff. 59'-67') somewhat reminiscent of William Byrd's contribution to this genre (if artistically not quite on the same level). Here too the movements have been published as independent pieces by Lincoln (*Chigi* II, 59, 62, 65 and 66), with no indication of their close interrelationships. The sequence consists of the usual battle episodes, with trumpet calls, drum rolls, and bullet volleys, alternating with more melodious sections; the latter presumably imitate the songs and marches heard from the warring troops. We shall see in fact that at least three of them can be identified as political or battle songs from various parts of Europe. In the first of these melodic sections (m. 36) one recognizes the sound of bagpipers. The second musical interruption of the battle is marked "Girometta" (m. 83); the melody corresponds to the popular song by that name. Its appearance in this context is not without precedent; Kirkendale, in his fascinating history of this tune, notes that it turns up in several musical portrayals of battles (*Franchesina*, 207). One assumes that it was heard also during real battles, as a soldier's song or marching tune. Kirkendale does not connect its appearance in the Chigi manuscript with the Battaglia tradition, but rather with that of the Pastorale.[86] As a result he explains the "unusually primitive style," i.e., the reiterated C-major triad in the left-hand accompaniment, in terms of this tradition and "its continuation and degeneration . . . by rustic musicians." However, in view of the battle context a more likely explanation is that the piece presents a bit of tone-painting imitating a fife-and-drum corps, much like Byrd's "The flute and the droome."

After further battle episodes the fife-and-drum corps (or perhaps the corps from the opposing troops) strikes up a new tune (m. 103); it is given a similar setting, with trills and C-major-triad drum beats. This is also an old song, but not one that ordinarily shows up in Italian sources: it is the "Wilhelmus," the song of the Netherlands' War of Independence, later to become the Dutch National Anthem. So far as I know, the appearance of the melody in this manuscript, complete with the traditional shift in meter, has not been noted before.[87]

Following the Wilhelmus the battle resumes (m. 121); we hear trumpet calls echoing across the fields—the markings "forte" and "piano" found here represent one of the rare appearances of indications for dynamics in the 17th-century Italian keyboard literature.[88]

The fife-and-drum corps makes another appearance (m. 151); the first part of the tune I could not identify, but the second part resembles the second half of the Ungaresca.[89] This is followed by a rendition of *Lanturlura*, another international tune (m. 161) known with a rather vulgar French text mocking the Huguenots;[90] it is set in octaves with trills (as was the repeat of the Girometta). After a final battle episode the sequence concludes with a setting of *O Clorida* (cf. Table 6, p. 42), a reference, perhaps, to the battle of Tancredi and Clorinda. This time the melody does not receive a drone accompaniment, but again the repeats of each strain are set in octaves, with trills added.

Unlike the earlier episodes of the *Battaglia, O Clorida* concludes in the manuscript with the zig-zag design that usually functions as final double bar. Nevertheless, it is possible that the following *Ciaconna* (f. 66') in C major, the key of the *Battaglia*, was meant to provide a victorious conclusion to the entire sequence.

CHIGI 29

(I-Rvat) Rome, Biblioteca Apostolica Vaticana, Ms. Chigi Q.IV.29.

Physical data:	16 × 22 cm; 101 ff. (ff. 51-100 blank).
Notation:	Two-staff keyboard score (2 × 6/7).
Attributions:	None.
Provenance:	Probably Rome (Chigi?), 1630-1650.
Literature:	Lincoln, *Manoscritti chigiani*, 76-77.
Edition:	Lincoln, *Chigi*.

The principal hand of Chigi 29 is described by Lincoln appropriately as "scrittura molto affrettata" (*Manoscritti chigiani*, 74). The writing is extremely undisciplined, with the stems of the notes slanted at times at an angle of almost 45 degrees, and with the beams crossing the stems as much as halfway along their lengths. There are a number of little fragments in other hands, including on f. 50' the first four measures of the fourth ricercare from Frescobaldi's RECERCARI (1615); no other concordances have been found.

The repertory consists of toccate, ricercari, canzoni (including two *Recercare-Canzona* pairs—see p. 46), a set of partite on la Monicha and two sets on the Ruggiero.

On ff. 100'-101 are recorded some payments to singers and instrumentalists without indication of dates or occasions. Here too the writing shows signs of great haste and some of it is difficult to decipher. Most musicians are identified only by their first names; the organist is listed simply as "organista."[91]

Because of the lack of attributions and concordances the dating of this collection is difficult. On the basis of style and repertory one can probably set 1630 and 1650 as outer limits.

CHIGI 205-206

(I-Rvat) Rome, Biblioteca Apostolica Vaticana, Ms. Chigi Q.VIII.205-206.

Since Chigi 205-206 consists of two folders containing fascicles and pages of varying dimensions and diverse provenance we shall not use the standard format for these entries, but will incorporate information on the individual items in the general discussion following below.

Literature:	Lincoln, *Manoscritti chigiani*, 77-80.
	MacClintock, *Giaches Fantasias*.
	Lowinsky, *Early Scores*, 135-136.
	Ladewig, *Frescobaldi*, 24-43.
Editions:	Lincoln, *Chigi*.
	Shindle, *Frescobaldi*.
	Shindle, *Pasquini*.

The collection Chigi 205-206 has become the subject of some scholarly dispute owing to the presence of a fascicle of scores apparently dating back to the 16th Century. Among the compositions in question are a set of Fantasie attributed to "Giaches." Lowinsky, who was the first to draw attention to the collection (*Early Scores*, 135-136), believed that "Giaches" stood for Jacques Brumel (organist in Ferrara from 1533 to 1564) and that the Fantasie were intended for organ. A few years later MacClintock published an article devoted entirely to these pieces (MacClintock, *Giaches Fantasies*); her contention— backed by a series of extended arguments—was that the compositions should not be attributed to Brumel but rather to Giaches de Wert (1535-1596) and that they were intended for instrumental ensemble—most likely for viols. MacClintock's case rests partially on her view of the provenance and the character of the entire collection of manuscripts assembled in Chigi 206;[92] her description of the collection is, however, not altogether accurate and to some extent misleading.

MacClintock states—correctly—that Chigi 206 is "a bundle of different manuscripts." She then proceeds under the assumption that these manuscripts belong together: "Probably they once formed part of an organist's collection." The latter statement is not supported by the varied content of the collection, which in addition to keyboard music, includes materials of diverse character and instrumentation, dating from a considerable time span (see below); furthermore, there is no a priori reason to assume that the items in this folder were brought together before the early years of the present century. As was observed in the general discussion of the Chigi collection (pp. 119-20), the librarian Baronci, when cataloguing the music manuscripts, gathered the loose fascicles and pages into a series of such folders and assigned them the numbers Q.VIII.196 to 206. He evidently attempted to sort the works at least roughly into chronologically homogeneous groups; thus, for example, Q.VIII.203 and 204 contain 18th- and 19th-century materials, and Q.VIII.205 and 206 for the most part contain 16th- and 17th-century compositions.[92] A modern stamped foliation runs continuously through Chigi 205 and Chigi 206, implying a (doubtless correct) conclusion on someone's part that the division of the items between the two folders is arbitrary (as is the order within each folder).

MacClintock states that the music in Chigi 206 spans a period from about 1560 to 1650. I would suggest adding the significant qualification that, with the exception of the fascicle containing the disputed scores, there is no reason to date any item from before c. 1610;[94] several other works, moreover, clearly date from the late 17th and from the 18th century (see Lincoln's inventory).

In stating her case for de Wert's authorship, MacClintock furthermore expresses the belief that the collection is of Ferrarese provenance, since "those named in the Chigi MS were . . . all connected in some way with Ferrara." I have been unable to confirm (and hence must question) this assertion with respect to most of the composers named in Chigi 205-206; the only ones known to have been resident in Ferrara are Luzzaschi, Frescobaldi, and Ercole Pasquini.[95] From the point of view of source tradition the use of the latter two names to support a Ferrarese provenance appears dubious (there are no other Ferrarese sources for their compositions).[96] Furthermore, we have no reason to assume that Chigi 205-206 departs significantly from the regional orientation of the Chigi collection as a whole. A cursory glance through the catalogue of the music manuscripts will show that the collection was throughout its history rooted in Roman musical life.[97]

In summary, although MacClintock's identification of "Giaches" as Giaches de Wert may well be correct, it cannot be supported on the basis of the provenance of Chigi 205-206.

Similarly, the case for an ensemble instrumentation—which in MacClintock's view supports de Wert's authorship—appears to me rather unconvincing. The fascicle containing the Fantasie also includes two cantus-firmus settings (of "la Spagna" and "Ave Maris stella") and five versetti (one of which is also based on "Ave Maris stella"), notated by the same hand and in the same fashion (i.e., four-staff score).[98] There is no evidence to associate such plainchant versets with any instruments but the organ in 16th-century Italy. Furthermore, the score notation itself remains a strong argument supporting keyboard performance.

I shall restrict my further discussion to the 17th-century keyboard materials in Chigi 205-206. These consist of a series of unbound fascicles varying in size from single papers to quaternions. In physical appearance the pages resemble those in the bound Chigi volumes. They use $2 \times 6/7$ staff ruling except for ff. 54-62' and 70-73, in which $2 \times 6/8$ is used. Some fascicles show signs of having been bound at one time (see p. 18), but with the majority this is not the case. From the variety of papers, watermarks, and dimensions even among papers in the same handwriting it is apparent that not even the keyboard portions of the manuscript ever constituted a single collection. Several hands can be distinguished, among which two predominate:

Hand A:	ff. 32-35', 92-92', 95-98', 128-131', 145-146', 150-150'
Hand B:	ff. 54-69', 74-91', 93-94', 99-115', 132, 135'
Hand C:	ff. 136-136'
Hand D:	ff. 137-138'
Hand E;	ff. 139-142
Hand F:	ff. 149-149', 182-187
Hand G:	ff. 192'-193'
Hand H:	ff. 194-195
Hand I:	f. 203
Hand J:	f. 203'
Hand K:	ff. 204-204'
Hand L:	ff. 205-206'

Hand A is also responsible for some of the ensemble parts included in Chigi 205 (ff. 16-30). Hand B shows some similarity to the hand of Chigi 29, but an actual identity between the two appears uncertain at best. The compositions in Hand A are without attributions and concordances, with the exception of the partial concordance to Frescobaldi's *Cento Partite* (see p. 64). Like several other compositions in Hand A, this version is incomplete.

The pieces in Hand B inlude four compositions with concordances to Frescobaldi's TOCCATE II (1627) and two with concordances to Ravenna 545 (both anonymous), as well as several compositions attributed to Frescobaldi that are not known from other sources. Among the pages by copyists other than the two principal hands are further attributions to Frescobaldi as well as to Ercole Pasquini.

The keyboard fascicles in Chigi 205-206 are close enough in appearance and contents to the keyboard volumes Chigi 24-29 to make it appear likely that they originated in the same period, i.e., 1630-1650.

VAT. MUS. 569

(I-Rvat) Rome, Biblioteca Apostolica Vaticana, Ms. Vat. mus. 569

Title:	Virginius Mutius sonabat Anno D [omi]ni/1661 (on flyleaf); Liber Virginij Mutij I.V.D. Discipulij D. Bonaventurae Mini, et Fabritij Fontanae respective 1663 (on top of p. 1).
Physical data:	16 × 22 cm; 59 ff.
Notation:	Two-staff keyboard score (2 × 6/7).
Attributions:	Pietro Arnò, G.B. Ferrini, Fabritio Fontana, and Bernardo [Pasquini?].
Provenance:	Rome, c. 1660-1665.
Literature:	Casimiri, *Frescobaldi*, 12. Kirkendale, *Fiorenza*, 73.

Vat. mus. 569 has only recently become accessible to scholarly investigators. It is an important manuscript that undoubtedly will play a key role in expanding our knowledge of Italian keyboard music after 1650. In addition to augmenting the number of known works by familiar figures such as Bernardo Pasquini (for whose keyboard music it is by several decades the earliest source) and Fabritio Fontana, it introduces the music of two virtually unknown composers, Giovanni Battista Ferrini and Pietro Arnò. But what is perhaps more important: it demonstrates the variety of musical currents running through Roman keyboard music of the 1660s.

The first reference to the manuscript appeared in 1933 in an article on unknown Frescobaldi works by Casimiri (*Frescobaldi*, 12). Casimiri, who at the time was the owner of the collection, describes it as "un codicetto manoscritto del sec. XVII . . . contenente musiche inedite per Organo e Cembalo di Gio-Batta Ferrini, di Bernardo (che è certamente il Pasquini), di Fabrizio Fontana, di Pietro Arnò (sic) e di Anonimo." According to a note on the inside cover of the manuscript Casimiri had bought it on 23 September 1927 (for 360 lire); upon his death in 1943 it was bequeathed, along with the rest of his music library, to the Biblioteca Apostolica Vaticana. The manuscripts remained uncatalogued and essentially inacessible until late 1972, when they were inventoried and catalogued under the *Fondo Vaticani musicali*.[99]

The collation shows no significant irregularities. All gatherings are quaternions except for the first, which consists of only two bifolios; the last quaternion lacks one page. The staff-ruling is uniform throughout; the watermark shows the common star-and-anchor pattern. There is a continuous pagination running from p. 1 to p. 118 (the final page of the manuscript).[100] The page numbers from p. 1 to p. 85 appear to have been entered by a 17th-century hand; those from p. 86 to p. 118 clearly are of 20th-century vintage. In addition pp. 88 to 113 contain a second, independent pagination, also in a (different) 17th-century hand, running from p. "1" (= p. 88) to p. "26" (= p. 113).

Although this section is not physically independent of the remainder of the manuscript (it commences and ends in the middle of gatherings and shows no discontinuities with respect to paper and staff-ruling), it is distinct in two respects. The music hand is different from that found in the surrounding portions of the manuscript (the latter hand is the principal music hand of the manuscript, responsible for pp. 33-87 and 114-118). Furthermore, whereas the majority of compositions are provided with attributions, only one inscription with a name is found in this portion; it appears above the opening composition (on p. 88 = p. "1"): "Dal Sig^r Pietro Arnò dall: 19 Novembre 1666." An almost identical inscription was entered on the preceding page, after the final bar of the composition concluded there (p. 87: "A di 19 Novembre 1663 dal Sig^r Pietro Arnò"). This could be interpreted as indicating that Arnò was responsible for all subsequent contributions (presumably up to the reappearance of the earlier hand) as copyist, and possibly also as composer or arranger.

The binding of the manuscript appears to have accommodated at one time a larger number of pages than are contained within it at present, judging by the width of its spine. In particular, a segment preceding the present p. 1 appears to be missing; the removal of a sizable portion is suggested not only by a gap between the flyleaf and the present p. 1, but also by the number "20" that appears in the upper left-hand corner of this page in front of the treble staff of the opening piece—presumably signifying that this was the 20th in a series. No further numbers are found within subsequent compositions; however, the later works are entered by different scribes.[101]

If the initial portion of the manuscript was indeed removed, the pagination and probably also the inscription on the present p. 1 were inserted after this removal had taken place. This could account for the two years' discrepancy between the dates on the flyleaf and on p. 1; presumably the first portion was taken out some time between 1661 and 1663.

Six names appear in the manuscript: Virginio Mutij, Bonaventura Mini, Fabritio Fontana, Giovanni Battista Ferrini, Bernardo, and Pietro Arnò. Nothing is known about Virginio Mutij; the inscription informs us that he was a pupil of Mini and Fontana and that he was a Doctor of Laws.[102] Several other Mutijs played, however, an important role in Rome's musical life during this period, both as music publishers and as musicians.

The publishing house of Mutij had flourished under Nicola (Nicolò) Mutij during the last years of the 16th century, issuing works of composers such as Palestrina, de Macque, Soriano, and Cavalieri (the *Rappresentazione di anima e corpo*). Shortly after 1600 it evidently ceased activities, but the family tradition was revived around 1670 by Giovanni Angelo Mutij, among whose publications are Fabritio Fontana's RICERCARI (Sa. 1677b) and the first editions of Corelli's *Sonate a tre* (Sartori, *Dizionario*, 108). In a note appended to some of his editions in which this Mutij advertises his publishing services to "li Sig.

Musici," he states that in his younger years he possessed some musical skills and received instruction from Girolamo Frescobaldi.[103]

Another Mutij, a son of Giovanni Angelo's predecessor Nicolò, rose to great eminence in Rome, becoming one of the leading keyboard players of the generation following Frescobaldi. Francesco Mutij (1602-1664) served as organist at S. Luigi dei Francesi, S. Maria in Aracoeli, and S. Maria Maggiore, and appears in the records of many sacred and secular performances in Rome from the 1620s to the 1660s.[104]

Fabritio Fontana (c. 1610-1695) is named twice in our manuscript: on p. 1, as teacher of Virginio Mutij, and on p. 30, as composer of a corrente. Fontana came to Rome from Turin around 1650, where he served as organist at S. Maria in Vallicella until 1657, and, subsequently, at St. Peter's until 1692. In addition to the aforementioned collection of ricercari published by Giovanni Angelo Mutij he is credited with a number of toccatas, appearing only in English sources, and with some vocal music.[105]

In Part Three of this study we shall deal with Ferrini, who is named as composer of twelve works in this manuscript, and with Bernardo Pasquini, who, as will be shown there, probably was the author of two compositions attributed to "Bernardo."

Nothing is known about either Bonaventura Mini, named in the inscription in p. 1, or of Pietro Arnò, whose name appears in the separately paginated segment described before. The latter may have been a Frenchman (Arnauld?), which would account for the accent on the last syllable of his name (not found in the spelling of the river Arno). Throughout this section one finds the sign $\sim$, the French indication for the trill, which appears nowhere else in 17th-century Italian keyboard sources (trills are generally indicated by "t" or "tr."). The segment opens with a composition which has the attribution to Arnò and a title *Capriccio*, to which another hand has added *Toccata*; Stylistically, this piece has little in common with Italian keyboard pieces of the period, showing closer affinity to a grand French fantasie, or an English voluntary. The segment includes, furthermore, some dances the titles of which use French spellings, "courante" and "branle" rather than their Italian equivalents, corrente and brando. Several are accompanied by doubles with the French designation "variation." Four dances in fact use French dance tunes, although the settings are unique to this manuscript:

p. 96: *Courante Lavignone* (La Vignon, one of the most popular of all 17th-century tunes; for a list of settings, see Gustafson, *Sources*, p. 10, to which can be added the settings in this manuscript, in Barb. Lat. 4182, f. 2, and one by Luigi Rossi in his opera *Il Palazzo incantato* [1642, Ms. Chigi Q.V.51, f. 170']).

p. 98: *Sarabanda* (many settings and attributions, see Gustafson, *Sources*, 20-21, 316 [No. 48a], 53 [f. 4].

p. 102: *Courante la Duchesse* (another setting appears in this manuscript, p. 27; for additional settings, see Gustafson, *Sources*, 351 [No. 67]).

p. 112: *Branle La Cocquille*, in Thomas Greeting, *The Pleasant Companion or New Lessons and Instructions for the Flagelet* [London: Playford, 1680]; for additional settings, see Gustafson, *Sources*, 533 [No. 13].

We see that Vat. mus. 569 contains the works of three composers who definitely can be placed within the Roman scene: Fontana, Ferrini, and Pasquini. There are in fact many professional ties between these three musicians. All three at one time served as organist at S. Maria della Vallicella, and during the period of our manuscript (1661-63) they frequently performed together in special festivities at churches and oratorios.[106] We also find Francesco Mutij appearing at these occasions, which often required several organists as well as harpsichordists. For example, for a polychoral performance at S. Luigi dei Francesi on 25 August 1661, four organists were employed: Fontana, Mutij, Pasquini, and Leonardo Castellani (the organist at S. Giovanni in Laterano).[107] During the same period we find these musicians performing in each other's company at S. Maria Maggiore and at the Oratorio di S. Marcello—Mutij usually on organ, Pasquini and Fontana sometimes on harpsichord, and Ferrini, almost always on "spinetta."[108]

Since Virginio Mutij calls himself a student of Fontana, it seems probable that the manuscript is in some way connected with this circle of Roman musicians. One of them may even have been responsible for the transmission of some pieces found in slightly older manuscripts. These concordances all involve Roman sources: Chigi 26, Chigi 28, Modena 491, and Vall. 121; in the case of Vall. 121 there is also a scribal concordance—see p. 140.[109] Since Pasquini was organist at S. Maria in Vallicella during the early sixties and both Fontana and Ferrini had served there earlier, any of these three musicians might have had some connection with Vall. 121 (as contributor or user), and hence might have transferred the pieces to Vat. mus. 569. Furthermore, the years 1661-1663 fell during the pontificate of Fabio Chigi (1655-1667) and it does not seem implausible that Fontana, who was organist at St. Peter's during most of Chigi's reign, or Pasquini, who in 1664 accompanied Chigi's nephew to Paris, had access to the pope's music collection.[110] Hence either may have played a role in the transmission of the compositions from the Chigi manuscripts.

Although Vat. mus. 569 is linked through concordances with these earlier manuscripts, its repertory is by and large representative of a new phase in Italian keyboard music. Unlike the older collections it no longer includes any works attributed to Ercole Pasquini and to Frescobaldi, but presents the work of a new generation of Roman composers, active during the 1660s. Indicative of the changing tastes is the absence of the Ruggiero and the Romanesca, the standbys of the earlier repertory. A few old-fashioned aria settings are still included, but side by side with these one finds such strikingly "modern" pieces as the *Toccata* by Ferrini (p. 1), with brilliant passagework of sixteenth- and thirty-second notes that foreshadow Alessandro Scarlatti's compositions in this genre.

VALL. 121

(I-Rv) Rome, Biblioteca Vallicelliana, Ms. Z. 121.

Title:	Libro d'intavolatura (on the flyleaf).
Physical data:	15 × 22 cm; 47 ff.
Notation:	Two-staff keyboard score (2 × 6/7).
Attributions:	None.
Provenance:	Probably Roman, c. 1650-1660.
Literature:	None.

This manuscript has remained undiscussed in the literature, probably owing to its lack of attributions.[111] On the flyleaf appears the inscription "Libro d'intavolatura," whose continuation (possibly in a different hand)—"da sonare o tasteggiare sopra li tasti del Manicordio"—has been crossed out. The foliation is recent; it does not account for a page missing between f. 27 and f. 28 (evidenced by the collation and by a discontinuity in the musical text). The manuscript consists of three segments, each in a different hand:

(1)	ff. 2-31:	hand A
(2)	ff. 31-39:	hand B
(3)	ff. 40-47:	hand C

The third segment uses a different paper of slightly larger dimensions and staff ruling of different width.

The pieces are grouped according to key and in some cases appear to form little suites consisting of a brief toccata followed by some dances and arie. Most of the compositions in the manuscript are in fact balli and arie, though only a few of these use traditional models: two Monica settings (one in hand A, f. 15, and one in hand C, f. 44), a *Ripresa di Romanesca* (f. 13), a *Ballo di Mantua* (f. 31), an untitled Fiorenza (f. 40), two Gagliarde (one in hand B, f. 33, one in hand C, f. 46), and a set of *Passacagli* (f. 12). The manuscript also contains a few liturgical compositions: *Sonata per l'elevatione* (f. 26) and four *Versetti del P[rimo] tono* (f. 37), the last of which is based on Palestrina's *"Vestiva i colli"* (f. 39).

Two consecutively placed pieces (f. 31, *Ballo di Mantua*, and f. 33, *Gagliarda*) also are found in Vat. mus. 569 (p. 39 and p. 29, respectively). A scribal as well as a musical concordance is involved: the versions in Vat. mus. 569 are in a hand that appears identical to hand B of this manuscript—the hand in which these two compositions are notated. This suggests that Vall. 121 is close in provenance to the Vatican manuscript (dated 1661-1663), although its repertory indicates that it may be somewhat older, perhaps from the 1650s. In the discussion of Vat. mus. 569 it was noted that three musicians named in that collection, Ferrini, Fontana, and Bernardo Pasquini, served as organist of S. Maria in Vallicella and hence might have had some connection with Vall. 121, and conceivably even with these concordances.[112] But regardless of whether such was the case, the concordances as well as the present location of the manuscript make a Roman provenance appear likely; such a conclusion is further supported by the general appearance of the manuscript (format, notation, etc.) and by the staff-line system.

CECILIA 400

(I-RSC) Rome, Conservatorio di musica Santa Cecilia, Ms. A/400.

Physical data:	21 × 27 cm; 76 ff.
Notation:	Single bass parts and two-staff keyboard score
	(4 × 5/5 and 2 × 6/8).
Attributions:	E. Pasquini, Frescobaldi, and Alessandro Stradella.
Provenance:	Probably Rome, first half of the 18th century.
Literature:	Jander, *Stradella*, 16.
	Apel, *Keyboard Music*, 747.
	Gustafson, *Sources*, pp. 143-45 and 547-50 (includes partial inventory).
	Anderson, *Cecilia* (includes complete thematic inventory).
Editions:	Shindle, *Pasquini* (compositions attributed to Pasquini).
	Anderson, *Cecilia* (edition of selected pieces).

Cecilia 400 is a manuscript of 18th-century origin; however, it contains much 17th-century repertory, including unica attributed to Stradella and to Ercole Pasquini.

Owen Jander, in his discussion of Stradella sources, gives a summary discussion of the manuscript (Jander, *Stradella*, 16).[113] He speculates that this volume might correspond to the "Piega di Sonate di Cembala, et Organo" listed in an inventory of Stradella manuscripts preserved in the Modena Archivio di Stato. We shall see, however, that this cannot be the case, since Jander dates the inventory c. 1682, and Cecilia 400 was compiled at the earliest during the second decade of the 18th century.

The manuscript is in a single hand; the writing is unusually graceful and shows a consistency of habits throughout the 76 folios. The latter observation suggests that it was copied during a comparatively limited time span. The collation is regular throughout, consisting of nineteen quaternions. The paper is uniform, but the staff ruling is not; the first sixty folios follow the "modern" 5/5 system, but the last two gatherings (ff. 61-76) use the old fashioned system of 6/8. This difference corresponds to a difference in musical content (see below) and also probably reflects the notation of the copyist's sources.

The manuscript divides into several segments:

(1) ff. 1-15: Untitled anonymous figured basses, probably partimento exercises, in progressive order of difficulty. The first fourteen pieces appear in fact in two partimento manuscripts with attributions to the Neapolitan composer Gaetano Greco (c. 1657-1728?); another piece appears in a third manuscript with an attribution to Gaetano's brother, Rocco Greco.[114]

(2) ff. 16-39: Untitled anonymous compositions, possibly written-out accompaniments to sonata or concerto movements (from c. 1700?).

(3) ff. 40-47: Anonymous organ pieces with French titles, ordered according to the eight tones. The genres are characteristic of the late 17th-century French organ repertory.

(4) ff. 47-54: A set of dances and other pieces with French titles, mostly for harpsichord. The pieces have no attributions, but several were apparently international favorites and are found in many other European sources. Among these are compositions attributed elsewhere to Monnard (d. 1646?),[115] to Lebègue,[116] and to François Couperin (le Grand),[117] as well as settings of popular airs and dances.[118]

(5) ff. 55-60: Untitled anonymous pieces in the style of early 18th-century violin sonatas.

(6) ff. 61-76: Keyboard compositions attributed to Alessandro Stradella, Ercole Pasquini, and Frescobaldi. The Frescobaldi pieces all appear in the AGGIUNTA (1637); the Stradella work is unique to this manuscript—in fact, it is the only surviving keyboard composition attributed to him, although he apparently wrote other music for the instrument (see Jander, *Stradella*, 16); the Pasquini compositions, some of which are also unique, are discussed in Part Three, pp. 180-82.

The chronological spread of the music in this collection is unusually wide, ranging from pieces attributed to Ercole Pasquini (d. 1620) to a composition by François Couperin first published in 1713, although most of the anonymous compositions stylistically appear to date from the end of the 17th and the beginning of the 18th century. Given the uniformity of paper and handwriting the entire volume probably was not compiled before c. 1715.[119]

SPELLO

(I-SPE) Spello, Archivio di Santa Maria Maggiore (no signature).

Physical data:	15 × 21 cm; 38 ff.
Notation:	Two-staff keyboard score (2 × 6/7).
Attributions:	Gio. Piccione.
Provenance:	Spello?, c. 1600.
Literature:	None.

This little volume appears to contain a typical church organist's repertory: organ Mass versets, ricercari, canzoni, toccate, and a capriccio. The pieces are brief and simple, and stylistically fall entirely within 16th-century practices. Only one composition has an attribution: *Toccata del p[rim]o tuono di Gio. Piccione* (ff. 28'-29'). A Giovanni Piccione was active as composer and organist in the region immediately north of Rome (where Spello is located). He was born around 1550 in Rimini, served as organist at the Duomo of Orvieto from before 1596 to 1619 and again in 1619, and was the composer of at least a dozen collections of sacred and secular vocal music published between 1577 and 1616.[120]

The manuscript probably belonged to one of the organists of S. Maria Maggiore, a church with a long musical tradition.[121] Many of the musicians working there were brought in from nearby Rome; it is therefore not surprising that in format and staff layout this manuscript follows Roman traditions. It probably was compiled near the end of the 16th or the beginning of the 17th century, as is suggested by handwriting style (e.g., tear-drop shaped noteheads, out of fashion by c. 1620), repertory, and the presence of the Piccioni attribution.

TRENT

(I-TR?) Trent, formerly in private library of Laurence Feininger (no inventory number). Present location unknown.

Physical data:	16 × 23 cm; 97 ff.
Notation:	Two-staff keyboard notation (2 × 6/7).
Attributions:	G. Gabrieli, E Pasquini.
Provenance:	Probably North-central Italian, c. 1600.
Literature:	Apel, *Keyboard Music*, 497.
Editions:	Shindle, *Pasquini*.

The Trent manuscript formed part of the private collection of Laurence Feininger.[122] It is briefly described by Apel (*Keyboard Music*, p. 497) and, being one of the principal sources of the keyboard music of Ercole Pasquini, is drawn upon extensively in Shindle's edition of Pasquini's works.

The collection contains several intabulations of 16th-century polyphonic compositions: an anonymous setting of Orlando di Lasso's "Susanne un jour" (f. 39'), a setting of Cipriano de Rore's "Anchor che col partire" (f. 69'), and some movements from Palestrina's *Missa O magnum mysterium* (f. 80'). "Susanne un jour" and "Anchor che col partire" are of course classical models for intabulations. "Susanne" settings are discussed by Levy, who gives a list of instrumental intabulations (Levy, *Susanne*, 379, n. 3). The list includes several Italian settings, all of which date from before 1600 (although the one by Andrea Gabrieli was not published until 1605). A similar discussion of settings of the de Rore madrigal is given by Ferand (*Anchor*); Italian instrumental settings date between 1568 and 1609, but the latest keyboard setting (again by Andrea Gabrieli) was published in 1596.[123] No other keyboard intabulations of Palestrina's Mass or, for that matter, of any other 16th-century Mass are found in 17th-century manuscripts. The presence of all these intabulations in Trent suggests, therefore, a close connection between the manuscript and late 16th-century traditions.

Three distinct hands appear in the manuscript. The first, occupying ff. 1-5, contributes an organ Mass and an untitled ricercare. The second hand is responsible for the major part of the manuscript, ff. 6-74. Among its contributions are a set of five Entrata-Recercare pairs, discussed in Chapter IX (p. 46). Beginning with f. 54, most of the pieces are attributed to Ercole Pasquini. A third hand appears on f. 74; this copyist continues with works attributed to Pasquini.

On f. 20 appears a piece in tablature marked "Teorba." At the top of f. 21 appears the inscription "Sonata di spinetta." Since no new piece commences on this page—it contains a continuation of an untitled composition beginning on f. 20'—this inscription is probably a later addition.

On f. 35' appears a "Toccata del signor Gio. P.G." This composition is also found in Diruta's TRANSILVANO (Sa. 1596b), and is attributed there to Giovanni Gabrieli. Although the manuscript version contains a number of minor variants, it seems probably that it was based on the text of Diruta's widely disseminated treatise. If such was indeed the case, the publication date 1593 would provide us with a terminus post quem, that appears plausible with respect to the remaining contents of the volume. Several aspects of the repertory suggest that the manuscript probably was not compiled much beyond the turn of the century: the presence of the intabulations (see above), the inclusion of compositions attributed to Ercole Pasquini along with the absence of any attributed to Frescobaldi,[124] and the lack of Ruggiero, Romanesca, and Fiorenza settings, found in large numbers in later manuscripts. The only partite included in this collection are those on the Passamezzo antico and on the Tenore di Napoli.

There are few clues to the regional origin of this manuscript. The many

Ercole Pasquini unica suggest a North or Central Italian provenance, since most of his work appears in sources from that region, and since, so far as we know, he worked only in Ferrara and Rome.[125]

VENICE 1227

(I-Vm) Venice, Biblioteca Nazionale Marciana, Cod. It. IV-1227 (Ms. 11699).

Physical data:	11 × 17 cm; 21 ff.
Notation:	Two-staff keyboard score (2 × 5/6).
Attributions:	None.
Provenance:	Probably Venice, c. 1530-1550.
Literature:	Jeppesen, *Tanzbuch.*
	Apel, *Keyboard Music,* 234-236.
Edition:	Jeppesen, *Balli* (complete edition).

This early 16th-century collection of aria and ballo settings is discussed in Chapter II, pp. 12-13.

VENICE 1299

(I-Vm) Venice, Biblioteca Nazionale Marciana, Cod. It. IV-1299 (Ms. 11068).

Title:	Canzoni, Capricci, Toccate, Ricercate ed altre Suonate per l'Organo, e/Clavicembalo del celebre Sig.[r] Geronimo Fresco Baldi/Organista della Pontifizia Basilica di S. Pietro in Vaticano di Roma/ridotte ad una moderna, e facile lettura da Bernardo Mantuaner (on f. [i]; Suonate/Girolamo/ Fresco Baldi/II (on cover).
Physical data:	22 × 31 cm; 88 ff.
Notation:	Two-staff keyboard score (5 × 5/5).
Attributions:	Frescobaldi.
Provenance:	Probably Venice, 19th century.
Literature:	None.

The manuscript was evidently acquired by the Marciana in 1928; it contains a note "Acquisto Canal 1928." The statement "ridotte ad una moderna, e facile lettura" probably refers to the use of "modern" 5/5 keyboard notations with F_4 and G_2 clefs, and with reduction of note values in some of the compositions copied from the Frescobaldi publications. The identity of Bernardo Mantuaner has not been established. The manuscript is in a single hand; the handwriting most likely dates from the 19th century.[126]

Of the 160 compositions included in the collection, 116 can be traced to Frescobaldi's published collections; almost the entire contents of the four major publications, TOCCATE I (1615) with the AGGIUNTA (1637), TOCCATE II (1627), CAPRICCI (1624) and FIORI (1635) are found here. The sequence in which the compositions appear is puzzling; pieces from the four publications follow each other in no discernible order. In some cases the musical text is simplified (for an example, see p. 63); in other cases the copied versions are incomplete. In several cases accidentals have been added, and copying errors are not infrequent.

Among Frescobaldi works are interspersed a number of compositions for which there are no known concordances. Most of these are simple dances in rather amateurish settings; stylistically they form a homogeneous group probably dating from the second half of the 17th century. In only one composition does an attribution appear in the text: on the upper left-hand corner of f. 10, a page containing a *Ballo del Granduca* (see p. 164), the name "G. Fresco Baldi" has been entered, possibly by a different hand (cf. p. 165).

VENICE 1727

(I-Vm) Venice, Biblioteca Nazionale Marciana, Cod. It. IV-1727 (Ms. 11425).

Physical data:	29 x 20 cm; 52 pp.
Notation:	Two-staff keyboard score (4 x 6/8).
Attributions:	Frescobaldi.
Provenance:	Probably Venice, second half of the 17th century or the 18th century.
Literature:	None.

This manuscript contains copies of compositions from Frescobaldi, TOCCATE I (1615) and TOCCATE II (1627), and an anonymous *Ballo di Mantova*.

VERONA MCXXIX

(I-VEcap) Verona, Biblioteca capitolare, Cod. MCXXIX.

Physical data:	Small oblong volume, 212 pp.
Notation:	Four-staff score.
Attributions:	Frescobaldi.
Provenance:	Dated 1703.
Literature:	Turrini, *Verona*, 38.

This manuscript is an early 18th-century copy of compositions from Frescobaldi's CAPRICCI (1626), FIORI (1635), and CANZONI IV (1645). On p. 212 appears the note "Copia fatta da me N.L.M. 1703"; the date 1703 also appears on p. 61. The manuscript apparently belonged to the collection of Prof. A. Suglia, which was donated by his heirs to the Biblioteca Capitolare.[127]

VICENZA 2.7.17.

(I-VIb) Vicenza, Biblioteca civica Bertoliana, Mus. Ms. FF 2.7.17.

Physical data:	31 × 23 cm; 276 pp.
Notation:	Four-staff score.
Attributions:	Frescobaldi.
Provenance:	Probably 18th century.
Literature:	Rumor, *Catalogo*, 17.

This manuscript contains copies of compositions from Frescobaldi's RECERCARI (1615) and FIORI (1635). A note on the back cover states: "prov. del Convento di S. Lucia in Vicenza."[128]

UCLA 51/1

(US-LAp) University of California at Los Angeles, Music Library, Ms. 51/1 (?).[129]

Physical data:	18 × 25 cm; 32 unnumbered ff. (ff. 29-32 blank).
Notation:	Two-staff keyboard score (2 × 5/8).
Attribution:	None.
Provenance:	North Italian, c. 1620-1660 (?).
Literature:	Hudson, *Fiorenza*, 344-45.

UCLA 51/1 was unknown to the literature prior to the appearance of Hudson's review of Kirkendale's *L'Aria di Fiorenza*. Hudson presents a transcription of a Fiorenza setting and lists the titles of a few other pieces, but gives no further description. The contents consist exclusively of arie and balli; among these are settings of the Monica, the Ruggiero, and the Passamezzo. The settings are extremely simple, with frequent parallels in the left-hand chordal accompaniments. The first twenty-one pieces (i.e., about two-thirds of the contents) all start with a G-major triad! No concordances were found for any of the compositions.

The notation, format and repertory leave little doubt that this collection is of Italian provenance. In content and type of setting the balli are closest to those in Bologna 360, with which the UCLA manuscript also shares the 2 × 5/8 staff-system. A piece entitled "Salluza di Modena" also suggests, but by no means proves, a provenance from the Emilia-Romagna region. In view of the absence of attributions and concordances it is difficult to establish a very precise dating. The repertory suggests that an origin from either before 1620 or after 1660 is unlikely; the earlier limit is based on stylistic considerations, the later limit on the decline of popularity of these arie and balli during the second half of the century.

GAROFALO

(US-NY?) New York, formerly in private collection of Carlo Giorgio Garofalo. Present location unknown.

Physical data:	30 × 14 cm; 134 pp.
Attributions:	Frescobaldi
Provenance:	Late 17th or early 18th century (?)
Literature:	Garofalo, *Scoperta*

According to Garofalo the collection contains "27 fughe a 3 e 4 voci, Sonata col flautino in la maggiore, Elevazione in sol minore, 19 canzoni, in capo alla P.a Frescobaldi."[130] Of the 19 canzoni apparently covered by a blanket attribution to Frescobaldi, three are in fact found among the published works: No. 12 corresponds to the *Capriccio sopra un soggetto* in CAPRICCI (1626), No. 14 to the *Canzona seconda setta la Sabattina* in CANZONI IV (1645), and No. 19 to the *Canzon undecima detta la Gardana* also in CANZONI IV (1645). The remaining canzoni are not known from other sources; in the judgement of Mischiati, Nos. 1, 2, 10, and 13 to 18 could conceivably be by Frescobaldi; the others definitely date from a later period, probably from the late 17th or early 18th century. Garofalo states that the manuscript originated no later than the beginning of the 18th century; whether it is of Italian provenance can at this point not be ascertained.

PART THREE

STUDIES OF INDIVIDUAL COMPOSERS

Introductory Note

The final segment of this work presents studies on the principal composers appearing in the manuscripts. The format of these studies varies somewhat, depending on the types of problems presented by the attributions. In most cases a brief biographical sketch is provided as background for the discussion of the sources and of the individual attributions. As elsewhere in this study the emphasis is on the relation between the composer and the works attributed to him, rather than on the intrinsic interest of these works.

GIOVANNI BATTISTA FERRINI (c. 1600-1674)

Vat. mus. 569 contains twelve compositions attributed to Giovanni Battista Ferrini (or to some abbreviated form of the name, such as G. B. F. or B. F. Fer.), a composer, organist, and harpsichordist active in Rome from c. 1620 to c. 1670.[1] One of these compositions also appears with an attribution to Ferrini in Modena 491 (see p. 105). The attributions in Vat. mus. 569 usually appear at the end of compositions; in the earlier pieces in the manuscript—from p. 32 to p. 48—they evidently were added by the copyist some time after he had copied the music, since for the attributions he used a pen and an ink color not found in the musical text until p. 49.

One of the attributions to Ferrini definitely is erroneous, since the composition is a *Balletto* from Frescobaldi's AGGIUNTA (1637). The *Balletto* is followed by an untitled "double" not known from Frescobaldi's works; this variation is also attributed to Ferrini. The mistaken attribution may be the result of a confusion of the two names or of their abbreviations (i.e., G. B. F. and G. F. B.); it is also possible that when the copyist found the variation attributed to Ferrini he assumed that the latter was also the author of the *Balletto*.

Kirkendale attributes an entire set of partite on la Fiorenza in Chigi 26 to Ferrini on the basis of the concordance of one partita to Vat. mus. 569 (see p. 55). If he is correct, at least one composition of Ferrini made its way to England, since Oxford 1113, of English provenance (see p. 55), contains a partita from the set in Chigi 26 (though not the one in Vat. mus. 569). This is of some interest since the name Ferrini, or rather Ferini, also appears in another English manuscript, London 31422.[2] The latter manuscript contains a set of pieces (*Sinfonie, Canzoni*) for "Violino, leuto, spinetta et organo" (the parts for the latter three instruments contain largely identical figured bass lines) attributed to "Bapt. Ferini." Fragments of several other works for instrumental ensemble attributed to Ferrini appear in Giuseppe Ottavio Pitoni's *Guida armonica* (Rome: c. 1695).[3]

GIROLAMO FRESCOBALDI (1583-1643)

The six volumes of keyboard music that Frescobaldi had published during his lifetime, and which presumably contained the canon of his works as he wished the world to know it, include a total of some 160 compositions.[4] About the same number of additional pieces are found ascribed to him in one way or another in various 17th-century manuscripts. The significance of this latter group of works is, however, in no way comparable to that of the music contained in the published volumes.

Frescobaldi spared neither care nor effort in the preparation of his publications; he sometimes financed them himself, even when this caused him hardship,[5] and he must have closely supervised their printing; the musical texts are remarkably free of misprints. The extensive prefaces are further signs of the value he attached to these works and the concern he felt about their proper performance.

These publications, which commenced in 1608, when, as a young man of twenty-five, he assumed his duties as organist at St. Peter's, and which continued until a few years before his death in 1643, provide a record of the paths he followed during most of his creative maturity. Their contents give every appearance of having been carefully planned and selected so as to offer supreme models of virtually every kind of keyboard music that might be needed or desired.[6] We are fully informed of their date and place of issue; the closeness of their musical texts to the intentions of the composer is practically beyond dispute.

The manuscript repertory inspires no such confidence. There is not a single work in it whose association with the composer can be established beyond a reasonable doubt. Furthermore, as was pointed out in Chapter X (p. 58), the fame of the composer and the quantity of the attributions give additional cause for treating these attributions with suspicion.

I shall not concern myself here with the many attributions in non-Italian (German, English, and French) manuscripts; these will be the subject of future study. The compositions in the Italian manuscripts can be divided into those for which concordances exist to his printed publications and those for which such is not the case. The former are listed in Table 8, the latter in Table 14.[7]

Many of the manuscripts containing concordances to the printed works date from many years after Frescobaldi's death; these late sources clearly are copies from his publications and generally reproduce their texts faithfully, although they occasionally contain some simplifications (as in Venice 1299—see p. 63). The only sources that may still have originated during his lifetime are Chigi 24, 27, 205-206, and Ravenna 545. The majority of the Frescobaldi compositions in these earlier manuscripts also appear to be copies; occasionally the captions explicitly identify them as such, for example, in Chigi 205-206, f. 54: "Toccata Prima del 2° Libro di Intavolatura di Geronimo Frescobaldi." The only works for which the question arises as to whether they possibly derive from a source other than the publications are those that contain substantial variants, i.e., some of the compositions in Chigi 27 and 205-206. In my discussion of these works in Chapter XI I showed that most of the variants consist of simplifications and probably represent adaptations from the printed versions for inexperienced students or faultily memorized versions. There are only two cases in which the variants cannot be accounted for in this fashion, chiefly because they contain musical material not found in the printed versions: the *Toccata* in Chigi 27, f. 70' and the *Passagalli* in Chigi 205-206, f. 95. With these the possibility that the alternative versions are based on sources stemming from the composer cannot be excluded, unlikely as I hold it to be.

Table 14
Compositions Attributed to Frescobaldi in Italian Manuscript Sources
(Compositions also found in 17th-century publications are not listed.)

Manuscripts		Editions[a]
Cologny T.II.1		
Blanket attribution on case containing manuscript		
ff. 78-79	Prima Toccata	n.p.
ff. 79'-80'	Seconda Toccata	n.p.
ff. 81-83'	Terza Toccata odi Canzona	n.p.
ff. 83'-85	Piva/Quarto Tocc.	n.p.
London 40080		
f. [i]	Blanket attribution: Fioretti di Frescobaldi.	
ff. 1-35	Canzona Prima . . . Canzona undecima	n.p.
ff. 35'-39	Toccata	n.p.
Bologna 360		
ff. 54'-55	L'Aria del Gran Ducha—del Freschobaldi	n.p.
Bologna 53		
ff. 1-3	Toccata p[a]—Del Sig. Frescobaldi	SK I, 3
Florence 2358		
f. [iii]	Blanket attribution: "Frescobaldi (1583-1644)" [sic]	n.p.
Ravenna 545		
ff. 37-39	Capriccio di G. F.	SF II, 17
ff. 39'-42	Capriccio di G. F.	SF II, 20
ff. 60'-64	Canzon di Girolamo Frescobaldi	SF II, 24
f. 64'	Verso di G. F.	SF III, 6
(f. 89	See Doria 250 B, f. 33'	)
Doria 250 B		
f. 33'	Corrente—del Sig. Girolamo Concordances in Chigi 205-206, f. 137' (anon.), and Ravenna 545, f. 89 (d'Hercol Pasquini)	SP 28a

Table 14—Continued.

Manuscripts		Editions[a]
Chigi 24		
ff. 51-52	Canzona D. Fr.	LC I, 35
ff. 52'-54	Fuga D. Fr.	LC I, 37
ff. 54'-55	Toccata di G . . . (?)	LC II, 8
Chigi 25		
f. [i']	Blanket attribution: del Sig. Girolamo	
	Frescobaldi	SF I, 1-29;
		II, 1-14;
		III, 6
Chigi 27		
ff. 70'-74'	Toc. del Signor Gierolamo Frescobaldi	SF I, 34
ff. 75-76	Corrente del Signor Ger. F. B.	SF III, 49
Chigi 205-206		
ff. 70-72'	Di Frescobaldi Toccata	SF I, 38
ff. 83-84'	Rugier del Sig. Frescobaldi	SF III, 10
ff. 105-106	Hinno per le Domeniche di tutto l'anno	
	Lucis Creator Optime G. F. B.	SF III, 1
ff. 107-108'	Hinno delli Apostoli. G. F. B.	SF III, 3
ff. 108'-110	Hinno di Natale G. F. B.	
	Xriste Redemptor omnium	SF III, 4
(f. 137	See Doria 250 B, f. 33'	)
Venice 1299		
f. [i]	Blanket attribution: del Sig[r]. Geronimo	
	Fresco Baldi	n.p.
p. 10	Ballo del Gran Duca—G. Fresco Baldi	

[a]Abbreviations: SK = Sandberger, *Kerll*; SF = Shindle, *Frescobaldi*; LC = Lincoln, *Chigi*; SP = Shindle, *Pasquini*; n.p. = not published (i.e., no modern edition).

Before discussing Frescobaldi's relation to the individual manuscripts listed in Table 14, I shall give a preliminary survey of the character of the attributions. Five of these take the form of blanket attributions: Venice 1299, Cologny T.II.1, Chigi 25, Florence 2358, and London 40080. In the latter three the attributions do not appear to have formed part of the original manuscript; they appear on a flyleaf and are in a hand different from that found in the manuscript proper. We shall see that for all these manuscripts, with the possible exception of Chigi 25, the attributions are for stylistic reasons highly implausible.

The attribution to Frescobaldi in Bologna 53 is certainly erroneous, since the composition has been positively identified as being by Kerll. The attribution in Doria 250 B to Sig. Girolamo is at least questionable, since there is a conflicting attribution to Ercole Pasquini in Ravenna 545. We shall see that the attribution appearing in Bologna 360 must be regarded as doubtful because of the nature of the setting; I shall also raise some questions with regard to Frescobaldi's association with L'Aria del Gran Duca (= la Fiorenza).

Only a small number of compositions remain for which Frescobaldi's authorship cannot be ruled out or brought into question a priori: a canzone in Ravenna 545, a toccata in Chigi 27, and a group of compositions in Chigi 205-206 (a toccata, a Ruggiero, and three hymn settings). Furthermore, three compositions in Ravenna and three compositions in Chigi 24 have attributions that, as we shall see, may or may not refer to Frescobaldi.

For the evaluation of these latter attributions the only available tool appears to be comparative stylistic study. Although I shall provide such a comparative analysis for only one of these compositions—the "Canzon di Girolamo Frescobaldi" in Ravenna 545, f. 60'—my investigation of the others, not reported here, has persuaded me that none of the attributions in this group is very plausible.

REVIEW OF THE FRESCOBALDI ATTRIBUTIONS IN THE INDIVIDUAL MANUSCRIPTS

Cologny T.II.1: As a result of Darbellay's investigations this manuscript, formerly believed to be a Frescobaldi autograph, can no longer be regarded as an authoritative source for Frescobaldi's works. Darbellay has in fact come to the conclusion that the four compositions not known from concordances do not stem from Frescobaldi—see p. 84.

London 40080: There are several reasons for being skeptical about a connection between Frescobaldi and this manuscript; if such a connection existed at all it must have been a rather remote one. Among these reasons are the following:

(1) The attribution is a blanket attribution on a flyleaf, in a hand not appearing in the body of the manuscript.

(2) The manuscript does not resemble 17th-century Italian manuscripts; it

uses a $3 \times 5/5$ staff system; the treble staff employs almost exclusively the G_2 clef, the bass mostly the F_4 clef; the handwriting is uncharacteristic of the period.

(3) The eleven canzoni differ from Frescobaldi's keyboard canzoni in several respects. They open with several measures of an unaccompanied and unfigured bass line moving predominantly in whole notes—see Example 16. This introduction is followed by a number of more conventional canzone sections in different meters; here the note values tend to be shorter than those found in most of Frescobaldi's keyboard canzoni: the duple-meter sections move almost exclusively in eighth- and sixteenth-notes, the triple sections in quarter- and eighth-notes. This "note picture" is more characteristic of Frescobaldi's toccate; yet the soggetti of the imitative sections leave no doubt about the appropriateness of the *Canzona* designation. The introductory measures of unaccompanied bass line might suggest that we are dealing with ensemble music notated in keyboard score. There are, however, many passages whose performance on anything but a keyboard instrument would be hard to conceive. On the other hand, if these canzoni are to be performed on keyboard, the player would undoubtedly have to "fill in" these first measures. Such a practice is certainly conceivable, but it is not found elsewhere in Frescobaldi's works (or for the matter in any 17th-century Italian keyboard music). A third possibility is that these pieces represent written-out keyboard parts for ensemble music. Such parts were common in English consort music and appear occasionally in Italian ensemble music—see, for example, the *Toccata per Spinettina, è Violino* in Frescobaldi, CANZONI I (1628i).

(4) In Chapter XI we discussed some partial concordances between this manuscript and some pieces attributed to Frescobaldi in London 36661. The latter manuscript was copied by an Englishman not before the late 17th century; it contains works attributed to Bernardo Pasquini as well as works attributed to Frescobaldi (actually to "Sigl. Freses Baldi"). The reliability of this manuscript is perhaps even more open to question than that of London 40080; at any rate its text is equally corrupt. The concordances between the pieces attributed to Frescobaldi in both manuscripts—one English and the other presumably Italian—would appear to strengthen the plausibility of the attributions. If, however, London 40080 also proves to be English rather than Italian, the value of the concordances for this purpose would be rather small.

(5) There is one thematic connection with an authentic Frescobaldi composition. The subject of the *Canzona Prima* (see Ex. 16, m. 3) is identical to the opening subject of one of his ensemble canzoni (*Canzona Prima* in CANZONI I [1628i] = *Canzon Seconda* in CANZONI I [1628j] = *Canzon Terza* in CANZONI I [1634]), except for the reduction of the note values by one half. The subject is treated in an entirely different fashion; there are no similarities between the counter subjects or between the subjects of subsequent sections of the two compositions. Although the noted thematic corre-

spondence at first might appear to plead for his authorship of the *Canzona* in London 40080, we do not know of other examples of this type of self borrowing in his authenticated works. Furthermore, as I suggested earlier (p. 60) the presence of authentic Frescobaldian material may in fact have lead someone to insert the attribution, the more so since in this case it appears at the beginning of the opening piece in this manuscript as well as in the same position in his CANZONI I (1628i). Nevertheless, the possibility that the canzoni in 40080 incorporate other fragments of lost Frescobaldi works cannot be altogether excluded.

Example 16

London 40080, f. 2:
[Frescobaldi?], Canzona Prima—Cimbalo Solo (mm. 1-8)

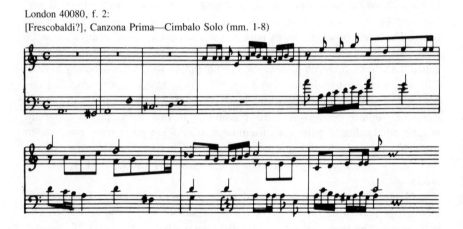

Bologna 360: Kirkendale rightly expresses doubts about the single setting of *la Fiorenza* attributed to Frescobaldi (Kirkendale, *Fiorenza*, 28); he goes on to say that it is "incompetently copied (or composed?)." Probably we are dealing with a bit of both: there are a few clear copying mistakes (e.g., not enough beats in a measure), but apart from that, the setting, whether incompetent or not, is far closer to the simple arrangements found in the aria and ballo collections than to the partite found in Frescobaldi's publications.

Bologna 53: The opening composition, ascribed here to Frescobaldi, is attributed to J. K. Kerll in all other sources and appears in Kerll's thematic index to his own works (see p. 97), so that there is no reasonable doubt about Kerll's authorship.

Florence 2358: We have seen in the discussion of this manuscript that for unkown reasons it was attributed to Frescobaldi by Gandolfi. The pencilled attribution on the flyleaf probably is in Gandolfi's hand; in any case, it appears to date from the beginning of the present century. The attribution includes the composer's dates; the death date is erroneous—1644 rather than 1643. The later date was mistakenly deduced by Haberl (*Frescobaldi*); it was corrected in 1908 by Cametti (*Roma*, 735-738). No further attributions appear in the manuscript. Stylistic analysis would probably place the contents towards the end of the 17th century (see p. 105).

Ravenna 545: There are no known ties linking Frescobaldi to the city of Ravenna. The compiler of Ravenna 545 was, to judge from his inclusion of works by Frescobaldi, Cifra and Ercole Pasquini, interested in the Roman composers. The manuscript contains three compositions attributed to G. F. and one canzone attributed to Girolamo Frescobaldi, as well as compositions known from the Frescobaldi prints. The initials G. F. have generally been interpreted as referring to Frescobaldi; this interpretation is not unreasonable since the same initials are used in the caption of a work known from his publications. On the other hand, one cannot exclude the possibility that the initials refer to a local composer, for example Gabriel Fattorini, who was Maestro di Cappella at the Duomo of nearby Faenza and of whose keyboard music other examples survive.

No strong case for Frescobaldi's authorship can be made on the basis of a stylistic comparison with his printed works. The compositions in Ravenna 545 bear closer resemblance to the anonymous works in the manuscript and to the works of Merula (who is also represented in this collection) than to the Frescobaldi compositions known from the prints. Atypical of the latter are, for example, the subjects with many tone repetitions (see Example 17; cf. p. 35). Without going into a detailed analysis I shall enumerate some features of one of these works, the *Canzon di Gerolamo Frescobaldi* (f. 60'), which give cause to question his authorship:

(1) The opening subject is uncharacteristic in that it has a tone repeated five times (see Example 17); in Frescobaldi's authenticated works no tone is reiterated more than three times in a subject.

(2) The composition consists of only two sections; the first section is of extraordinary length, containing 99 measures. Frescobaldi published only one canzone consisting of as few as two sections: the *Canzon Dopo la Pistola* in the FIORI (1635); in that work, however, the small number of sections is commensurate with the simplicity and brevity of the entire piece. The individual sections in Frescobaldi's canzoni usually have from ten to twenty or at most twenty-five measures. The length of the Ravenna canzone seems entirely at odds with the basic conception of the Frescobaldian canzone: a succession of brief imitative sections of contrasting mensuration.

(3) Frescobaldi's canzoni are invariably in four voices, even if one or two voices may occasionally drop out. The Ravenna canzone seems to have been conceived essentially in three voices; much of the time only two voices are present, frequently moving together in parallel thirds or tenths, as in mm. 6, 9, 13, 23-24, 40-41, 46-47, 49, 54, 61, 88, 101, 105, and 107. Only in a few places does the texture thicken to four or five—or even to six—voices.

(4) The lack of rhythmic variety is particularly uncharacteristic of

Frescobaldi, who never sustains any specific pattern for very long. The figure ♪♪♩♩♩♩ appears in thirty-three consecutive measures; in fact, the alternation of the figure with the figure ♫♫♩♩♩♩ provides virtually the only rhythmic variety in the entire extended first section.

(5) The upper voice extends to c′′′, exceeding by a third the highest note used by Frescobaldi in his keyboard music (a′′).

It seems evident that the departures from Frescobaldi's customary procedures are far more substantial than can be reasonably expected in a composition of his authorship.

Example 17

(a) Ravenna 545, f. 35:
    Capriccio di G. F.
    (mm. 1-2, 29-31)

(b) Ravenna 545, f. 39′:
    Capriccio di G. F.
    (mm. 1-2)

(c) Ravenna 545, f. 60′:
    Canzon di Girolamo
    Frescobaldi (mm. 1-2)

The Chigi Manuscripts: Although we have no knowledge of any connections between Frescobaldi and Fabio Chigi, both men lived in Rome during the years 1626-28 and both had associations with the Barberini. The Chigi manuscripts probably originated at a somewhat later time, but it is nevertheless conceivable that they contain material that Chigi received from Frescobaldi. In other words, there are no external factors that argue conclusively against the acceptance of these manuscripts as a reliable source for Frescobaldi's works. What is lacking, however, is any evidence in their favor.

With the exception of the manuscript bearing the blanket attribution—Chigi 25, to be discussed below—the collection includes only a few attributed works that cannot be identified as copies or adaptations of compositions appearing in Frescobaldi's printed editions. The authenticity of these unique works appears dubious at best; they are written in a much simpler and more predictable style than any of Frescobaldi's printed works. The latter observation applies particularly to the three sets of versets in the folder Chigi 206 (ff. 105, 107, 108').[8] Compared with the settings in Frescobaldi's TOCCATE II of some of the same hymns, the Chigi settings are rather simple; if they are not the work of a beginning composer, they must at least have been written for a beginning performer.

In addition to stylistic considerations, some pieces of external evidence seem to cast doubt on Frescobaldi's authorship. In Chigi 24, the second of two compositions bearing Frescobaldi's (?) initials (see p. 123) is entitled "Fuga," a term not known to have been used by Frescobaldi; the piece has all the characteristics of a canzone. The upper voice of the "Corrente del sig. F.B." in Chigi 27 (f.75) extends to b'' and hence exceeds the range used in Frescobaldi's printed works. It is my belief, furthermore, that the appearance in the Toccata in Chigi 27 (f. 70') of two passages from a printed toccata (see p. 66) pleads against rather than for his authorship of the manuscript toccata. The printed version was first published in 1615 and appeared in every subsequent edition of TOCCATE I—the last one from 1637—without any revisions. If the Chigi Toccata were also by Frescobaldi, it probably would have been composed before 1615, since Frescobaldi was not likely to borrow from a composition already widely circulated in print. On the other hand Chigi 27 dates from the 1640s, and it seems improbable that in those years a youthful version, superseded by the printed Toccata, would still be circulating in Italy. More likely the borrowed passages are merely another example of the common 17th-century "pasticcio" practice.

In spite of the problematic form of the attribution in Chigi 25, it has traditionally been taken for granted that Frescobaldi is the author of the works contained in this volume; they appear under his name in two modern editions (Santini, *Frescobaldi*; Shindle, *Frescobaldi*). The only writer who apparently has not been willing to accept Frescobaldi's authorship of at least one of the compositions is Gustav Leonhardt; in an article on Johann Jacob Froberger he suggests that Froberger is the composer of the *Toccata 3ᵃ* (f. 63).[9] No reason is given for this supposition; it may be merely an intuitive guess. Nevertheless, coming from a sensitive musician, who has studied and performed the music of Froberger and of Frescobaldi for many years, the suggestion deserves some consideration.

Although Froberger's works are found in manuscripts scattered throughout Northern Europe,[10] the only work positively known to have been disseminated in Italy is the *Fantasia sopra ut, re, mi, fa, sol, la* quoted in Kircher's *Musurgia universalis* (Rome, 1650). Nevertheless, the idea that other compositions of his are preserved in Italian manuscripts is by no means far fetched. Froberger made at least two extended visits to Rome: he stayed there from 1637 to 1640 (or 1641) to study with Frescobaldi, and returned for a second visit of undetermined length lasting until early 1649, possibly to work with Carissimi. The facts of this second sojourn have only recently come to light with the discovery of some correspondence between Froberger and Kircher (Scharlau, *Froberger*). Kircher also had close relations with Fabio Chigi (see p. 119); hence it is conceivable that through him some of Froberger's music might have entered the Chigi collection. I shall return to Froberger's possible authorship of some of the works in Chigi 25 below.

If my theory about Frescobaldi's relation to la Fiorenza is correct (see pp. 164-65), the presence of partite on this aria does little to strengthen the case for his authorship of the contents of Chigi 25; at the same time, its appearance as opening piece in the manuscript might provide an explanation for the attribution of the collection to Frescobaldi. Froberger is an even more unlikely candidate as composer of these partite, since no setting of any of the popular Italian arie is found among his known works.

The collection contains three strikingly similar toccate in the D mode, each entitled "Toccata per organo," (ff. 5', 13, and 31). In the second and third of these toccate the pedal tones follow a simple D-A-D progression; in the first one the pedal also progresses through D and A, but then moves to several other tones before returning to D. The three works open with similar motives (Example 18). Although these opening formulas can be found elsewhere in toccate in this mode, they do not appear in any of Frescobaldi's printed toccate. The texture above the pedal tones consists almost exclusively of two voices moving predominantly in parallel thirds, sixths, or tenths. In these respects the works are much simpler than the two pedal toccate in Frescobaldi's TOCCATE II—his only contributions to this particular branch of the genre. In the two published works the pedal-tone progression is more complex, and the contrapuntal texture above the pedal is much denser and more varied. Another feature shared by the pieces in the manuscript, and also by a fourth toccata in the collection (f. 37')—but not by any of Frescobaldi's printed toccate—is that they are followed by a canzone or its equivalent.[11]

The second of the pedal toccate (f. 13) has a second title—"Capriccio sopra Vestiva i colli"—added in what appears to be a different hand, but subsequently crossed out. Its inclusion in Shindle's edition (*Frescobaldi* I, 7) as a subtitle must be questioned, because the deletion may well represent a recognition of error: there are in fact no traces in this toccata of Palestrina's frequently intabulated madrigal, nor are there any in the untitled following movement (headed "Capriccio" by Shindle). It is conceivable that the title belongs to the next composition in the manuscript (f. 19); this work has the caption *Capriccio*, and uses a subject that shows some resemblance to the alto entry of Palestrina's madrigal—see Example 19.

The last portion of the manuscript is physically quite distinct from the earlier part. It contains three toccate, called, respectively, "Toccata p^a,"

Example 18

(a) Chigi 25, f. 5': Toccata Per organo (mm. 1-2)

(b) Chigi 25, f. 13: Toccata Per organo (mm. 1-2)

(c) Chigi 25, f. 31: Toccata Per organo con Pedali (mm. 1-2)

Example 19

(a) Chigi 25, f. 19. Capriccio (mm. 9-10)

(b) Palestrina, "Vestiva i colli," alto part (mm. 2-5), transposed, note values reduced (Il desiderio, II libro dei Madrigali à 5, Venice, 1566, p. 8).

"Toccata 2ᵃ," and "Toccata 3ᵃ"; the third of this set is the composition singled out by Leonhardt as possibly being the work of Froberger. These compositions are artistically far superior to the other works in the collection—indeed to much of the manuscript repertory. They fall squarely within the tradition of the flamboyant harpsichord toccate of Frescobaldi and Froberger and one would like to think that they are indeed the work of a composer of that stature. Stylistically they stand in many ways between Frescobaldi's last published examples in this vein, those in his TOCCATE II of 1627,[12] and the earliest dated toccate by Froberger, those in the latter's *Libro secondo* of 1649.[13] They contain more and longer canzone–like imitative sections than are found in the Frescobaldi toccate, though these sections are not as fully worked out as those in Froberger's. The individual subjects occasionally hint at motivic relationships—common with Froberger but never found in Frescobaldi's toccate. In terms of key the third of the Chigi toccate ventures further than any of Frescobaldi's toccate: its tonality is C minor, and it makes frequent use of the pitch D-flat. They key of C minor and the pitch D-flat are used by Frescobaldi only in the *Cento partite* in his AGGIUNTA (1637), and then only in passing.

We do not know in what direction Frescobaldi steered the genre between 1627 and his death in 1643; nor do we have any information on the nature of the keyboard music Froberger wrote between, say, 1634, when he became organist at the Imperial Court in Vienna, and 1649, the date of his *Libro secondo*. It seems therefore clear that stylistic considerations alone would never suffice to tell us whether we are dealing with late works of the former composer or early works by the latter—assuming that they were indeed by one or the other.

There are, to be sure, several striking resemblances between some passages in Froberger's toccate and some passages in the Chigi set—see Example 20. However, Froberger frequently borrowed figures from his master, and hence these resemblances are not particularly helpful in settling the issue.

In conclusion, we have at present no firm basis for attributing these works to either Frescobaldi or Froberger, and hence will have to classify them along with the rest of the anonymous repertory as compositions whose authorship has not been established.

Venice 1299: The compositions covered by the blanket attribution but not authenticated by concordances to the printed works appear to date from the second half of the 17th century; the thin, at times rather sketchy textures are among several factors that make Frescobaldi's authorship unlikely. On the "Ballo del Gran Duca," p. 10, which has an attribution in the manuscript to G. Fresco Baldi, see the following remarks on Frescobaldi and the *Aria di Fiorenza*.

Frescobaldi and the Aria di Fiorenza

During the earlier 17th century the Aria di Fiorenza, also known as Ballo del Granduca, rivaled in popularity the traditional arie such as the Romanesca and the Ruggiero.[14] It was, however, never employed by Frescobaldi in any of his published works. This is curious, since he made use of most of the other popular arie—some in several different types of settings or genres: the Ruggiero (three settings for keyboard, in CAPRICCI, in TOCCATE I, and in the AGGIUNTA; one for instrumental ensemble, in CANZONI I [1628j]; and one for voice and continuo, in ARIE MUSICALE I), the Romanesca (one setting for keyboard, in TOCCATE I; one for instrumental ensemble, in CANZONI I [1628j]; and one for voice and continuo, in ARIE MUSICALE II), and the aria "Or che noi rimena" (in CAPRICCI, and, as *Aria detto Balletto*, in TOCCATE II). In view of the general popularity of la Fiorenza, one might have expected it to appear in one of his collections; it would have been particularly appropriate for him to include a setting in the ARIE MUSICALI, the product of his Florentine years—the first volume of which is dedicated to Grand Duke Ferdinand II (the grandson of the Duca of the Ballo)—since, as Kirkendale has shown, the Fiorenza was traditionally associated with Florence and with the Medici. Nevertheless, despite the presence in this collection of settings of other popular arie—the Ruggiero, the Romanesca, the Ciaccona and the Passacaglia— the Fiorenza itself does not appear. This suggests—whatever the reason may have been—that Frescobaldi was not willing to accept the Fiorenza among the traditional arie. Paradoxically, there seems to have been a tradition associating Frescobaldi with la Fiorenza; as we have seen, pieces of this genre are attributed to him in Venice 1299, pp. 10 and 111, in Bologna 360, f. 54', and in Chigi 25, f. 1.[15] It is clear from the foregoing discussion of Frescobaldi's printed works, however, that the Fiorenza compositions must be of dubious authenticity. We have seen that the age and character of the attributions provide no evidence to contradict this conclusion. None is demonstrably contemporary with Frescobaldi; they all may even be interdependent. Although the ultimate source of the tradition linking the aria with Frescobaldi remains unknown, the available evidence gives us every reason to question both its age and its validity.

GIOVANNI DE MACQUE (c. 1550-1614)

De Macque was born c. 1550 at Valenciennes. He was employed as early as 1563 at the Imperial Court in Vienna; by 1568 he was living in Rome, and by 1586 he had moved to Naples, where he remained until his death in 1614.[16] Much of his vocal music was published during his lifetime, but his printed output of instrumental music appears to have been much more limited. A tenor part book is all that is preserved of the RICERCATE E CANZONI FRANCESE A 4, published in Rome in 1586 by Gardano; a 19th-century manuscript score of two ricercari apparently from a lost *Secondo Libro de Ricercari* survives in Berlin (Deutsche Staatsbibl. 13320).[17] So far as we know, no other ensemble or keyboard music appeared in print.[18] Fortunately, a good number of de Macque's keyboard compositions survive in manuscript collections—see Table 15;

Example 20

(a) Chigi 25, f. 51: Toccata p^a (m. 20)

(b) Froberger, Toccata IV (Adler, *Froberger* I, 11), (m. 16)

(c) Chigi 25, f. 56: Toccata 2^a (mm. 36-38)

(d) Froberger, Toccata IX (Adler, *Froberger* I, 24) (mm. 31-33)

(e) Chigi 25, f. 56: Toccata 2^a (mm. 64-65)

(f) Froberger, Toccata XVIII (Adler, *Froberger* III, 16), (mm. 12-14)

Example 20—Continued.

(g) Chigi 25, f. 63: Toccata 3^a (mm. 86-87)

(h) Froberger, Toccata VII (Adler, *Froberger* I, 20), (mm. 35-36)

although all of these manuscripts may date from after his death, at least one, London 30491, can in all probability be regarded as reliable with respect to attributions as well as to text. We saw in the discussion of this manuscript that it seems to have been compiled a few years after de Macque's death by his pupil Luigi Rossi (although some uncertainty remains with respect to this dating and perhaps even with respect to Luigi Rossi's role).

The works attributed to de Macque in this collection have a number of similarities to those in a publication by another pupil of de Macque: Trabaci's RICERCATE I, Sa. 1603c. In the latter one finds many of the same genres represented; both collections contain *Canzoni francese, Capricci, Gagliarde, Toccate, Consonanze stravaganti* (*(Stravaganze* in London 30491) and *Partite sopra Ruggiero*. At times the similarity extends beyond the titles; for example, in Trabaci's *Capriccio sopra la, fa, sol, la* and de Macque's *Capriccio sopra rè, fà, mi, sol*: the two compositions introduce their four-note motives in almost identical fashion—see Example 21—and further resemblances can be found in the subsequent treatments. If one assumes that de Macque's pieces served as models for Trabaci—de Macque being the older man and Trabaci's teacher—one has to conclude that they were composed before 1603, the date of Trabaci's publication.

One genre found in Trabaci's RICERCATE I but not in London 30491 is the ricercare itself. One can, however, draw analogous comparisons between the Trabaci print and the ricercari attributed to de Macque in Florence 106b (see p. 102). Both sources contain a set of twelve pieces ordered according to the twelve tones and bearing only the designations *Primo tono, secondo tono*, etc., without

Example 21

(a) London 30491, f. 23: Capriccio di Gio: de Macque sopra re, fa, mi, sol (mm. 1-3)

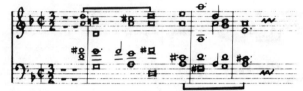

(b) Trabaci, RICERCATE I (Sa. 1603c), p. 63: Capriccio sopra la, fa, sol, la (mm. 1-4)

Example 22

(a) Florence 106b, f. 9′: P[rimo] del Macque (mm. 1-4)

(b) Trabaci, RICERCATE I (Sa. 1603c), p. 1: Primo Tono con tre fughe (mm. 1-5)

Table 15
Compositions Attributed to de Macque
in Italian Manuscript Sources

Source		Watelet Edition
London 30491		
ff. 4'-6'	Partite sopra ruggiero di Gio: Macque	p. 50
ff. 8'-9'	Capriccietto di Giovan de Macque	p. 55
ff. 17-18'	Canzon di Gio: de Macque chiamate le due Sorelle	p. 57
f. 19	Prime S[t]ravaganze di Gio: de Macque	p. 60
f. 20'	Prima Gagl[i]arda di Gio: de Macque	p. 61
f. 21'	Seconda Gagliarda di Gio: de Macque[a]	p. 61
ff. 23-26'	Capriccio di Gio: de Macque sopra rè, fà, mi, sol	p. 33
ff. 29-30	p[a] Canzon di Gio: de Macque	p. 62
ff. 30'-31'	S[a] Canzon di Gio de Macque	p. 65
ff. 31'-32'	Toccata di Gio: de Macque a modo di Trombette	p. 67
ff. 33-35	Seconde S[t]ravaganze di Gio. de Macque	p. 69
Naples 48		
ff. 55-57'	Intrata d'organo di Giov. Macque	not publ.
Naples 73		
ff. 120-120'	Consonanze stravaganti del Sigr. Gio. de Macque	p. 37
ff. 121-122'	Durezze, e ligature di Gio. Macque	p. 38
ff. 122'-124'	Capriccio sopra un sogetto. Macque	p. 39
ff. 125-126'	Capriccio sopra tre soggetti. Macque	p. 41
ff. 127-128'	Canzona francese di Gio. Macque	p. 43
Florence 106b		
ff. 9'-34'	p[o] del Macque, Secondo Tono . . . Duodecimo Tono. On f. 34: Joannis de Macques Psalmodiare.	not publ.

[a]Concordance (transposed) in Naples 55 (set of part books), p. 3: *Gagliarda seconda* (anon.).

genre name (although in Trabaci's print the name *Ricercare* is clearly implied by the listing of contents on the title page). There are internal similarities as well; compare, for example, the beginnings of the first ricercari of both sets (Example 22). Here, too, it appears likely that one set served as model for the other. Since the part book of de Macque's RICERCATE of 1586 has not been available to scholars, we do not know whether these correspond to those in Florence 106b; if such correspondence is found, the priority of de Macque's *Ricercari* as models will be established.

Naples 73, compiled some sixty years after de Macque's death, appears to be a less trustworthy source. If the compositions attributed to de Macque in this manuscript are in fact his, they represent a phase in his work, or a manner, distinct from that found in London 30491. More likely these works have been modernized and smoothed out; they show few of the extravagances of the London pieces and the fantastic colorature are missing altogether (compare, for example, the *Stravaganze* in both manuscripts, or, for that matter, the *Canzoni*). Some of the pieces in Naples 73 may also have been shortened, for example the brief *Canzona francese* (f. 127), which ends, contrary to common practice, with a section in triple meter.

The idea that the pieces in Naples 73 represent modernized adaptations receives some support from a comparison of the *Durezze e ligature* in this manuscript with two pieces attributed to de Macque in earlier sources: the *Intrata d'organo* in Naples 48, f. 55, and the *Prime S[t]ravaganze* in London 30491, f. 19. The first few measures of the three compositions are almost identical except that Naples 48 introduces ornamentation and additional chromaticism and that London 30491 has the inner voices inverted (T to A, A to S, S to T): see Example 23. The further development of the Naples 48 *Intrata*—given in its entirety in Example 24—is strikingly similar to that of the London 30491 *S[t]ravaganze* (both, for example, have coloratura sequences over G-D-A pedal chords), leaving little doubt that both works follow the same model. The *Durezze* piece in Naples 73 appears, however, to follow the later, retrospective "Durezze" tradition, adhering to stile antico practice with motion predominantly in half notes.

TARQUINIO MERULA (1590-1665)

Several collections of Merula's ensemble music were published during his lifetime, but no keyboard music appeared in print. Curtis has published a volume of the keyboard compositions surviving in manuscripts (Curtis, *Merula*); however, of the thirteen works contained in this edition, six have no attributions in the sources and were included on the basis of style and of placement in the manuscripts, and another piece included in the edition is a Polish intabulation (in the Pelplin Tablature) of an ensemble canzone from Merula's CANZONI I (Sa. 1615d). Of the remaining six compositions only three appear in Italian sources:

(1) Bologna 53, f. 86': "Sonata Cromatica di Tarquinio Merula." Apel judges the work "poor artistically, but stylistically rather advanced," and asks: "Is it possible that this composition is spurious and is really the work of a musician who lived fifty years later?" (Apel, *Keyboard Music*, 483-484). Considering the date of the manuscript (after c. 1720) and the fact that the other composers named in the collection worked principally during the second half of the 17th century, it is not unlikely that his question should be answered in the affirmative.

(2) Ravenna 545, f. 71': "Canzon di Tarquinio Merula." The opening subject is identical with that used in the Canzona "la Lugarina" in Merula's CANZONI IV (Sa. 1651a), f. 46.

(3) Assisi, f. 23: "Canzon di Tarquinio Merula." This manuscript dates from the second half of the 17th century. The composition was added by a different hand on the last two pages of the manuscript; the earlier portion consists of excerpts from Frescobaldi's FIORI. This canzone appears to be a parody of the one entitled "La Loda" in Merula's CANZONI IV (Sa. 1651a), f. 42; the first seven measures are nearly identical, but after that the two pieces proceed on different courses. Two other compositions use motivic material from the opening of these two works: a "Capriccio del Sig: Tarquin: Merula" in Leipzig, Städtische Musikbibliothek II.2.51, p. 36, and the *Canzona Prima* in Fasolo, ANNUALE, Sa. 1645d.[19]

We see that the number of Merula's surviving keyboard works is too small and the status of the attributions too doubtful to allow us to form an assessment of his significance as a keyboard composer. Certainly these works cannot support Crocker's evaluation: "Merula's small quantity of extant keyboard music rivals that of Frescobaldi in quality and has greater clarity in outline and style, an indication of the prevailing direction of stylistic development towards 1650" (Crocker, *History of Style*, 248).

Example 23

(a) Naples 73, f. 121: Durezze, e ligature di Gio. macque (mm. 1-4)

(b) Naples 48, f. 55: Intrata d'organo di Giov. Macque (mm. 1-6)

(c) London 30491: f. 19: Prime S[t]ravaganze di Gio: de Macque (mm. 1-4)

Example 24

Naples 48, ff. 55-57': Intrata d'organo di Giov. de Macque

Example 24—Continued.

Example 24—Continued.

BERNARDO PASQUINI (1637-1710)

There exists at present no complete survey of Pasquini's keyboard works and their sources, in spite of the fact that his keyboard music forms the subject of two recent dissertations.[20] The principal sources are the autographs Berlin L.215 and London 31501; the latter consists of three volumes of which the second is only partially autograph. Many compositions in this autographs are accompanied by a date; the dates in Berlin L.215 range from 1697 to 1702, those in London 31501 from 1703 to 1704.[21] Heimrich believes that these dates represent not merely copying dates, but correspond to the dates of composition (Heimrich, *Pasquini*, p. 37).

The manuscript Vat. mus. 569, dated 1661-1663, contains two compositions attributed to "Bernardo." In the discussion of that collection we noted that Pasquini had many professional ties to two other musicians associated with the manuscript: Ferrini and Fontana (both are named in attributions; furthermore, Fontana was the teacher of Virginio Mutij, the owner of the collection). In various lists and payment records Pasquini often is listed as Bernardo, and there seems no reason to doubt that the two attributions to this name in Vat. mus. 569 refer to the same person.[22] This supposition is further strengthened by the titles of these compositions: *Tastata arpeggiata longa* and *Tastata 2ᵃ*. Although Vat. mus. 569 also contains a few anonymous compositions entitled "Tastata," this designation appears not to have been in general use during the period; its only appearance outside this manuscript is in the Pasquini autograph, Berlin L.215, which includes several compositions called "Tastata" and "Tastata arpeggiata."

The discovery of compositions attributed to Pasquini in Vat. mus. 569 is of considerable interest. Since the autographs have generally been regarded as the earliest sources for his keyboard works—the other sources probably all date from the 18th century—and since the dates in these autographs are believed to correspond to the time of composition, it has been suggested that in his earlier years Pasquini concerned himself exclusively with vocal music, and that in the 1690s his interest shifted to keyboard music (see Kast/Crain, *Pasquini*, c. 865). However, this theory is now untenable since Vat. mus. 569 appears to antedate the sources of any of his vocal compositions (the earliest datable compositions are from the 1670s). Transcriptions of the two pieces included in this manuscript follow in Examples 25a and 25b.

Example 25

(a) Vat. mus. 569, pp. 45-46: Bernardo [Pasquini?], Tastata arpeggiata longa

Example 25—Continued.

(b) Vat. mus. 569, p. 47: Bernardo [Pasquini?], Tastata 2[a]

ERCOLE PASQUINI (c. 1550—before 1620)

Recent interest in the keyboard music of Ercole Pasquini stems largely from speculations on his role as a significant formative influence on Frescobaldi. His "collected works" have been made available (Shindle, *Pasquini*) and have been dealt with at some length in the literature (Apel, *Keyboard Music*, 421-23). A recent dissertation examines his contributions towards the development of imitative genres in Rome during the first decades of the 17th century (Ladewig, *Frescobaldi*). Nevertheless, it remains unclear whether the available information on the chronology of his life and works is sufficient to assess his importance as an innovator and as an influence on Frescobaldi.

Biographical data on Pasquini are scarce and allow us to account securely for his whereabouts for little over twenty years.[23] He evidently was living in Ferrara by the middle 1580s, where he studied with Alessandro Milleville (d.1589). Sometime after 1594 he was appointed organist to the Accademia della Morte in Ferrara;[24] in 1597 he moved to Rome to become organist at the Cappella Giulia. In 1608 he was dismissed from this post, to be succeeded by Frescobaldi (who earlier, in Ferrara, had succeeded him at the Accademia della Morte). From 1604 to 1608 he also was organist at S. Spirito in Saxia, a position in which Frescobaldi did not follow him until 1620. By 1620 he apparently was no longer alive; according to Superbi he had died in Rome under unfortunate circumstances. In summary, all we know is that he was in Ferrara from sometime before 1589 until 1597, and in Rome from 1597 until 1608, and that he died in Rome between 1608 and 1620. We have no proof that he was born in Ferrara,[25] nor can we be sure that he remained in Rome during the entire period between his dismissal from the Cappella Giulia in 1608 and his death.

We see that Pasquini's career had several parallels to Frescobaldi's, and that in at least two positions he was the latter's immediate predecessor. Although there is no documentary evidence that they maintained a teacher-pupil relationship at any time,[26] or any other form of personal contact, the circumstances of their lives were so close as to make some mode of interaction more than likely.

No keyboard music of Ercole Pasquini survives in 17th-century publications. A good number of compositions are credited to him in Italian manuscripts; indeed, he probably fares better in this respect than most of his contemporaries with the exception of Frescobaldi. This in itself attests to the interest that must have existed in his works. Furthermore, judging from the provenance of his sources, this interest was far from regional and was sustained throughout the century.

Unfortunately, the nature of the sources is such that we cannot hope to obtain a fair picture of Pasquini's keyboard music. The problem of the credibility of the attributions is probably not so severe as with his famous colleague, although it must be considered, especially for the attributions appearing in geographically and chronologically more remote sources. A greater obstacle is the problem of the musical text, which in these sources often is corrupt and incomplete—sometimes unintentionally, the result of carelessness, sometimes intentionally, the result of parody and pasticcio procedures. Copying errors can usually be recognized, but the extent of recompositional treatment and shortening cannot be determined when reliable sources are not available for comparison.

There are altogether some thirty distinct compositions with attributions, distributed over five main sources (see Table 16a, b): Trent (11 compositions), Ravenna 545 (9 compositions), Chigi 27 (3 compositions), Naples 73 (3 compositions)[27] and Cecilia 400 (5 compositions). Concordances, some anonymous and one with a conflicting attribution, appear in five additional sources: Naples 48 (1 composition), Doria 250 B (1 composition), Berlin 40615 (1 composition), Chigi 205-206 (3 compositions). The attributions taken to refer to Ercole Pasquini appear in several different forms:

H, E, He P	Trent
H. P.	Ravenna 545
hercole	Trent, Chigi 205-206
Ercole	Berlin 40615
Hercol P.	Ravenna 545
Hercol Pasquino	Ravenna 545
Ercole Pasquino	Cecilia 400, Naples 73
Ercole Pasquini	Chigi 27, Naples 48

Since in the Trent manuscript the last name is never spelled out, it might be questioned whether the attributions refer to Pasquini. However, Trent also contains an anonymous composition that is attributed to "Hercol Pasquino" in Ravenna 545, and the forms "hercole" and "HP" are similar to those appearing in other sources in which, because of concordances or other considerations, they can be believed to refer to Pasquini. In fact, the reference to the composer by his initials and first name could be regarded as an indication that his name was quite familiar to the users of the manuscript. Taken together with the dating of the collection (c. 1600) and with the large number of attributions, it suggests that the composer was close to the circles in which the manuscript was compiled.

The second half of the manuscript, from f. 54 to f. 97, is largely devoted to works attributed to Pasquini. Since at least one of the anonymous pieces in this segment of the manuscript appears elsewhere under his name, it is possible that the other anonymous compositions found here should also be credited to him. Indeed, some of these (f. 47: "I[ntrada] de"; f. 49′: "I[ntrada] di n[apoli]"; f. 58: "T[occat]a de"; f. 59′: "c[anzon]a de") show a number of musical resemblances to the attributed works, suggesting at the very least that a careful comparative study might be fruitful.

Although Ravenna 545 was probably compiled one or more decades after Pasquini's death, it seems to have originated in a city close to Ferrara (where as late as 1620 Pasquini was still remembered and honored—see Superbi,

Table 16a
Compositions Attributed to Ercole Pasquini
in Italian Manuscript Sources
(Compositions in which the attribution appears
in a concordance are given in parentheses.)

Manuscript	Composition	Shindle Edition No.
Berlin 40615		
f. 228'	See Table 16b.	16c
Naples 48		
ff. 10-12	See Table 16b.	not in Shindle
Naples 73		
(ff. 22'-23'	See Chigi 205-206, f. 137'.	18a)
ff. 135-137	See Table 16b.	16b
ff. 137'-141	Durezze e ligature del detto	7
Ravenna 545		
ff. 2'-3'	Toccata di H. P.	6
ff. 69'-71	Canzon di'Hercol Pasquino	14
ff. 74'-76'	Canzon D. H. P.	15
ff. 77-78'	H. P.	25
ff. 78'-80	H. P. (continuation of preceding composition?)	26
ff. 85-85'	B.[allo] D. H. P.	30
ff. 89-89'	Corrente d'Hercol Pasquino. Concordances in Chigi 205-206, f. 79 (anon.) and Doria 250 B, f. 33' (Sig. Girolamo).	28a
ff. 98'-100'	Pass'e mezzo d'Hercol Pasquino. Concordance in Trent, f. 86' (anon.).	23b
ff. 101-107'	Romanesche d'Hercol Pasquino	24
ff. 109-111	Romanesche d'Hercol P.	25
ff. 114-114'	Gagliarda d'Hercol Pasquino	29
Doria 250 B		
(f. 33'	See Ravenna 545, f. 89.	not in Shindle)

Table 16a—Continued.

Manuscript	Composition	Shindle Edition No.
Cecilia 400		
ff. 61-62	Durezze di Ercole Pasquino	8
ff. 62-62'	Corrente di Ercole Pasquino	27
ff. 63-64	Primo tono di Ercole Pasquino	19
ff. 64'-66'	Canzona francese di Ercole Pasquino	13
ff. 67-68	See Table 16b.	17
Chigi 27		
ff. 66'-67'	Toc. del Sig: Ercole Pasquini	3
ff. 87'-89'	Tocchata del Sig: Ercole Pasquini	4
ff. 90-92'	Tocchata del Sig: Ercole Pasquini	5
Chigi 205-206		
(ff. 79-80	See Ravenna 545, f. 89.	28a)
f. 137	Canzona d'Hercole. Concordance in Naples 73 (anon.)	18b
(ff. 137-138'	See Table 16b.	16a)
(ff. 205-206	See Table 16b.	16a)
Trent		
ff. 54'-55'	C[anzona] d'H	9
ff. 56-57'	I[ntrad]a di H	1
ff. 64-67'	R[uggiero] di H	10
ff. 68-69	C[anzona] di H	22
ff. 69'-72	Ancor che col partire di H	21
ff. 72'-74	Fuga di H	11
ff. 74'-76	T[occata] di E	not in Shindle
ff. 76'-78	di H P	2
ff. 78'-79	di H P	20
(ff. 86'-92	See Ravenna 545, f. 98'.	23a)
f. 95'	d'hercole, canzona	12

Table 16b
Sources For The Canzona, Shindle No. 16–17.
(A, B, and C refer, respectively, to the first, second, and third
sections of this canzona.)

1. Chigi 206, ff. 205-205′ — Beginning missing, hence no title, anon., begins with last 7 mm. of A; B and C complete.

2. Chigi 206, ff. 138, 138′, 137 (bound in wrong order) — No title, anon., A only, but seems complete; version not related to 1 above, see text.

3. Naples 48, ff. 10-12 — "Canzona francese d'Ercole Pasquini. 1600" Inscription probably in recent hand. A, B, C complete, but binding error, see text.

4. Naples 73, ff. 135-137 — "Canzona del Ercole Pasquino." A, B, C complete. Several corruptions and omissions.

5. Cecilia 400, f. 67-68 — "Altra Sonata di Ercole Pasquino." Note values doubled. Many other variants.

6. Berlin 40615, f. 228′ — "Can: 3: To: Au: di Ercole." A only.

7. "Foglio ms. senza luogo ne data," in Torchi, *Arte*, 257-260 — "Canzona Fràzese per cembalo." A, B, complete; C: see text.

8. Ravenna 545, f. 99′ — Uses same subject; no further similarities.

Apparato, 132). His appearance in this collection in several ways parallels that in Trent: he is one of the principal "contributors," represented by an almost equally large number of works, most of which appear in close proximity, in the second half of the manuscript. A link is formed between the Pasquini repertories in the two manuscripts by a set of passamezzo variations included in both collections. Actually, only the first two variations are shared; Trent continues with three further variations, none of them similar to the final (third) variation in Ravenna 545.[28] Even the first two variations show a number of variants between the versions. Since in most cases the reading in Trent is clearly superior, it appears unlikely that the text in Ravenna 545 represents a later revision by the composer. There is, however, an example in Ravenna 545 of a "revision" by the copyist: the opening of the first variation was visibly altered from a half-note D-minor chord, as it appears in Trent, to two quarter-note chords, respectively, in D minor and A major—see Example 26.

Chigi 27, probably dating from the 1640s, contains three toccate (in the first, second, and third tone) attributed to Pasquini amidst a group of works credited to Frescobaldi. The apparent corruptions in some of the latter pieces (cf. pp. 63, 66) casts doubt on the reliability of this manuscript for the transmission of musical texts.

Naples 73 was compiled in Naples in the 1670s. Because of its geographical and chronological provenance, this source may appear problematical. However, of the three compositions it contains, two are credited to Pasquini in earlier sources. It may seem farfetched to connect an interest in his music at this late date with the Neapolitan musicians visiting Ferrara some seventy years earlier (see Newcomb, *Gesualdo*), but it is conceivable that some contact between Ercole and this city was maintained or re-established at a later date.

The appearance of attributions in the 18th-century manuscript Cecilia 400 is perhaps even more remarkable. A confusion with his namesake, Bernardo Pasquini, is possible, but not likely; one would expect such a mix-up to go in the other direction, Bernardo being presumably a more familiar name to an early 18th-century copyist. Furthermore, a concordance provides some connection with the attributions in the other sources.

In summary, of the principal Pasquini sources only Trent is likely to have been compiled during Pasquini's lifetime. Ravenna 545 and Chigi 27 probably date from several decades after his death; Naples 73 and Cecilia 400 are appreciably more recent. Most of Pasquini's allegedly innovative procedures, including all but one of those described by Apel (*Keyboard Music*, 421-23), appear in the later manuscripts. Hence, when such novel features are found in Frescobaldi's compositions as well as in Pasquini's, the chronology of the sources cannot confirm that the older rather than the younger composer was the first to introduce them.

One canzone attributed to Ercole Pasquini appears in at least six sources; we have seen in Chapter IX that such wide dissemination is highly exceptional in this repertory. Table 16b summarizes the manner in which it appears in these manuscripts. Unfortunately, the composition is not found in the three important early Pasquini sources—Trent, Ravenna 545, and Chigi 27—although Ravenna 545 contains a canzone attributed to him that uses an identical subject.

The two versions in Chigi 205-206 are both incomplete; in fact, they "overlap" for only eight measures. This has allowed Shindle to construct a composite version with two alternate endings for the first part. Nevertheless, it is doubtful that any connection existed between the two segments; they are found in different (unbound) fascicles and are in different hands (cf. the discussion of Chigi 205-206 in Part Two). Furthermore, the version starting on f. 205, although it contains only the A section, was clearly regarded as complete by the copyist; it ends with a double bar and a fermata, and is followed by a blank staff.

The canzone is reprinted in Torchi, *Arte*, 257. Shindle notes that "[Torchi's] version is inferior to the above versions [in the known sources]. The authenticity of the final section is questionable. Unfortunately Torchi does not mention his source." Shindle certainly appears justified in questioning the final section as it appears in Torchi. Three measures after the beginning of the third (C) section this version suddenly diverges completely from all the other versions. Harmonically, and even in terms of voice-leading, the music seems to proceed correctly at this point: nevertheless, one has the feeling of a musical non sequitur: see Example 27. After a few measures this section is followed by a second triple section, which is not related motivically to the earlier sections and which concludes in G major rather than in A minor, the key of the rest of the canzone.

Torchi does give a "source," but his indication is not very helpful: "Foglio ms. senza luogo ne data." The basis of Torchi's "unauthentic" version becomes clear upon a careful examination of Naples 48 (apparently not consulted by Shindle). This manuscript would provide a seemingly good and complete text of the canzone, except that it became scrambled as the result of a misbinding. The canzone runs from f. 10 to f. 12, but f. 9, which contains the concluding section of an *Intrata in G sol re ut* commencing on f. 7', is inserted between f. 11 and f. 12. As fortune—or rather misfortune—would have it, the beginning of f. 9 provides a superficially acceptable musical continuation to the end of f. 11' (even though the custodes do not match) and the unwary copyist of this Canzona might simply continue copying from f. 11' to f. 9 and bring the piece to the conclusion in G. appearing on f. 9'. On the next page (f. 12) he would encounter a "fragment" of another piece, which in actual fact is the conclusion of the canzone.

It appears likely that Torchi based his version either directly on Naples 48, or on an intermediary copy. There are some indications that a now-lost source possibly played a role in that transmission. In the first place, even though Torchi's version is closer to the text of Naples 48 than to any of the other versions, there are a number of variants between the two. In all these variants the version in Naples 48 is superior to that of Torchi. Some differences appear to be

Example 26

(a) Ravenna 545, f. 98':
    Pass'e mezzo
    d'Hercol Pasquino
    (mm. 1-2)

(b) Same, reconstruction
    of original

(c) Trent, f. 86':
    [untitled composition]
    (mm. 1-2)

Example 27

(a) Torchi, *Arte*, p. 254: Ercole Pasquini, Canzona Frāzese per cembalo (mm. 49-53)

(b) Naples 48, ff. 11'-12: Canzona francese d'Ercole Pasquini. 1600 (mm. 42-45)

(c) Naples 48, ff. 8'-9: Intrata in G sol, re,
    ut (mm. 18-22)

copying errors for which Torchi may indeed be to blame (similar errors appear throughout his edition). Other variants seem more typical of 17th-century corruptions than of 20th-century sloppiness, for instance, the missing entry in measure 10 of the second section. Furthermore, Torchi gives as title, "Canzona Fräzese per cembalo," but the caption in Naples 48 reads "Canzona francese d'Ercole Pasquini. 1600," without the superscript *n* and without mention of "cembalo." On the other hand, considering the general carelessness of Torchi's editing, none of these variants may be significant.

As a final note I should mention another "variant" version in a modern edition: the version included by Mario Vitali in his *Clavecembalisti italiani*, I, 12-13. Vitali's version, although heavily edited to make it suitable for the modern pianist, clearly is based on Torchi's text (it includes a number of Torchi's corruptions). It seems, however, that Vitali could not stomach the incorrect final section, with its conclusion in G major; consequently he replaced it with a written-out "da capo" of the first section!

MICHEL'ANGELO ROSSI (1602-1656)[29]

Today Michel'Angelo Rossi is generally regarded as the most significant keyboard composer of the generation following Frescobaldi.[30] There is no evidence that his contemporaries accorded him such a position; no copies survive in Italian manuscripts of the compositions from his single known keyboard publication, TOCCATE, Sa. 1657a (which, however, did go through several editions), and, except for a little *Ballo* in the Antoniano manuscript, the only other keyboard works attributed to him are the seven compositions in Bologna 258. This manuscript was copied almost fifty years after his death from unknown sources; affirmation of the reliability of the attribution is wanting.

Some of the compositions in Bologna 258 contain mannerisms reminiscent of Rossi's printed works; but in others (e.g., in the prosaic fourth *Toccata*) not a glimmer of his fiery style is discernible. On the whole these works appear less dense and more predictable than those in the publication. Apel accounts for the stylistic differences by postulating that the compositions in the manuscript are late works; such an explanation, however, cannot substitute for a more substantive support of their authenticity.

Notes

INTRODUCTION

1. Sartori, *Bibliografia*.

2. Published studies on individual manuscripts include: Tagliavini, *Kerll* (on Bologna 53), Oncley, *Conservatorio* (on Naples 73), Lincoln, *Manoscritti chigiani* (on Chigi 24-29 and 205-206), and Darbellay, *Manuscrit frescobaldien* (on Cologny T.II.1). These studies will be reviewed in the discussions of the respective manuscripts in Part Two.

3. A comprehensive bibliographic survey of the sources of French keyboard music, limited however to music intended for harpsichord, is Gustafson, *Sources* (see Preface). Information on many English sources can be found in Caldwell, *Keyboard Music* and Cooper, *Keyboard Music*. Two detailed studies have appeared on German sources: Schierning, *Überlieferung* (dealing with sources from before c. 1650), and Riedel, *Beiträge* (covering sources from the second half of the century). These last two monographs, although differing somewhat in scope and format from my undertaking (they consider printed as well as manuscript collections and do not attempt to catalogue all surviving sources) have, nevertheless, served in many ways as models for this study, and have provided me with several valuable insights.

4. The catalogue includes a few post-17th-century manuscripts (some in the past erroneously dated to the 17th century) that contain 17th-century repertory.

5. The significance of this omission is even more apparent when one considers that Apel includes in his survey virtually every collection of Italian keyboard music that appeared in print. It should be added that Apel played a major role in awakening interest in the manuscript sources; he was the first to draw attention to many of the manuscripts and to point to their significance—see Apel, *Überlieferung* (on some Frescobaldi sources), Apel, *Clavierschule* (on Naples 73), and, especially, Chapters 16 and 20 of his *Keyboard Music*.

6. Modern editions of the works of individual composers and of individual manuscripts (none, unfortunately, complete) are listed in the corresponding sections in Part Three and Part Two. Virtually all these editions lack adequate critical commentary; most are unsatisfactory in other respects. A few of the compositions not included in these editions will be presented here in transcription.

7. As an example one could mention the studies on individual composers in Apel's *Keyboard Music*. Although Apel does include a discussion of the composers' works surviving in manuscripts, he fails to consider the validity of the attributions; nor does he, when dealing with the composers' stylistic developments, take into account the dating of these manuscripts—see, for example, his discussion on Frescobaldi, pp. 482-483.

8. See, for example, the stile antico ricercare collections of Battiferri (Sa. 1669h) and of Fontana (Sa. 1677) or Strozzi's CAPRICCI (Sa. 1687h)—modelled on the early 17th-century Neapolitan publications.

9. See Part Three, Bernardo Pasquini.

10. See Rostirolla, *Catalogo*, 537-38, and Sartori, *Scarlatti*, 140-43.

11. A recent study of Scarlatti's toccate in Neapolitan manuscripts (Pestelli, *Toccate*) discusses the musical contents of these sources, but is not concerned with their provenance.

CHAPTER I

1. Most of these and the following data on Italian publications were compiled with the aid of Sartori, *Bibliografia*.

2. cf. RISM, A/I/3, 114-115.

3. No complete listing of manuscript copies is available, although a large number of German copies are listed in Riedel's valuable treatment of Frescobaldi's influence in Germany (*Beiträge*, 54-55, 117-20). A similar investigation of the Frescobaldi tradition in England would be of considerable interest.

4. In interpreting these statistics it should be remembered that they are based on the number of surviving publications (or, in one or two cases, on references to lost publications) and that we do not know to what extent these represent the actual number published. There are, however, some indications that the number of lost publications, at least from the later 16th century onward, is small. Virtually all of the keyboard-music publications listed in a 1649 sales catalogue of Vincenti, including editions from several publishers dating between 1593 and 1645 (Vincenti, *Indice*), have survived in one or more copies or, in a few cases, in manuscript copy. References to titles of lost publications are rare; among the few examples are the two collections of Scipione Giovanni (Sa. 1650d and Sa. 1652), listed in the catalogue of the Civico museo in Bologna but no longer extant.

5. Publishers do not seem to have interfered to any substantial degree with the material that they received. One of them, in fact, specifically disclaims responsibility for the musical text of his publications, blaming all errors on the handwritten copies provided him (although he does not state whether these copies were obtained from the composers or from less authoritative sources): "E se ritrovate qualche errore nel Cantar le Opere stampate non date la colpa al stampatore perche ogni giorno se ne ritrova nella originale a penna" (Vincenti, *Indice*, 3).

6. Most of the works contained in CANZONI I also appear in an edition published by Frescobaldi during the same year, CANZONI I (1628j), but the curious and rather uncharacteristic pieces for "Spinettina" appended to the former publication are not found in the composer's edition. The eleven canzoni in the posthumous collection of 1645, "raccolte d'Alessandro Vincenti"—which, according to Vincenti's preface, did not fall into his hands until after

the composer's death—show several departures from Frescobaldi's usual practice. The sections in triple meter do not use the old-fashioned mensuration signs 0 3 and ℭ 3/2 frequently encountered in the canzoni published during the composer's lifetime; none, in fact, uses tempus-perfectum notation, still much favored by Frescobaldi. The *Canzon Terza detta la Crivelli* is altogether untypical of the compositions entitled "Canzon" by Frescobaldi; it lacks sections in contrasting meter and has all the characteristics of a stile-antico ricercare. Even if the original texts of these works derive from Frescobaldi, one suspects at least the presence of Vincenti's editorial hand. In any case, the titles given pieces in both Vincenti's and Grassi's editions—e.g., "La Gardana," "La Scacchi"— surely do not stem from the composer. As Sartori has pointed out (*Pratique*), the titles found in Grassi's publication do not appear in the composer's own edition of the same works; moreover, Sartori notes that the practice of naming canzoni after prominent families or persons was common only in Northern Italy.

7.   The only exceptions are the CAPRICCI PUERILI of Pistocchi (Sa. 1667c), a set of forty variations on the Ballo di Mantova, supposedly by an eight-year-old child prodigy, and the very late anthology of sonatas by various composers, Arresti, SONATE (Sa. 1697?m).

CHAPTER II

1.   See Plamenac, *Keyboard Music*, and Kugler, *Tastenmusik*, for editions and literature. Two intabulations similar in notation and character to those in Faenza 117 and probably of contemporary origin appear in Paris 6771 (the Reina Codex). Whether this repertory should be regarded as keyboard music has been a matter of some dispute, but at present most scholars appear to agree with Plamenac's conclusion that it was in fact intended for keyboard instruments.

2.   On association of the toccata with the madrigal, see Chapter VII.

3.   Perhaps this difference from the two-part Faenza settings is more apparent than real; it is quite conceivable that performers filled in the texture by a voice moving at thirds and fifths with the bass.

4.   From the second half of the 15th century all we possess are a few measures of an intabulation of a Spanish villancico, appearing as a theoretical example of "intavolature del canto de organo" in a fragmentary manuscript in the library of the University of Bologna. The fragment was described recently by Fallows, who concluded that it probably is Neapolitan in origin (*Tablatures*, 18-28 and Pl. 8). Despite its brevity this intabulation is of some interest, since it is notated in what is known today as old German organ tablature (to be sure, the early usage of this notation appears not to have been restricted to Germany, and its 16th-century survival there may represent merely a conservative feature of that country's notational practice).

5.   For the history of the passamezzo, etc., and for the history of such settings in general, the dating of this allegedly earliest source is crucial. No other passamezzi, labelled as such, appear before c. 1540, although dances with similar harmonic progressions can be found in earlier music, for example, in some of the Attaingnant tablatures of 1530.

CHAPTER III

1. In my discussion of the provenance of the manuscripts I shall anticipate here some of the conclusions arrived at in Part Two.

CHAPTER IV

1. As a consequence the format can furnish some help for determining the origin of a manuscript; for example, Berlin 40316, which Apel (*Keyboard Music*, 339) believes to be the work of an Italian copyist, is in upright format, and hence is more likely to be of Northern provenance.

2. These exceptional cases are: two volumes in four-staff score notation, for which the oblong format might not allow sufficient space (Florence 106b and London 30491—the latter, however, contains a fascicle in two-staff keyboard notation, which is in oblong format); two volumes that contain texted vocal settings and perhaps were not conceived exclusively as keyboard collections (Florence 138 and Barb. lat. 4288); and one volume that consists almost entirely of copies from printed collections and appears to follow the format of its exemplars (Bagnacavallo; the upright format is in fact quite common among Italian printed collections).

3. According to Krummel (*Oblong Format*, 312) this oblong quarto format was common in printed 16th-century part-books; towards the end of the century it gradually was replaced by upright quarto format.

4. The manuscripts Barb. lat. 4181 and 4182 have the golden Barberini bees stamped on their covers, but such decoration is exceptional. The parchment coverings are missing from Chigi 26 and Chigi 27; the present cardboard covers of those manuscripts are, however, of the same kind as those found under the parchment of the other volumes of the Chigi collection.

5. Florence 2358 has a Medici coat of arms; the coat of arms on London 40080 has not been identified.

CHAPTER V

1. The only known example of the use of a Spanish-type number tablature is in the Neapolitan publication, Valente, INTAVOLATURA (Sa. 1576); letter notation is used for the pedal part in Annibale Padovano's TOCCATE (Sa. 1604e). The former may be a consequence of Spanish influence, the latter of following German models. Neither practice survived in Italian keyboard notation.

2. For a list and description, see Lowinsky, *Early Scores*.

3. See Riedel, *Beiträge*, 35, 36; Schierning, *Überlieferung*, 81.

4. The national classification can even lead to somewhat circular evidence for establishing the provenance of manuscripts: the manuscripts classified as "niederländische Handschriften" by Schierning (*Überlieferung*, 79-81), partially on the basis of their common notational style, are in fact all German.

5.   See Wolf, *Notationskunde* I, 292.

6.   The FROTTOLE (Sa. 1517) use 5/5, but in Italian keyboard music this system is exceptional.

7.   For a 17th-century reference to this practice, see Riedel, *Beiträge*, 7.

8.   This may account for the fact that in a portion of Trent the lowest line of the bottom staff, which originally had eight lines, is crossed out, reducing the staves to the "Roman" 6/7 system (see below).

9.   For a discussion of the meaning and use of these two signs in the early 17th century, see Dahlhaus, *Entstehung*; Dahlhaus, *Taktlehre*; and Brainard, *Diminution*.

10. The interpretation of the various triple-mensuration signs appearing in 17th-century sources forms a complex problem to which there are probably no solutions valid for the entire literature. A discussion of the implications of the mensuration signs in Frescobaldi's keyboard music is given in Darbellay, *Liberté*. The author explored Frescobaldi's practice from a somewhat different point of view in a paper "Meter and Tempo in the Keyboard Music of Frescobaldi," prepared at Brandeis University, 1971, which he hopes to revise for publication in the near future.

11. Dots are also found in Barb. lat. 4288, but in that manuscript they apparently indicate ornaments.

12. UCLA 51/1 contains a single piece with a signature of two sharps: f. 24', *Ballo di Ungheria*. Elsewhere in the manuscript sharp key signatures are not used, even when their use would have been convenient.

CHAPTER VI

1.   The appearance of text underlay in keyboard settings is, of course, not unique to the Italian manuscripts; examples can be found in printed sources, such as Facoli, INTAVOLATURA II (Sa. 1588c) and Strozzi, CAPRICCI (Sa. 1687h), and in foreign keyboard collections such as Henestrosa, *Libro de cifra nueva . . .* (Alcala: 1557), and the Elizabeth Rogers Virginal Book.

CHAPTER VII

1.   Bradshaw (*Toccata*) has suggested that the toccata—especially in its earlier, Venetian manifestations, but to some extent during its entire history—was essentially a cantus firmus setting of a psalmtone (the cantus firmus being "ideal," i.e., not physically present in the score). I find this thesis altogether unconvincing. The earlier toccate as well as the canzoni and ricercari, do partake of the modal language paradigmatically represented by the psalmtones; I do not believe, however, that they depend structurally on them. Bradshaw's hypothesis implies a freedom, in fact capriciousness (in terms of segmentation, fragmentation, reordering, rhythmic weight, voice leading, and dissonance treatment), entirely beyond the procedures followed during the period, whether in real or in "ideal" cantus-firmus settings.

2. In the tables appearing in this chapter the manuscripts are listed in approximately chronological order.

3. Mattheson, in his *Kern melodischer Wissenschaft* of 1737 (quoted in Bradshaw, *Toccata*, 42), states that although toccate sound as if they are improvised, they are mostly written-out.

4. Bradshaw (*Toccata*, 35, 45 ff.) goes to considerable lengths in an attempt to refute the notion of the toccata as an improvisational composition; he states that ''the composer or organist was guided throughout his composition by one of the most solid of all compositional techniques—a cantus firmus.'' However (leaving aside the issue whether the toccata is in fact a cantus-firmus setting—cf. n. 1 above), the cantus-firmus setting is also one of the most ancient and most basic of all improvisational techniques. There is a tendency today to associate the so-called ''free style,'' consisting of chords and running passages, with improvisation, but we have every reason to assume that the well-trained 17th-century organist was just as capable of improvising simple counterpoint to a given cantus firmus.

5. When explaining the manner of performance of his toccate in the Preface to TOCCATE I he also refers to ''i Madrigali moderni.'' Riedel in fact sees the roots of the Italian toccata in madrigal and chanson intabulations and also mentions Frescobaldi's intabulation in this connection (Riedel, *Einfluss*, 23).

6. See also p. 46 on the role of imitative sections within the toccata.

7. In a paper presented at the 1975 national meeting of the American Musicological Society (''The independent instrumental canzone, does it exist?'') Floyd Sumner showed that a large number of late 16th-century canzone and ricercare subjects are derived from the subject la-sol-mi-fa-sol-la or its inversion.

8. Some of the openings of these triple-meter canzoni are reminiscent of the gagliarde of the same period. It is curious that Trabaci, another Neapolitan, in his RICERCATE I (Sa. 1603) includes several pieces entitled *Gagliarda* which open like the more conventional canzoni, i.e., in duple meter, with an imitative exposition of a typical canzone subject (e.g., the Gagliarda terza and the Gagliarda quinta).

9. Mayone in his printed collections CAPRICCI I (Sa. 1603b) and CAPRICCI II (Sa. 1609f) uses the term in a more generic sense; it appears only in the titles of the publications, which in fact contain a wide variety of genres. Actually, Frescobaldi in a few of his printed capricci also uses the term in a more general manner, that is, to denote a keyboard composition based on some compositional idea (Cromatico, *Durrezze*) or character (Pastorale, Battaglia).

10. Mr. Louis Bagger has suggested to me in connection with Frescobaldi's setting of the Arcadelt madrigal that the specific figures (or ''affetti,'' as Frescobaldi calls them in his preface) appearing in the intabulation of a madrigal might bear some relation to the mood or image of the corresponding line of text. It would be interesting to examine the settings in the light of his suggestion; but whether or not the practice existed does not affect the observation that from the musical point of view the intabulations are essentially new compositions.

11. See also the discussion of compositions "per l'elevatione" in the preceding section on the toccata.

12. They appear in the Pasquini segment of the manuscript (see p. 179).

13. I have avoided the term ostinato-setting since it very rarely is appropriate.

14. See Alaleona, *Laudi*, 7-8 for further bibliographical information and more detailed description.

15. See, for example, Hudson, *Ripresa*, 366, and Flotzinger, *Gagliarda*, 94.

16. The situation is somewhat analogous to that of modern American blues. The blues also tends to follow a harmonic scheme (subject to many individual variations—as is the case with the Italian arie), but blues compositions contain many other characteristic features that allow one to recognize the genre long before the harmonic scheme has been perceived.

17. Some of the ideas presented here regarding the aria settings were discussed at greater length in a paper *Oral Tradition and the Ostinato Variation of the Late Renaissance*, given by the author at the 1977 Spring meeting of the Midwest Chapter of the American Musicological Society at Champaign-Urbana, Illinois.

18. The "Gagliarda" entry refers not to the dance-type composition, but rather to an aria in duple time found under this name in the sources. The appearance of settings of this aria in the manuscripts confirms the supposition by Flotzinger that the title of a composition in a lute manuscript, "La Galiarda Italjana," refers to a standard model rather than to the dance-type (*Gagliarda*, 95; Flotzinger was not familiar with other settings of this aria).

19. See notes 8 and 18 above for two other types of compositions also called gagliarda, but apparently not related to the dance.

CHAPTER VIII

1. An extreme example of organizational mania can be found in the Turin manuscripts—of German provenance, c. 1640—in which a repertory of nearly 2,000 compositions is grouped and subgrouped according to genre (adhering in basic outline to the standard order); the copyists went to the point of extracting imitative sections from the toccate and placing these excerpts in the "Fuga" section (see Mischiati, *Torino*).

2. As a matter of fact, the *Recercare-Motet* sequences in Cavazzoni, RECERCHARI (Sa. 1523), which are remarkably like prelude-and-fugue pairs, could be regarded as prototypes.

3. See p. 121, where it is suggested that these pairs form part of a complete set in all the modes.

CHAPTER IX

1. The 18th-century manuscripts Bologna 53 and Cecilia 400 will be excluded from most of this discussion, since they relate to an altogether different group of sources (see the discussions of the individual manuscripts).

2. Note that the Frescobaldi four-staff score publications, RECERCARI, CAPRICCI, and FIORI, which later gained such wide distribution in manuscript copies in Italy as well as elsewhere (presumably for their value in contrapuntal studies), were rarely drawn upon in the earlier Italian manuscripts.

3. For a discussion of this manuscript and its dating—about which there has been some disagreement—see Silbiger, *Tradition*.

CHAPTER X

1. Von Dadelsen, *Echtheitskritik*.

CHAPTER XI

1. Lincoln, apparently unaware of the connection between the two compositions, has included the manuscript version in his edition of the anonymous repertory from the Chigi manuscripts (Lincoln, *Keyboard Music*, II, 48).

2. Ward, *Henestrosa*; Reimann, *Pasticcios*.

3. Included in Lincoln, *Keyboard Music* II, 48 (See comment in note 1, above.)

4. There are, in fact, some curious partial concordances among the compositions attributed to Frescobaldi in foreign sources—for example, the "Trio de Frescobaldi" in the Bauyn Ms. in which a passage from his *Toccata duodecima* in TOCCATE I (1615) is transformed into a typical French "Trio d'orgue" by means of the transposition of an inner voice to a higher octave.

5. Ward, *Henestrosa*; Reimann, *Pasticcios*.

6. Several of the ensemble canzoni in Frescobaldi's CANZONI (1628j) appear in his CANZONI (1634) in versions that might be called "self-pasticcios." Furthermore, the versions of the partite on the Romanesca and on the Ruggiero in the two editions of TOCCATE I, 1615 and 1616, show substitutions of variations similar to the substitutions found in variation sets in the manuscripts.

CHAPTER XII

1. See, for some examples, the illustrations in Testi, *Seicento* II, between pp. 172 and 173.

2. Such notated examples are hence somewhat similar to editions of jazz music on the market today: improvisations by great artists taken down from recordings, and simpler—often inferior—imitations specifically written for less accomplished players.

3. Again London 30491 appears as an exception; the de Macque compositions it contains may very well have been obtained directly from the composer since the copyist, Luigi Rossi, is known to have been de Macque's pupil. The text of these compositions appears much more reliable than that of the other de Macque sources (see Part Three, Giovanni de Macque).

4. Of course, these considerations do not apply to the few manuscripts no longer residing in Italy, such as those in the British Library in London.

PART TWO

1. See the Introduction to this study for a more detailed discussion of the criteria by which manuscripts were selected.

2. The order followed in Benton, *Research Libraries*, has been observed for those libraries and collections listed there.

3. For a few manuscripts the exact dimensions were not available to me at the time of writing and hence are not given. Other information on physical aspects of the manuscript frequently follows in the annotations.

4. See the note on *Abbreviations and Other Conventions* for the system followed to indicate the staff ruling.

5. Editions that include only one or two compositions—usually duplicated in the listed editions— are omitted, as are editions not based on the manuscripts (e.g., editions based on 17th-century publications containing the same works).

6. The article "Frescobaldi" in MGG (Reimann, *Frescobaldi*, 913) contains a photographic reproduction of a page from this manuscript; the legend describes this page as "Autograph."

7. Modern edition in Osthoff, *Composizioni vocali*, 10; not included in the Malipiero edition of the complete works.

8. The viola bastarda was probably a small bass viola da gamba, the Italian equivalent of the English division viol (not of the English lyra viol, nor of the Italian lira da gamba, according to Lejeune, *Lyra-viol*). The small but not negligible surviving repertory for this instrument (most of it in pedagogical publications, e.g., dalla Casa, MODO DI DIMINUIR II, Sa. 1584e, and Rognoni, SELVA II, Sa. 1620d) has not yet been systematically investigated. It is similar to the English division viol repertory in its exploitation of an extended melodic range with many large leaps, but differs from this repertory in that it does not make use of chords.

9. The "double-stops" in individual lines and the figuration leave little doubt that this repertory was intended primarily for keyboard, or possibly for harp. The "Prima Gagliarda di Gio. di Macque," f. 20', appears in transposed form in Naples 55, a set of part books; however, the latter version may represent an adaptation for ensemble of the keyboard version. Such an adaptation is suggested for specific pieces in several Neapolitan keyboard publications (e.g., Salvatore, RICERCARI, Sa. 1641c, Canzon Francese Seconda: "Queste Canzona può sonarsi con il Concerto di Viole"). In some compositions the writing is occasionally difficult to negotiate on a keyboard instrument because of voice crossings or large stretches (e.g., the final partita on Ruggiero by de Macque, f. 6'). These pieces may have been intended either for a harpsichord or organ with pull-down pedals, or for harp. Other Neapolitan publications of the time include compositions for harp (e.g., Mayone, CAPRICCI, Sa. 1609f, Trabaci, RICERCATE II, Sa. 1615c); Rossi was well-known as a harp virtuoso.

10. Scipione Stella, active c. 1580-1605, in Gesualdo's service 1593-c. 1603—see Prota-Giurleo, *Napoli*, 69-70.

11. See p. 165.

12. Rinaldo dell'Arpa, in Gesualdo's service—see Jackson, *Neapolitan Composers*, ix, and Newcomb, *Gesualdo*, 414-415.

13. Francesco Lambardo (1587-1642)—see Prota-Giurleo, *Napoli*, 82-83.

14. Jackson (*Neapolitan Composers*, ix) suggests this refers to Ippolito Tartaglioni (d. 1582).

15. Fabritio Fillimarino, member of Gesualdo's *Accademia*, accompanied Gesualdo to Ferrara in 1594—see Watkins, *Gesualdo*, 67-69.

16. See note 39 below.

17. Presumably Gesualdo—see Watkins, *Gesualdo*, 291-295.

18. Cerreto (*Prattica musica*, 1601) lists "oratio detto del Violone per antichità Napolitano" among Neapolitan players of the Viola d'arco no longer living (in 1601).

19. Muzio Effrem, in Gesualdo's service 1593-1616, still alive in 1626—see Prota-Giurleo, *Napoli*, 71. The passaggi attributed to Effrem are listed in the *Tavola* but are missing in the manuscript (see p. 89).

20. A good description of the different appearances of 16th- and 17th-century music writing is given in Lowinsky, *Early Scores*, 134-135.

21. The attribution does not appear in the caption, but is given in the *Tavola*.

22. This probably refers to Don Luigi Gaetano, Duke of Traietto, who accompanied Gesualdo in the latter's visit to Ferrara in 1594 and who evidently took an interest in musical activities at the Ferrarese court (Newcomb, *Gesualdo*, 415-416).

23. See Gustafson, *Sources*, 470.

24. See Osthoff, *Composizioni vocali*, iv-v.

25. "Biblioteca Con[ven]tus s. Francisci Ord. Min. Conv."

26. Pacchioni, *Balli*, includes an edition of 21 of these pieces.

27. Among these are tunings of the violin, the lute, and the Spanish guitar, as well as the *spinetto*. The instructions for the latter provide the tuning sequence (from E-flat to G-sharp by fifths and fourths) but do not specify the tempering.

28. See p. 112.

29. A set of six *Preludio-Sonata* pairs appearing in a mid-18th century manuscript in Dresden (Sächsische Landesbibliothek, Ms 1/T16) is mentioned in Riedel, *Beiträge*, 139; apparently the first Sonata of this set is also identical with the Sonata in Arresti's collection. I strongly suspect that the two sets are in fact identical throughout, which would confirm my supposition about Pollaroli's authorship, but I have not yet been able to verify this.

30. Lowinsky describes the first three pieces as a *Romanescha*, a *Canzona*, and a *Ricercare con 7 fughe e rovesci*. The first piece is indeed entitled *Romanescha*; however, the second is called *Ricercare* (furthermore, it has all the characteristics of that genre), and the third is called merely "2^O" (presumably implying "2^O Ricercare"). At the end of the latter piece is written "3° ricercare con 3 [not 7] fughe, e rovesci"; this title must refer to a following piece, since it does not describe the preceding *Ricercare*. However, no third ricercare was entered into the manuscript; the staves follow this title are blank.

31. Lowinsky writes of del Rio: "an otherwise unknown Flemish musician living in Italy, where he probably Italianized his name." Actually del Rio may be a Spanish rather than an Italianized Flemish name; there was a prominent Antwerp family by this name, of Spanish origin (see *Biographie nationale*, V, 468-491).

32. Watkins traces some individual madrigals to before 1604, but even that is of course not sufficiently early to establish Nenna's primacy.

33. He states that the de Macque *Ricercari* have not been examined or discussed by anyone (*Gesualdo*, 215, n. 7).

34. A printed tenor part of a Book of ensemble *Ricercari* by de Macque published in 1586 survives in private hands in Turin (see p. 165). This part book has not been available to scholars for examination; whether it contains any concordances to Florence 106b is not known.

35. According to Gandolfi, *Catalogo*, 260, it was also attributed to Frescobaldi in Gandolfi, *Indice di alcuni Cimeli* (Florence: 1913); the author was unable to examine this publication.

36. Information on this manuscript is based on a description and inventory furnished me by Prof. Francesco Degrada of the Milan Conservatorio; the dating follows Degrada's estimate.

37. The composition is, however, mentioned in Apel, *Keyboard Music*, 224; see p. 172 for a transcription.

38. Cited in Cerreto, *Prattica musica* (Naples, 1601) in a list of organists living in Naples (p. 157) as "Pietro d'Alem Flamengo, e per antichità Napolitana" (see also Prota-Giurleo, *Napoli*, 69). "Alem" may be an Italianization of Haarlem.

39. Giovanni Maria Trabaci (b. Montebelasco, c. 1575, d. Naples 1647).

40. Fabrizio Gaetano, organist of the Real Capella di Napoli from 1555 to 1598—see Prota-Giurleo, *Trabaci*, 191.

41. Possibly a relative of Trabaci, since it corresponds to the maiden name of Trabaci's mother—see Prota-Giurleo, *Trabaci*, 185.

42. There is no f. 20—presumably a numbering mistake, since the collation shows no missing page.

43. It is conceivable that the segments in hands A and B are in fact the work of a single copyist; but if so these segments must date many years apart.

44. The model evidently was not known to Debes; see *Merulo*, 351.

45. A *Canzona Francese* on f. 42' has an opening almost identical to that of the *Fantasia Seconda* in Frescobaldi's FANTASIE, (1608); the similarity does not extend beyond the first three measures (i.e., the first two entries of the soggetto). If this resemblance is taken to mean that Frescobaldi's *Fantasia* served as a model, a somewhat later dating would result. However, the use of an identical soggetto does not necessarily imply such a relationship.

46. Debes mistakenly lists this attribution as being to Erbach—a rather unlikely composer to appear in this Neapolitan manuscript.

47. Another composition apparently written in imitation of a folk instrument is found in Chigi 28—see p. 129; both pieces are discussed at greater length in an article by the author forthcoming in *The Galpin Society Journal*: "The Colascione and the Zampogna: Imitations of Folk Instruments in 17th-Century Keyboard Music."

48. Francesco Antonio Boerio (second half of the 17th century). Apel (*Clavierschule*, 128) and Oncley (*Conservatorio*, 6) state that no other compositions by Boerio are known; several of his liturgical compositions are preserved, however, in the Archivio dell'oratorio del Filippini—see article "Boerio" by the author in the forthcoming sixth edition of *Grove's*.

49. Giovanni Salvatore (c. 1605-1688?); see Hudson, *Salvatore*. The toccata on f. 108 is a shortened and slightly simplified version of the *Toccata primo* in Salvatore, RICERCARI (Sa. 1641c); the other works are unique to this manuscript.

50. Giacinto Ansalone (1605-1657), maestro di capella at the Conservatorio della Pietà dei Turchini—see article "Ansalone" by the author in the forthcoming sixth edition of *Grove's*.

51. Oncley, *Conservatorio*, 2.

52. See Oncley, *Conservatorio*, 7.

53. Gallico, *Canzoniere*, 69-73. I wish to thank Professor Joshua Rifkin of Brandeis University for bringing Gallico's study and the references to Joseph of Ravenna to my attention.

54. The Monastery of Classe was located on the site of the present Biblioteca Comunale—see Benton, *Research Libraries* III, 240.

55. For a bibliography of studies on 18th-century materials in the collection see Benton, *Directory* III, 245. Incidentally, Benton is incorrect in stating that Holschneider, *Musiksammlung*, gives a complete listing of the Doria-Pamphilj holdings; only a selected number of volumes are listed (the keyboard volumes are not mentioned). On the role of members of the Pamphilij family as patrons of music and the arts in 17th-century Rome, see Montalto, *Pamphilij*.

56. They do receive a passing mention in Holschneider, *Römische Handschriften*, in which they are described as "zwei Bände mit Musik für Tasteninstr." Doria 250 A was apparently examined by Holschneider, who compiled a thematic inventory of this volume. The inventory has not been published, but a copy was made available to me by Oscar Mischiati.

57. See Prunières, *Barberini*, 120.

58. The original owner probably was Nicolò Maria Barberini, born in 1632, a son of Urban's nephew, Taddeo.

59. Heawood does include a number of similar watermarks from 16th- and 17th-century Italian publications, e.g., Nos. 1104-1123 (star-and-crown), and Nos. 2610-2616 (three mounts).

60. This catalogue apparently was to contain a complete listing of the vocal and instrumental manuscripts, but did not get further than providing a list of opera scores.

61. Now kept in the *Sala di consultazione dei manoscritti* in the Biblioteca Vaticana.

62. The information on the Chigi family is derived in part from Pastor, *Popes* and from Sestan, *Chigi*.

63. Prince Chigi-Saracini was the founder of the *Accademia musicale Chigiana* and of the *Settimane musicali senesi*.

64. Montanelli, *L'Italia*, 471.

65. On Alexander's artistic patronage see Haskell, *Patrons*, 150-155.

66. A contemporary testified that the gift of a valuable manuscript formed an assured way of gaining his favor (Gachard, *Bibliothèque Chigi*, 220).

67. Wessely-Kropik, *Colista*, 43-44. According to Wessely-Kropik, Boccalini is recorded as performing on lute, theorbo, violin, viola bastarda, violone, and lira (*Colista*, 32, 52). In addition, he apparently was an organist; the records of a Vespers performance for Easter 1657 at S. Maria Maggiore list a "Boccalino organista" (Arch. S. Maria Maggiore, Capp. Mus., Giustificazione I, n. 67), and a Francesco Boccalini is listed as *Guardiano degli organisti* of the Congregazione di S. Cecilia for 1670-72 (Giazotto, *Cecilia*, 375). Such professional versatility is uncommon among Roman 17th-century musicians.

68. Witzenmann, *Marazzoli*, 54-55.

69. Documents in the Archivio Chigi (now also in the Vatican Library) record numerous payments to Colista during Alexander VII's pontificate, mostly for expenses connected with these occasions, such as reimbursements to other musicians and music copyists (Arch. Chigi 456, 457, 537, 576, 685, 9044, 9057, 9083).

70. Wessely-Kropik (*Colista*, 64-65) states that none of the French and Italian sources related to this mission lists the musicians accompanying Flavio, and that the earliest reference to Pasquini's presence in the delegation is found in the composer's biography in Cresimbeni, *Notizie istoriche degli arcadi morti*, Vol. II (Rome: 1720), p. 232. I did come across two documents listing the personnel accompanying the Cardinal on his mission (Archivio Chigi 3310 and 9057); both lists include Lelio Colista and Pietro Paolo Cappellini, but Pasquini is not named in either one. Furthermore, throughout the period of the mission (May-October 1664) Pasquini continued to receive monthly payments as organist of S. Maria Maggiore (see Silbiger, *Tradition*). On the other hand, no autograph receipts exist at S. Maria Maggiore, and it is possible that a substitute served during this period. A manuscript report on the mission (Fondo Chigi, Ms. E.II.38) contains a reference to a "Bernardo excellente suonator di tasti" (f. 267), suggesting that Pasquini was indeed in Chigi's entourage.

71. Golzio, *Documenti*, pp. 185, 241, 243, 250, 252.

72. Chigi's relation to Kircher is of possible significance in connection with the authorship of Chigi 25—see p. 162.

73. A selected list of 17th-century manuscripts "by authors most worthy of being mentioned" is given in Golzio, *Chigi*, 375-76. It should be noted that the Chigi manuscript probably best known to scholars today, the choirbook C.VIII.234, is not catalogued with the music manuscripts, but rather under the C signature, as are a few chant books.

74. On Agostini and Cardinal Chigi, see Golzio, *Chigi*, 373-74; on the singers of the Sistine Chapel, see Celani, *Cantori*, 55-61.

75. Witzenmann, *Marazzoli I* and *Marazzoli II*.

76. Lincoln includes some of these dances in his edition of the anonymous pieces. The *Corrente* on f. 11' appears in Lincoln, *Chigi* II, 36, as "Corrente del (Illegible)." The manuscript reads clearly "Corrente del Baletto," which in Lincoln's edition would, to be sure, not make much sense, since the corresponding balletto has been separated from its mate and put into the *Balletto* section.

77. See p. 56. The dances of LaBarre apparently enjoyed a considerable vogue during the middle of the 17th century; they appear in French, English, German, Spanish, Danish and Dutch manuscripts (see Gustafson, *Sources*, 100-104, 1167, 1316-1317). Several members of the LaBarre family were active as musicians during this period, mostly at the French court; it is not clear to which member the attributions in this manuscript refer. Only one other work attributed to La Barre has been found in an Italian source: a "Menuet di Monsu la barra" for violin in Bologna 360 (f. 67').

78. For concordances, see Gustafson, *Sources*, 544, No. 30; and 545, No. 32.

79. In Lincoln's inventory the second half of the double of the second corrente is incorrectly listed as a separate composition—f. 49: [corrente].

80. Similar abbreviations appear in other manuscripts, for example, Ravenna 545, f. 74': Canzon D. H. P. (= di Hercole Pasquini).

81. Lincoln notes that the Balletto is a variation on the same theme used by Frescobaldi. This theme, also known as "More palatino" and as "Or che noi rimena," was in fact set by many North- and South-European composers; a second set of variations on the aria was included by Frescobaldi in his CAPRICCI (1624).

82. Hudson, *Further remarks*, 312.

83. Rossi visited Paris in 1647 in connection with the production of his *Orfeo*. A *Passacaille* attributed to him in four northern keyboard sources (see p. 90), is very similar to the pieces in Chigi 27.

84. The *Passacaglia* and the *Ciaccona* found in the 1627 edition of TOCCATE II were in fact deleted from the 1637 edition of that collection, perhaps because they were "superseded" by those in AGGIUNTA.

85. For a further discussion of this composition and another related "Colascione" piece, see the author's forthcoming article referred to in Part Two note 47.

86. He probably was misled by Lincoln's edition of the work, in which it appears as an independent composition. That he believes it to be an isolated piece is evident from his reference to the "keyboard Girometta" and to "the 77 measures of this piece" (Kirkendale, *Franchesina*, 208).

87. On the history of this tune see Curtis, *Klaviermuziek*, xxxviii. Curtis believes the setting in the Gresse manuscript to be the earliest keyboard setting of the tune. Since he dates the corresponding part of the manuscript from shortly after 1650, the setting in Chigi 28 very likely anticipated it, or, at least, was contemporary with it. The Wilhelmus appears in another Battle—this one in a more likely source: Jacob van Eyck, *Der Fluyten Lust-Hof* (Amsterdam, 1646) II, "Batalia."

88. The "f" signs appearing earlier in the *Girometta* in Lincoln's edition (p. 62) are actually misreadings of .s., i.e., repeat signs, indicating that the latter part of the tune is to be played again.

89. See Mainerio, BALLI, Sa.1578b, f. 15.

90. The tune and text of "Contre les Huguenots" with the refrain "Lanturlu" appear in Barlier, *Histoire*, p. 125; its source is given as Paris, Bibliothèque Nationale, Ms. Ars 3118. Other settings of the tune appear in van Eyck, *Der Fluyten Lust-Hof* I, 35 and Marco Ucellini, SONATE (Sa. 1642a), p. 44.

91. As a result of my recent studies on Roman musicians I now can associate several of the names listed in the payment records with singers and instrumentalists working in Rome during this period. I am confident that with further research in this area we will be able to pinpoint more precisely when, and perhaps even where, this performance took place. Hopefully this will enable us to determine who the organist was and, hence, to discover who compiled this volume.

92. "The contents of the manuscript [sic] as a whole also support our theory" (*Giaches Fantasias*, 380).

93. Baronci either erred or departed from his scheme in including some 18th-century items in Chigi 205-206—see the dating of individual works in Lincoln, *Manoscritti chigiani*, 75-80. To be sure, I am not in agreement with all of Lincoln's datings. Judged by handwriting and musical content, some of the items he assigns to the 19th century more likely are from the 18th (e.g., f. 230); others assigned by him to the 18th century probably belong to the 17th (e.g., f. 151).

94. Even the possibility of a later copying date for this fascicle cannot be excluded; at least, a dating before 1607 may be incompatible with MacClintock's assumption of a Ferrarese provenance (see note 98 below).

95. Two composers named in the vocal segments—Vincenzo de Grandis and Lorenzo Ratti—can definitely be associated with Rome (on the former, see Wessely-Kropik, *Colista*, 51, 63, on the latter, Cametti, *Roma*, 745). Incidentally, it seems stretching a point to call Frescobaldi (1583-1643) a "younger contemporary" of Giaches de Wert (1535-1596). Their association appears more unlikely than the association questioned by MacClintock as part of her main thesis: that of Brumel (died after 1564) and Luzzaschi (1545-1607).

96. We might note, furthermore, that Luzzaschi visited Rome in 1601 (Ladewig, *Frescobaldi*, 12).

97. Fabio Chigi was papal vice-legate in Ferrara from 1631 to 1635 and might have acquired the "Ferrarese" fascicle during this period.

98. The first cantus firmus setting is entitled "Lucciasco [Luzzaschi?] a 4"; the second one carries the inscription "Era attaccato al precedente e però si crede esser del Lucciasco." This last comment, which appears to have been made by the copyist, indicates a remoteness from this composer, and suggests that either these pieces were not copied in Ferrara or they were copied after his death in 1607. At any rate, Newcomb considers Luzzaschi's authorship of both pieces doubtful on stylistic grounds (Newcomb, *Modo*, 38, n. 2).

99. At the time of my visit to the Library (1972) the Casimiri collection had not yet been processed. However, Mons. Ruysschaert of the library staff kindly arranged for me to examine the Casimiri manuscripts.

100. When I examined this manuscript in 1977 it had been rebound and a stamped foliation had been added. The foliation commences on what was originally the opening flyleaf (additional flyleaves were inserted upon rebinding), so that p. 1 corresponds to f. 2. On the spine of the original parchment cover—now replaced—appeared an inscription reading "Sonate di cembalo."

101. This paragraph describes the state of the manuscript when I examined it in 1972. As a result of subsequent rebinding (see note 100 above) this gap is no longer visible—an example of how well-intentioned restoration can destroy potentially valuable evidence for determining the history of a manuscript.

102. I.V.D. = Iuris Utriusque Doctor—see Capelli, *Dizionario*, 194.

103. See, for example, Domenico Scorpione, *Motetti* . . . (Rome, 1675).

104. For further information on Francesco Mutij and on other musicians named Mutij, see Silbiger, *Tradition*.

105. Additional information on Fontana and a list of the sources of his music can be found in Silbiger, *Tradition*.

106. See Silbiger, *Tradition*.

107. Wessely-Kropik, *Colista*, 51.

108. Rome, Arch. S. Maria Maggiore, Capp. mus., Giustificazione I (1650-1696), and Arch. Segreto Vaticano, Fondo S. Marcello, H.XIV.67. Pasquini does not appear at S. Marcello until 1664, when he succeeds Mutij as organist for the first choir. For further discussion of this group of musicians and their professional associations, see Silbiger, *Tradition*.

109. We are disregarding the previously listed concordances in the "French" section, since these represent concordances of the melodies but not of the settings, which are unique to this manuscript (cf. p. 56).

110. I am assuming here that the keyboard manuscripts already formed part of the collection during this period—see p. 120.

111. The only reference to the manuscript appears in Rubsamen, *Italian Libraries*, 550.

112. The Biblioteca Vallicelliana formerly belonged to the Congregazione dell'Oratorio, associated with S. Maria in Vallicella. Ferrini also received a pension from the Oratorians from at least 1660 until 1674; see Silbiger, *Tradition*.

113. Since the completion of my dissertation two detailed descriptions of the manuscript by Anderson and Gustafson have appeared (see above under *Literature*).

114. Naples, Conservatorio di musica S. Piètro a Majella, Ms. P103 and Ms. P226, and Milan, Conservatorio di musica Giuseppe Verdi, Ms. Noseda Z.16-13; see Anderson, *Cecilia*, 11-13 and 71-76.

115. f.47': *Sarabande*, also found in Paris 674, f. 42' and in St^e. Geneviève 2348, f. 14; for other concordances, see Gustafson, *Sources*, 549.

116.   f. 47: *Gavotte*, in his *Premier Livre de Clavecin* (Paris: 1677), p. 17; for other concordances, see Gustafson, *Sources*, 548.

117.   f. 54: *Canaries*, in his *Pièces de Clavecin, Premier Livre* (Paris: 1713), p. 24.

118.   f. 52: "Marche du Prince d'Orange" (= Lilliburlero), and f. 52, "Dessent dopolon" (= Descent d'Apollon, from Lully, *Le Triomphe de l'Amour* of 1681).

119.   Some of the contents of Couperin's *Premier Livre* were, according to the composer's preface, composed at an earlier time. A few compositions—although not the piece included in Cecilia 400—appeared, in fact, anonymously in an anthology published by Ballard in 1706 (see Tessier, *Couperin*). Nevertheless, it appears unlikely that any of the unpublished compositions would have fallen into the hands of the scribe of our Italian manuscript before 1713.

120.   See "Piccioni, Giovanni" in *Enciclopedia della musica Rizzoli Ricordi*, V, p. 41. This encyclopedia also lists a Giovanni Maria Piccioni, from Brescia, who was in the service of Vincenzo Gonzaga in Mantua, and in 1630 became organist at the Duomo in Brescia. He seems like a less plausible candidate because (aside from working in a different region) he was a priest, and hence probably would not be referred to as "Sig. Giovanni Piccioni."

121.   A description of the musical activities at this church and a list of musicians known to have worked there are given in Fausti, *Cappella*, and Pomponi, *Memorie*. Piccioni is not mentioned in either article.

122.   Father Feininger informed me that the manuscript was acquired from Ottorino Respighi; he had no other information on its history. I have been told that upon Father Feininger's death in 1976 the volume was donated to the Biblioteca Comunale in Trent, but have not yet received verification of this.

123.   Neither Levy nor Ferand lists the settings in Trent.

124.   With the exception of Naples 48—another early source—all manuscripts containing Pasquini attributions also contain Frescobaldi attributions.

125.   To be sure, a few attributions appear in two Neapolitan manuscripts (Naples 48 and Naples 73), but both are otherwise heavily devoted to works credited to Neapolitan composers. Because this is not the case with the Trent manuscript, a Neapolitan origin can probably be ruled out.

126.   This is also the opinion of Oscar Mischiati, with whom I discussed this manuscript.

127.   Information from Turrini, *Verona*, and from Oscar Mischiati (private communication).

128.   Information from Oscar Mischiati (private communication).

129.   The call number 51/1 was given in Hudson, *Fiorenza*; it does not appear anywhere on the manuscript.

130. All information on this manuscript is derived from the description provided by its one-time owner (Garofalo, *Scoperta*), and from a transcription of the nineteen canzoni in the possession of Oscar Mischiati.

PART THREE

1. His specialty apparently was playing the spinetta and he is referred to as "Giovanni Battista Ferrini detto della spinetta." For more detailed information on the life and works of this musician, who is not included in any musical reference works, see Silbiger, *Tradition*.

2. On this manuscript, see Holman, *Suites*, 25-30.

3. Additional fragments appear in a more extended manuscript version of the *Guida armonica*, Biblioteca Apostolica Vaticana, Mss. Capp. Giulia I.4 to I.44; see Silbiger, *Tradition*.

4. This count does not include the eleven canzoni collected and published posthumously by Alessandro Vincenti in CANZONI IV (1645)—cf. Chapter I note 6.

5. See letter by Frescobaldi of 29 July 1608, letters by Facconi of 22 November 1614 and of 7 February 1615 (Cametti, *Roma*, 708, 718-720), and the preface to Frescobaldi, CANZONI I (1628i).

6. The comprehensiveness of his printed *oeuvre* was already recognized by his pupil Bartolomeo Grassi, who writes in 1628: "Consiglio dunque ogni studioso, che faccia provisione di tutte le opere del Signor Girolamo, cominciando dal primo libro delle Toccate in Rame [1615], & seguendo il secondo dato adesso in luce [1627]. . . . più copioso di diversita di opere, si da Organo, come da Cimbalo, & ogni sonatore di tasti havendo questidue libri in materia di Toccate, Galanterie, & riposte necessarie à tutti li bisogni per la Chiesa. . . . ma per pigliar vivacità, & motivi allegri si di fughe, come d'altri passage, si proveda in ogni maniera della presenta opera [1628i] che la troverà in questo genere, come in gravita e dottrina perfettissima; aggiunga anco i Capricci, & Ricercari del medesimo [1626] se vuole gravità di stile" (Preface of CANZONI I, 1628i).

7. I have not included in Table 14 nor considered in my discussion the Frescobaldi attributions in the Garofalo Ms, since I was not able to examine this manuscript (its present whereabouts are not known), and, hence, could not verify the nature of the attributions, or, for that matter, ascertain that it is of Italian provenance. The authorship problems, however, would seem to be similar to those encountered with other manuscripts having blanket attributions.

8. A fourth set, on *Veni Creator Spiritus* (f. 106), has no attribution; it has been included in Shindle's edition (Frescobaldi III, 2) probably because it appears to be part of the group.

9. *Froberger*, 28. Leonhardt has nevertheless recorded this composition under Frescobaldi's name (Frescobaldi, *Toccaten* . . ., Telefunken SAWT 9463.B).

10. Adler, *Froberger*; Leonhardt, *Froberger*.

11. The composition following the second of the three Chigi toccate has no title, nor is its soggetto particularly canzone-like; but structurally it is similar to the canzoni.

12. The restrained organ toccate in the FIORI (1635) really belong to a different genre.

13. Autograph, Vienna, Österreichische Nationalbibliothek, Ms. 18706 (no *Libro primo* survives).

14. See p. 42 for its appearance in the keyboard manuscripts; a more general discussion of its background and diffusion is given in Kirkendale, *Fiorenza*. Some of the considerations presented here also appeared in my review of Kirkendale's book (Silbiger, *Fiorenza*).

15. Furthermore, Casimiri has suggested that Frescobaldi was the composer of an eight-voice anonymous *Missa sopra l'Aria di Fiorenza* in a manuscript in San Giovanni di Laterano (Rome)—a proposal questioned by Kirkendale (*Fiorenza*, 34), but accepted by Mischiati and Tagliavini in their edition of the Mass (Mischiati, *Messe*, VIII-IX).

16. Prota-Giurleo, *de Macque*.

17. On the 1586 part book, see Part Two note 34.

18. Intabulations of four of his madrigals for lute and harpsichord are included in Verovio's LODI DELLA MUSICA (Sa. s.a. 1595), but the arrangements were probably not de Macque's work. Four *Canzoni* appeared posthumously in Woltz, NOVA MUSICES (Sa. 1617e), notated in German organ tablature.

19. Not considered in the Curtis edition are some pieces attributed to Merula in Vienna, Musikarchiv des Minoritenkonventes, Ms. XIV.717. The attributions in this manuscript, copied around 1700 in Austria, are, however, highly suspect (including one attribution to Frescobaldi that on stylistic grounds is altogether implausible).

20. Haynes, *Pasquini*; Heimrich, *Pasquini*; see also the review of Heimrich's dissertation by Tagliavini (*Pasquini*) in which additional sources are listed.

21. The earliest date in Berlin L.215 (p. 194) is generally quoted as 1691 (Haynes, Heimrich, etc.); however, this is probably a misreading, since the following composition in the manuscript is dated 1697 and the subsequent dates are separated by comparatively short time intervals (cf. Tagliavini, *Pasquini*).

22. In a file I have compiled of musicians active as keyboard players in Rome during the 17th-century, which contains over one hundred names, there appears not a single other musician named Bernardo.

23. The following information is based on Superbi, *Apparato*, 132; Cametti, *Roma*, 709, 710; and Allegra, *Saxia*, 30. The most comprehensive survey of our present knowledge on this composer is given in Ladewig, *Frescobaldi* (pp. 43-49). Ladewig notes that in 1593 Pasquini was referred to as a "buon vecchio" and hence probably was born already during the 1540s.

24. "Catalogo dei maestri di Cappella dell'Accademia della Morte. . . ," Ferrara, Biblioteca comunale Ariostea, Coll. Antonelli 22, f.2'.

25. Although documentary support for the generally-held belief that he was born in Ferrara c. 1560 (e.g., Apel, *Keyboard Music*, 421) is lacking, the fact that he studied there with Milleville makes it likely that he came from that area. A further indication might be his somewhat uncommon first name, possibly honoring Ercole II d'Este (d. 1559). This would suggest that he was born before or during 1559.

26. Frescobaldi seems to recognize only Luzzasco Luzzaschi as his master; see his prefaces to CAPRICCI (1624) and to ARIE MUSICALE II (1630).

27. A composition from Naples 73 (f. 141'), included in Shindle, *Pasquini*, in an Appendix, will not be considered here, since it has no attribution other than the blanket attribution in a table of contents of recent origin; see p. 59.

28. Since the set in Trent has no attribution it is questionable whether Pasquini's authorship should be assumed for these additional variations—see our discussion of the "wandering variation," p. 55.

29. Rossi died on 7 July 1656 in Rome, rather than—as is generally stated in the literature—c. 1670 in Faenza. For a revised biography of this composer, incorporating recent findings, see Silbiger, *Tradition*.

30. See, for example, Apel, *Keyboard Music*, 487. Apel states—as others have done—that Frescobaldi was Rossi's teacher; so far as I know this has not been documented.

Bibliography

Abbiati, Franco. *Storia della musica*, 3 vols. Milan: Garzanti, 1941.

Adler, Guido, ed. *Johann Jakob Froberger: Orgel-und Klavierwerke*, 3 vols. (*Denkmäler der Tonkunst in Österreich*, IV/1:8; VI/2:13; X/2:21). Vienna: Breitkopf & Härtel, 1893-1903.

Alaleona, Domenico. "Le laudi spirituali italiane nei secoli XVI e XVII e il loro rapporto coi canti profani." *Rivista musicale italiana* XVI (1909), 1-54.

Allegra, Antonio. "La Cappella Musicale di S. Spirito in Saxia di Roma." *Note d'archivio* XVII (1940), 26-38.

Anderson, Lyle J. "Cecilia A/400: Commentary, Thematic Index, and Partial Edition." M.M. Thesis, University of Wisconsin-Madison, 1977.

Apel, Willi. "Die handschriftliche Überlieferung der Klavierwerke Frescobaldis." In *Festschrift Karl Gustav Fellerer*, edited by Heinrich Hüschen. Regensburg: Bosse, 1962, pp. 40-45.

Apel, Willi. *The History of Keyboard Music to 1700*. Translated and revised by Hans Tischler. Bloomington: Indiana University Press, 1972.

Apel, Willi. "Die süditalienische Clavierschule des 17. Jahrhunderts." *Acta musicologica* XXXIV (1962), 128-41.

Becherini, Bianca. *Catalogo dei manoscritti musicali della Biblioteca Nazionale di Firenze*. Kassel: Bärenreiter, 1959.

Benevuti, Giacomo, ed. *Marco Antonio Cavazzoni: Ricercari, Mottetti, Canzoni; Jacobo Fogliano, Julio Segni ed anonimi: Ricercari e Ricercate*. Milan: I classici musicali italiani (Fondazione Eugenio Bravi), 1941.

Benton, Rita, ed. *Directory of Music Research Libraries*, 3 vols. Iowa City: University of Iowa, 1967-72.

Biographie nationale (l'Academie Royale des sciences, des lettres et des beaux-arts de Belgique), vol. V. Brussels: Bruylant-Christophe, 1876. Articles "del Rio," cc. 468-91.

Bonta, Stephen. "The Uses of the Sonata da Chiesa." *Journal of the American Musicological Society* XXII (1969), 54-84.

Bradshaw, Murray C. *The Origin of the Toccata*. American Institute of Musicology, 1972.

Brainard, Paul. "Zur Deutung der Diminution in der Tactuslehre des Michael Praetorius." *Musikforschung* XVII (1964), 169-74.

Brown, Howard M. *Instrumental Music Printed Before 1600*. Cambridge: Harvard University Press, 1965.

Caldwell, John. *English Keyboard Music Before the Nineteenth Century*. Oxford: Blackwell, 1973.

Caluori, Eleanor. *Luigi Rossi (ca. 1598-1653)*, 2 vols. (*Wellesley Edition Cantata Index Series*, fasc. 3). Wellesley College, 1965.

Cametti, Alberto. "Girolamo Frescobaldi in Roma." *Rivista musicale italiana* XV (1908), 701-52.

———. "Organi, organisti, ed organari del Senato e Popolo Romano in S. Maria in Aracoeli (1583-1848)." *Rivista musicale italiana* XXVI (1919), 441-85.

Cappelli, Adriano. *Dizionario di abbreviature latine ed italiane*, 6th edition. Milan: Hoepli, 1973.

Casimiri, Raffaele. "Girolamo Frescobaldi, autore di opere vocali sconosciute ad otto voci." *Note d'archivio* X (1933), 1-31.

———. "Oratorii del Masini, Bernabei, Melani, Di Pio, Pasquini e Stradella in Roma, nell'Anno Santo 1675." *Note d'archivio* XIII (1936), 157-69.

Celani, E. "Canzoni musicate del secolo XVII." *Rivista musicale italiana* XII (1905), 109-50.

———. "I Cantori della Cappella Pontificia nei secoli XVI-XVIII." *Rivista musicale italiana* XVI (1909), 55-112.

Cerreto, Scipione. *Della prattica musica vocale e strumentale*. Naples, 1601.

Cooper, Barry A. R. "English Solo Keyboard Music of the Middle and Late Baroque." Ph.D. Dissertation, Oxford University, 1974.

———. "The Keyboard Suite in England Before the Restoration." *Music & Letters* LIII (1972), 309-19.

Crocker, Richard L. *A History of Musical Style*. New York: McGraw-Hill, 1966.

Curtis, Alan. *Nederlandse Klaviermuziek uit de 16e en 17e Eeuw (Monumenta Neerlandica* III). Amsterdam: Vereniging voor Nederlandse Muziekgeschiedenis, 1961.

Curtis, Alan. "L'opera cembalo-organistica di Tarquinio Merula—Note introduttive." *L'Organo* I (1960), 141-51.

———, ed. *Tarquinio Merula: Composizioni per organo e cembalo*. Brescia: L'Organo, 1961.

D'Accone, Frank. "The 'Intavolatura di M. Alamanno Aiolla'." *Musica disciplina* XX (1966), 151-74.

von Dadelsen, Georg. "Methodische Bemerkungen zur Echtheitskritik." In *Musicae scientiae collectanae, Festschrift Karl Gustav Fellerer*, edited by Heinrich Hüschen. Cologne: Volk, 1973, pp. 78-83.

Dahlhaus, Carl. "Zur Entstehung des modernen Taktsystems in 17. Jahrhundert." *Archiv für Musikwissenschaft* XVII (1961), 223-40.

Dahlhaus, Carl. "Zur Taktlehre des Michael Praetorius." *Musikforschung* XVII (1964), 162-69.

Darbellay, Etienne. "Liberté, variété et 'affetti cantabili' chez Girolamo Frescobaldi." *Revue de musicologie* LXI (1975), 197-243.

———. "Un manuscrit frescobaldien à Genève." *L'Organo* XIII (1975), 49-69.

Debes, Louis H. "Die musikalischen Werke von Claudio Merulo, 1533-1604; Quellennachweis und thematischer Katalog." Ph.D. dissertation, Würzburg, 1964.

Enciclopedia della musica Rizzoli-Ricordi, vol. V. Milan: Rizzoli, 1972. Articles "Giovanni Piccioni," "Giovanni Maria Piccioni," p. 41.

van Eyck, Jacob, Jr. *Der Fluyten Lust-Hof*, 3 vols. (Amsterdam: 1646), edited by Gerrit Vellekoop. Amsterdam: Ixijzet, 1957.

Fallows, David. "15th-Century Tablatures for Plucked Instruments: A Summary, a Revision, and a Suggestion." *The Lute Society Journal* XIX (1977), 7-33.

Fausti, Luigi. "La cappella musicale della Collegiata di S. Maria di Spello." *Note d'archivio*, X (1933), 136-44.

Ferand, Ernest T. "Anthor che col partire. Die Schicksale eines berühmten Madrigals" In *Festschrift Karl Gustav Fellerer*, edited by Heinrich Hüschen. Regensburg: Bosse, 1962, pp. 137-154.

Flotzinger, Rudolf. "Die Gagliarda Italjana." *Acta musicologica* XXXIX (1967), 92-100.

Gachard, M. "La bibliothèque des princes Chigi à Rome." *Compte rendu des séances de la Commission Royale d'histoire*, 3 series, X (1869), 219-20.

Gallico, Claudio. *Un canzoniere musicale italiano del cinquecento. ("Historiae musicae cultures" biblioteca* XII). Florence: Olschki, 1959.

Gandolfi, Riccardo [et al.]. *Catalogo delle opere musicali . . . Città di Firenze. Biblioteca del R. Conservatorio di musica*. Parma: Fresching, 1929.

Garofalo, Carlo G. "Una scoperta importante di musiche inedite e ignorate," *Rivista nazionale di musica* III (1922), pp. 307-09.

Ghislanzoni, Alberto. *Luigi Rossi: Biografia e analisi delle opere*. Turin: Bocca, 1954.

Giazotto, Remo. *Quattro secoli di storia dell'Accademia Nazionale di Santa Cecilia*, 2 vols. Rome: Accademia Nazionale di Santa Cecilia, 1970.

Golzio, Vencenzo. *Documenti artistici sul seicento nell'Archivio Chigi*. Rome: Palombi, 1939.

Grove's Dictionary of Music and Musicians. Sixth Edition, edited by Stanley Sadie. London: Macmillan, in preparation.

Gustafson, Bruce. "Sources of Seventeenth-Century French Harpsichord Music." Ph.D. dissertation, University of Michigan, 1977.

Haberl, Franz X. "Hieronymus Frescobaldi," *Kirchenmusikalisches Jahrbuch* II (1887), 67-82.

Haskell, Francis. *Patrons and Painters*. New York: Harper & Row, 1971.

Haynes, Maurice B. "Keyboard Works of Bernardo Pasquini (1637-1710)." Ph.D. dissertation, Indiana University, 1960.

Heawood, Edward. *Watermarks, Mainly of the 17th and 18th Centuries*. Hilversum: Paper Publications Society, 1950.

Heimrich, Werner. "Die Orgel- und Cembalowerke Bernardo Pasquinis." Ph.D. dissertation, Berlin, 1958.

Holman, Peter. "Suites by Jenkins Rediscovered," *Early Music* VI (1978), 25-30.

Holschneider, Andreas. "Römische Handschriften, C. 9: Bibl. der Fürsten Doria-Pamphilj." *Die Musik in Geschichte und Gegenwart* XI (1963), c. 770.

Holschneider, Andreas. "Die Musiksammlung der Fürsten Doria-Pamphilij." *Archiv für Musikwissenschaft* XVIII (1961), 248-64.

Hudson, Barton, ed. *Giovanni Salvatore: Collected Keyboard Works*. American Institute of Musicology, 1964.

Hudson, Richard. "The Development of Italian Keyboard Variations on the Passacaglio and Ciaccona from Guitar Music in the 17th Century." Ph.D. dissertation, University of California at Los Angeles, 1967.

―――. "Further Remarks on the Passacaglia and Ciaccona," *Journal of the American Musicological Society* XXIII (1970), 302-14.

―――. "The Ripresa, the Ritornello, and the Passacaglia." *Journal of the American Musicological Society* XXIV (1971), 364-94.

―――. Review of Warren Kirkendale, *La Fiorenza* (q.v.). *Journal of the American Musicological Society* XXVI (1973), 344-50.

Hughes-Hughes, Augustus. *Catalogue of Manuscript Music in the British Museum*, 3 vols. London: British Museum, 1906-09.

Jackson, Roland, ed. *Neapolitan Keyboard Composers*. American Institute of Musicology, 1967.

Jander, Owen. *Alessandro Stradella, 1644-1682*, 2 vols. (*Wellesley Edition Cantata Index Series*, fasc. 4a, 4b). Wellesley College, 1969.

Jeppesen, Knud. "Ein altitalienisches Tanzbuch." In *Festschrift Karl Gustav Fellerer*, edited by Heinrich Hüschen. Regehsburg: Bosse, 1962, pp. 245-63.

―――, *Die italienische Orgelmusik am Anfang des Cinquecento*, 2 vols., 2nd edition. Copenhagen: Hansen, 1960.

―――, ed. *Balli antichi veneziani*. Copenhagen: Hansen, 1962.

Kast, Paul and Gordon Crain. "Pasquini, Bernardo." *Die Musik in Geschichte und Gegenwart* X (1962), cc. 861-67.

Kirkendale, Warren. *L'aria di Fiorenza id est il ballo del Gran Duca*. Florence: Olschki, 1972.

Kirkendale, Warren. "Franchesina, Girometta, and their Companions in a Madrigal 'A diversi linguaggi' by Luca Marenzio and Orazio Vecchi." *Acta musicologica* XLIV (1972), 181-235.

Klemm, Johann. *Partitura seu Tabulatura Italica*. Dresden, 1631.

Krummel, Donald W. "Oblong Format in Early Music Books." *The Library*, Fifth Series, XXVI (1971), 312-24.

Kugler, Michael. *Die Tastenmusik im Codex Faenza*. Tutzing: Schneider, 1972.

Ladewig, James L. "Frescobaldi's *Recercari et canzuni franzese* (1615): A Study of the Contrapuntal Keyboard Idiom in Ferrara, Naples, and Rome, 1580-1620." Ph.D. dissertation, University of California at Berkeley, 1978.

Lejeune, Jerome. "The Lyra-Viol: An Instrument or a Technique?" *The Consort* No. 31 (1975), 125-31.

Leonhardt, Gustav. "Johann Jacob Froberger and his Music." *L'Organo* VI (1968), 15-40.

Levy, Kenneth J. " 'Susanne un jour.' The History of a 16th-century Chanson." *Annales musicologiques* I (1953), 375-408.

Lincoln, Harry B. "I manoscritti chigiani di musica organo-cembalistica della Biblioteca Apostolica Vaticana." *L'Organo* V (1967), 63-80.

————, ed. *Seventeenth-century Keyboard Music in the Chigi Manuscripts of the Vatican Library*, 3 vols. American Institute of Musicology, 1968.

Lodi, Luigi. *Catalogo dei codici e degli autografi posseduti del Marchese Giuseppe Campori*, vol. I. Modena: 1875.

Lowinsky, Edward. "Early Scores in Manuscript." *Journal of the American Musicological Society* XIII (1960), 126-71.

MacClintock, Carol. "The 'Giaches Fantasias' in Ms. Chigi Q. VIII. 206: A Problem in Identification." *Journal of the American Musicological Society* XIX (1966), 370-82.

Mischiati, Oscar, "L'intavolatura d'organo tedesca della Biblioteca Nazionale di Torino." *L'Organo* IV (1963), 1-154.

Mischiati, Oscar and Luigi F. Tagliavini, eds. *Girolamo Frescobaldi: Due messe a otto voci e basso continuo* (*Opere complete*, vol. I). Milan: Suivini Zerboni, 1975.

Monroe, James F. "Italian Keyboard Music in the Interim Between Frescobaldi and Pasquini." Ph.D. dissertation, University of North Carolina, 1959.

Montalto, Lina. *Un mecenate in Roma barocca, il Cardinale Benedetto Pamphilij*. Florence: Sansoni, 1955.

Montanelli, Indro and Roberto Gervaso. *L'Italia del seicento*. Milan: Rizzoli, 1969.

Newcomb, Anthony. "Carlo Gesualdo and a Musical Correspondence of 1594." *Musical Quarterly* LIV (1968), 409-36.

————. "Frescobaldi." Typescript submitted to *Grove's Dictionary of Music and Musicians* (q.v.).

————. "*Il modo di far la fantasia*: An Appreciation of Luzzaschi's Instrumental Style." *Early Music* VII (1979), 34-38.

Oncley, Lawrence A. "The Conservatorio de Musica San Pietro a Majella Library Manuscript No. 34.5.28: Transcription and Commentary." Master's thesis, Indiana University, 1966.

Ortiz, Diego. *Tratado de glosas sobre clausulas y otros generos de puntos en la musica de violones* (Roma, 1553). Edited and translated by Max Schneider. Kassel: Bärenreiter, 1961.

Osthoff, Wolfgang, ed. *C. Monteverdi: 12 composizioni vocali profane e sacre (inedite)*. Milan: Ricordi, 1958.

Pacchioni, Giorgio, ed. *Balli italiani del XVII secolo*. Wilhelmshaven: Heinrichshofen, 1975.

Pastor, Ludwig, Freiherr von. *The History of the Popes, from the Close of the Middle Ages*, vol. XXX. Edited and translated by Ernest Graf. London: Kegan Paul, 1940.

Pestelli, Giorgio. "Le toccate per strumento a tastiera di Alessandro Scarlatti nei manoscritti napoletani." *Analecta musicologica* XII (1973), 169-92.

Plamenac, Dragan, ed. *Keyboard Music of the Late Middle Ages in Codex Faenza 117*. American Institute of Musicology, 1972.

Pomponi, Luigi. "Memorie musicali della Collegiata di S. Maria Maggiore di Spello." *Note d'archivio*, XVII (1940), 179-222.

Porter, William V. "The Origins of the Baroque Solo Song: A Study of Italian Manuscripts and Prints from 1590-1610." Ph.D. dissertation, Yale University, 1962.

Praetorius, Michael. *Syntagma musicum*, III (Wolfenbüttel 1619). Facs. ed. (*Documenta musicologica*, Ser. I, 15). Kassel: Bärenreiter, 1958.

Prota-Giurleo, Ulisse. "Giovanni Maria Trabaci e gli Organisti della Real Cappella di Palazzo di Napoli." *L'Organo* I (1960), 185-96.

————. "La musica a napoli nel seicento." *Samnium* I (1928), fasc. 4, 67-90.

————. "Notizie sul musicista Belga Jean Macque." In *Report of the First Congress for the International Society of Musical Research* (Liège, 1930), pp. 191-97.

Prunières, Henry. "Les Musiciens du Cardinal Antonio Barberini." In *Mélanges de musicologie offerts à M. Lionel de la Laurencie.* Paris: Droz, 1933, pp. 119-22.

Reimann, Margarete. "Frescobaldi, Girolamo." *Die Musik in Geschichte und Gegenwart* IV (1955), cc. 912-26.

Reimann, Margarete. "Pasticcios und Parodien in norddeutschen Klaviertabulaturen." *Musikforschung* VIII (1955), 265-71.

Riedel, Friedrich W. "Der Einfluss der italienischen Klaviermusik des 17. Jahrhunderts auf die Entwicklung der Musik für Tasteninstrumente in Deutschland während der ersten Hälfte des 17. Jahrhunderts." *Analecta musicologica* V (1968), 18-33.

————. *Quellenkundliche Beiträge zur Geschichte der Musik für Tasteninstrumente in der zweiten Hälfte des 17. Jahrhunderts.* Kassel: Bärenreiter, 1960.

RISM A/I/3 (*Einzeldrücke vor 1800*, vol. 3). Edited by Karlheinz Schlager. Kassel: Bärenreiter, 1972.

RISM B/VI/2 (*Écrits imprimés concernant la musique*, vol. 2). Edited by François Lesure. Munich: Henle, 1971.

Rostirolla, Giancarlo. "Catalogo generale delle opere di Alessandro Scarlatti," in R. Pagano and L. Bianchi, *Alessandro Scarlatti.* Turin: Edizione RAI, 1972, pp. 319-595.

Rubsamen, Walter H. "Music Research in Italian Libraries." (Second installment) *Notes* Series 2, IV (1949), 543-69.

Rumor, Sebastiano. *Biblioteca Bertoliana, città di Vicenza: Catalogo delle opere musicali.* Parma: Fresching, 1923.

Sandberger, Adolf, ed. *J. K. Kerll, Ausgewählte Werke*, vol. I (*Denkmäler der Tonkunst in Bayern*, II, 2). Leipzig: Breitkopf & Härtel, 1901.

Santini, P. O., ed. *G. Frescobaldi: XIV composizioni inedite . . .* Rome: Psalterium, 1940; revised edition, 1955.

Sartori, Claudio. "Bibliografia," in *Alessandro Scarlatti: Primo e secondo Libro di Toccate*, edited by Ruggero Gerlin. Milan: I classici musicali italiani (Fondazione Eugenio Bravi), 1943, pp. 134-43.

————. *Bibliografia della musica strumentale italiani.* 2 vols. Florence: Olschki, 1952-68.

————. *Dizionario degli editori musicali italiani.* Florence: Olschki, 1953.

————. "Madrigali del Passerini e Ricercari di Macque e Gesualdo," in *Testimonianzi, studi e ricerche in onore di Guido M. Gatti (1892-1973).* Bologna: Antiquae musicae italicae studiosi, 1973, pp. 181-86.

————. "Une pratique des musiciens Lombards (1582-1639)," in *La musique instrumentale de la Renaissance*, edited by Jean Jacquot. Paris: Centre National de la Recherche Scientifique, 1955, pp. 305-312.

Scharlau, Ulf. *Athanasius Kircher (1601-1680) als Musikschriftsteller (Studien zur hessischen Musikgeschichte*, vol. 2). Marburg, 1969.

————. "Neue Quellenfunde zur Biographie Johann Jacob Frobergers." *Musikforschung* XXII (1969), 47-52.

Schierning, Lydia. *Die Überlieferung der deutschen Orgel- und Klaviermusik aus der ersten Hälfte des 17. Jahrhunderts.* Kassel: Bärenreiter, 1961.

Sestan, Ernesto, ed. *Dizionario storico-politico italiano.* Florence: Sansoni, 1971. Article "Chigi," pp. 343-44.

Shindle, W. Richard, ed. *Girolamo Frescobaldi: Keyboard Compositions Preserved in Manuscript.* 3 vols. American Institute of Musicology, 1968.

Shindle, W. Richard, ed. *Ercole Pasquini: Collected Keyboard Works.* American Institute of Musicology, 1966.

Silbiger, Alexander. "The Roman Frescobaldi Tradition: 1640-1670." *Journal of the American Musicological Society*, forthcoming (1980).

————. Review of Warren Kirkendale, *L'aria di Fiorenza* (q.v.). *Nuova rivista musicale italiana*

VII (1973), 272-77.

Slim, H. Colin. "Keyboard Music at Castell'Arquato by an Early Madrigalist." *Journal of the American Musicological Society* XV (1962), 35-47.

————. "The Keyboard Ricercar and Fantasia in Italy, ca. 1500-1550, with Reference to Parallel Forms in European Lute Music of the Same Period." Ph.D. dissertation, Harvard University, 1961.

————, ed. *Keyboard Music at Castell'Arquato*, vol. I. American Institute of Musicology, 1975.

Superbi, Agostino. *Apparato de gli Huomini illustri della città di Ferrara*. Ferrara: Suzzi, 1620.

Tagliavini, Luigi Ferdinando. "Un importante fonte per la musica di J. K. Kerll." *Collectanea historiae musicae*, vol. IV. Florence: Olschki, 1966, pp. 283-93.

————. Review of Werner Heimrich, "Die Orgel-und Cembalowerke Bernardo Pasquinis" (q.v.). *L'Organo* I (1960), 272-76.

Tessier, A. "Attribution à Couperin le Grand d'une pièce anonyme d'une recueil de Ballard." *Revue de musicologie* III (1922), 69-78.

Testi, Flavio. *La musica italiano nel seicento*, 2 vols. Milan: Bramante, 1972.

Torchi, Luigi. *L'arte musicale in Italia*, vol. III. Milan: Ricordi, n.d.

Turrini, Giuseppe. *Il Patrimonio musicale della Biblioteca Capitolare di Verona dal Sec. XV al XIX*. Verona: La tipografica Veronese, 1952.

Varotti, A. *Tomaso Fabri: Toccata del primo tono per organo*. Assisi: Edizioni Capella Musicale S. Rufino, 1970.

Vincenti, Alessandro. "Indice di tutte le opere di musica. . ." [Venice, 1619 and 1649]. Reprinted in *Monatshefte für Musikgeschichte* XIV (1882), Beilage 1-50.

Vitali, Mario, ed. *Clavicembalisti Italiani*, vol. I. Milan: Ricordi, n.d.

Walker, Thomas. "Ciaccona and Passacaglia: Remarks on Their Origin and Early History." *Journal of the American Musicological Society* XXI (1968), 300-20.

Ward, John. "The Editorial Methods of Venegas de Henestrosa." *Musica Disciplina* VI (1952), 104-13.

Watelet, Joseph, ed. *Charles Guillet, Giovanni de Macque, Carolus Luyton: Werken voor Orgel (Monumenta Musicae Belgicae*, IV). Antwerp: De Ring, 1938.

Watkins, Glenn. *Gesualdo: The Man and his Music*. Chapel Hill: The University of North Carolina Press, 1973.

Wessely-Kropik, Helene. *Lelio Colista, ein römischer Meister vor Corelli: Leben und Umwelt. (Österreichische Akademie der Wissenschaften, Philosophisch-Historische Klasse, Sitzungsberichte*, 237. Band, 4. Abhandlung). Vienna: Böhlaus, 1961.

White, John R., ed. *Michelangelo Rossi: Keyboard Works*. American Institute of Musicology, 1966.

Willetts, Pamela J. *Handlist of Mss Acquired 1908-1968*. London: Museum Trustees, 1970.

Witzenmann, Wolfgang. "Autographe Marco Marazzolis in der Biblioteca Vaticana (I)." *Analecta musicologica* VII (1969), 36-86.

————. "Autographe Marco Marazzolis in der Biblioteca Vaticana (II)." *Analecta musicologica* IX (1970), 203-94.

Wolf, Johannes. *Handbuch der Notationskunde*, 2 vols. Leipzig: Breitkopf & Härtel, 1913-19.

Index

Manuscript short titles are in boldface. Page references to manuscript entries in Part Two and composer entries in Part Three are in italics.

Cover illustrations: watermark examples selected from the *French Harpsichord Music of the 17th Century* by Bruce Gustafson, published by UMI Research Press.

DATE DUE